"I HAVEN'T A THING TO WEAR!"

JUDITH KEITH

ILLUSTRATIONS BY LEE WYDRA

AVON
PUBLISHERS OF BARD, CAMELOT, DISCUS AND FLARE BOOKS

AVON BOOKS
A division of
The Hearst Corporation
959 Eighth Avenue
New York, New York 10019

Copyright © 1980 by Judith Keith
Cover photography Copyright © 1981 by Kathie A. McGinty
Styling by Sandy Lopes
All jewelry by "Kenneth Jay Lane"
Black high heel sandals and two-tone blue high heel by "Nina"
Tan sling back pump by "Life Stride"
Tan espadrille by "Wimzees"
Published by arrangement with Tandem Press
Library of Congress Catalog Card Number: 76-57886
ISBN: 0-380-55574-3

The Tandem Press edition contains the following Library of Congress Cataloging
in Publication Data:

Keith, Judith.
    "I haven't a thing to wear!"

    1. Clothing and dress. 2. Beauty, Personal.
I. Title.
TT507.K38   1980   391

First Avon Printing, September, 1981

10 9 8 7 6 5 4 3 2 1

*To the women at my shows
whose warmth and laughter
have made the years a pleasure*

Acknowledgments

The author gratefully acknowledges the editorial advice of Elisa B. Fitzgerald. When an author past the speed limit is lucky to have an editor not yet twenty-one, her work becomes more effective. How wonderfully tough and perspicacious young people are! Miss Fitzgerald's contemporary touch, twentyish eye and ear, plus her enthusiasm and perception have indeed added a youthful dimension.

Contents

Contents

Part Three—Winning!

Part 1

The Concepts

1

The Concepts . . . The Answer To Timeless Fashion

I was the original *"IT"* girl.

Mama gave birth at home, and when Grandma took me to be cleaned, Mama heard shrieks. Not from her newborn, but from her mother.

"Gott in himmel, what is *IT?"* Silence. And then a resigned sigh, "Well, thank God, at least *IT's* healthy!"

My mother was beautiful. Grandma said I looked just like my father. She hated him. At five I dropped a toad into Grandma's neckline as my pretty cousins June and Ray climbed into her lap. She wailed to Mama, "What will become of *IT?"*

At seven, I jumped from our third floor apartment window with an umbrella because I wanted to "parachute." Grandma stomped down the stairs. Her ponderous breasts parted the hedges as she dragged me, scared, scratched but unscathed from the soft earth. She shook me to make sure I was alive and screamed up at Mama hanging out the window, "If you don't do something about *IT,* no one will ever marry *IT*!"

Hey Grandma, up there in the sky. Stop stirring chicken soup and listen . . . IT has been married more times than both of ITs cousins put together!"

When you have a long nose, big ears, stringy hair, myopic eyesight, crooked teeth and a figure all too human, you decide early on, *it isn't*

3

what you have, it's what you do with what you have that counts!

What counts most for a woman, or a man, is to be perfectly comfortable with themselves, and to *love* what they are doing!

My premise is simple. Any person can ignite their imagination, their ingenuity, to become a creative, interesting individual. *You can be what you want to be.* You can do what you enjoy best. All it takes is to be *realistic* about your goals, and then *work at it!* It is never too early or too late to begin.

How does all this relate to "I HAVEN'T A THING TO WEAR!", the subject of my show for 22 years and this book? It is the basis of a fashion philosophy that has enabled me to illustrate how one can stay timelessly in style and save substantial amounts of money on clothes. Since 1958 I have entertained audiences in the United States, Canada, England and Ireland in a simple black dress and with a suitcase of accessories. I have shown how *easy* it is to make an individual fashion statement in a ready-to-wear-world . . . and spend very little money!

I do it by approaching fashion in a conceptual manner, using concepts to save time and money. The concepts will ease your frustration over what you know you can wear best, and what is being designed. The concepts will help you swing from trend to trend so that what you buy today will not be outdated next month.

The concepts are:

COMFORT—CONTOUR—COLOR—CLASSICS—
COORDINATION

We discuss each of these in detail later on.

Despite having performed for more than 3,000 audiences in a fashion program, I have no connection with the fashion industry. I am as unknown in the showrooms of Seventh Avenue as I am in Paris and I choose it that way. For me to successfully communicate concepts which relate to the *average* person, I do not wish to be unduly influenced by high fashion whose designers create for the perfect figure, the perfect face.

Clothes, accessories and makeup are art forms, expressions of talented people who want the products of their creative energies displayed in the most ideal manner, and they design for *"models."* Since few of us are *"tens"* we need to individualize trends to fit our frame, our face, our finances and our lifestyles. My show is an extension of the way I live. It translates the creativity of design to

4

the practical, everyday needs of the average person. Its purpose is to *save you money,* and to show you how to be comfortable, chic and unique!

My audiences have ranged from the wives of top management at companies such as Ford, Exxon, Kodak and Xerox to women inmates of Kansas State Prison and New York's Bedford Correctional Facility, a maximum security institution. I have also appeared for farm women in home extension workshops throughout Middle America; crisp, competitive young corporate executives; supportive military and corporation wives; the wives of blue collar workers and high school and college students.

Disparate in background and life-style, these women all express a common interest, a common need. They want to be loved and they equate being loved with being beautiful.

And beauty is possible for all! Knowing what to wear when, feeling healthy and looking attractive is the antidote for all the hellish situations that surface in everyone's life. Throughout this book you will find ways to enhance your looks, for beauty is an attainable goal if you will but reach for it. Women of all ages have more opportunity for beauty than ever before, just as they have more options when it comes to love.

Even in the most isolated areas I find women testing new lifestyles, experimenting with ideas, changing not only their *look,* but their *outlook.* They are aware, creative, adventurous; adopting and adapting alternatives. I also find them dressing with a flair and style which reflects these new found freedoms for chic women are not confined by geography. The antagonist to chic is not where one *lives,* but how one *thinks.* I have seen unattractive, dowdy looking women in the smartest cities and in the smartest places. And I have seem supremely stylish women in communities so small they still don't have direct dialing.

Women do not resent changes in style; they look *forward* to them, *providing* they can coordinate them easily and economically with what they have. They want new looks! They enjoy wearing exciting new designs which mirror their changing and growing attitudes, but the high cost bothers them. Money is tight, especially for those who must dress in the latest trends because of business and social needs.

The high cost of clothes puts particular strain on young women: students, careerists, homemakers. This strain can be eased by using the conceptual approach to fashion . . . the CONCEPTS . . . which make it easy and economical to stay in style.

No matter how varied the clothes in your closet. No matter how cleverly you coordinate. No matter how skilled you may be with a needle. No matter how "up" you are on the latest news from the salons of New York, Paris, Milan and Rome. No matter how much money you have . . . there will always be that special moment, that special occasion when you honestly say. . . . "I HAVEN'T A THING TO WEAR!"

The concepts: COMFORT—CONTOUR—COLOR— CLASSICS—COORDINATION—are for those moments.

COMFORT comes first, because without your being totally comfortable, nothing is going to work for you. The ultimate of style is the ability to put something on and wear it so comfortably that you forget it . . . and, at the same time look chic, smart and in step with the vitality of life.

Never sacrifice comfort for fashion. Not only the familiar aspect of comfort as it regards fit, but the subtle psychological, social, and financial considerations that encompass the full spectrum of what comfort truly means, such as:

How do I *feel* in it?

Is it *suitable?*

Does it make me look *lovely?*

How will *he* like it?

Can I *afford* it?

Comfort is being honest with yourself; natural, in tune with your likes, your dislikes and your needs. Trust yourself, your instincts, your intuition. Do not be impatient. It takes time to establish style because it takes time to understand what you are all about. And your style will change as you change. Be prepared for all kinds of reactions when you try the outrageous, the unpredictable, the non-conforming. But that is the fun of trying new ideas. Just make sure that the essential, the honest YOU is always visible, for you know yourself better than anyone.

Allow your personality, your energies, your vitality, your wit to well up from within and reflect themselves in what you wear, in how you look, for then you will be most comfortable. Comfortable people set their own style. They are unique. They are creative. They are special!

Understanding and incorporating all the other concepts enables you to achieve comfort in clothes, cosmetics, hairstyles, and in the way you live. Your comfort underlies all that we discuss in this book. Every chapter is intended to help you achieve comfort; to cope comfortably not only with changing fashions, but with your own changing needs and desires.

When you accept what works best for you, what is most comfortable, you will create the unusual, expressing a fashion image that is your own, carefree and assured. Comfort makes you confident, and confidence unleashes the power of your creative potential!

Comfort in clothes is a balance of mind and body thinking. To understand your body best, we explore the second concept . . . CONTOUR.

2

Contour . . . or . . . Does the End Justify the Jeans?

When the shape you are in, is not the shape you want to be . . . *be very careful of the shapes you buy,* or to put it more succinctly, *does the end justify the jeans?*

If you want to look terrific in clothes, know your body and its proportions. Use contour and camouflage to compensate for figure faults.

Your body is the result of generations of genes; your mother's pre-natal diet; your adolescent nutrition and exercise habits, and your current life-style. If you are disciplined and dedicated, you can improve this heritage with diet and exercise, but those unseen, unalterable, and unforgiving genes have made your essential shape, and while genetic engineering in the future may create perfectly proportioned people . . . WHAT DO YOU DO IN THE MEANTIME?

You perfect the art of balance, harmony, line, so that what you wear creates an illusion of beauty, and of perfect proportion.

Very few women are perfect. More than 50 percent need extensive alterations in ready-to-wear and in patterns for home sewing, yet some know themselves so well, the clothes they wear create an aura of perfect proportions.

A young woman named Sandi, phoned one day to ask if I would rent my mother's chalet which is adjacent to my ski cabin. Living in the country, one becomes casual about clothes. I had been busy all morning reading manuscripts before the fire and was dressed in jeans and a cotton turtleneck shirt. Sandi's appearance that blustery spring morning was a welcome surprise. I had expected another jeans-clad person. She wore a handsome beige wool suit with a small patterned beige and brown silk shirt and a smartly tied silk scarf. Elegant leather boots and a rakishly tilted hat completed the attractive ensemble. She was warm, outgoing, immensely attractive and we chatted animatedly. I learned of her interest in clothes. Her overall look was so splendid, I was startled when I realized she was not a particularly pretty girl. Her features were irregular, her hair and skin poor, yet she was lovely to look at. I rented the chalet to Sandi and as we became friends, my admiration for her grew. A single girl in her mid-twenties, earning only a modest salary, Sandi is one of the best dressed women I know. Her figure is unproportioned with narrow shoulders, small bosom, slender waist, heavy hips, thighs and buttocks. Dressed, Sandi gives the *illusion* of a perfectly proportioned figure because she knows just what looks best on her and is brutally honest about her figure faults. She is uncompromising in her choice of line, color, texture, balance and fit.

The best way to know your figure is to get down to *bare* facts: the barer, the better, although a bathing suit will do for the more timid. Stand in front of a good quality, full length mirror. Cheap mirrors are distorting, and a three-way mirror is expensive. But a quality, single pane, full length mirror is a necessary fashion investment for any woman.

To compare oneself with the ideal figure is unimportant, but since so many are curious to see just how close they can come to what is considered "ideal" I offer an outline of the perfectly proportioned body:

It is a symmetrical "T" with the distance from the hipbone to the top of head equalling the distance from the hipbone to feet. Knees, evenly divide the lower half.

Bust and hip measurement are the same, with waist ten inches less. Elbows meet waistline; fingertips touch mid-thigh.

Width across shoulders equals distance from neck to waist.

Well formed shoulders mark the "T." If clothes are to fit well across shoulders and back, posture must be erect.

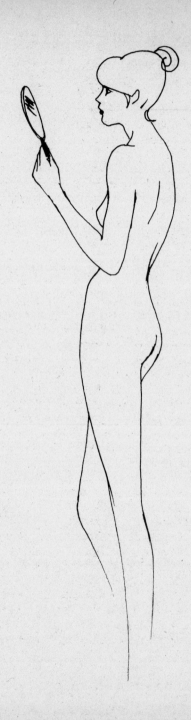

If you are interested in making comparisons with the foregoing, you can take the following measurements:

Hipbone to top of head—hipbone to feet—knees up to hipbone —knees down to feet—nape of neck to back of waist—width across shoulders—width around bust, waist, hips, wrist.

A wrist measurement of six inches or less connotes a small to medium boned person; over six inches generally means one is large-boned. Mirror analysis of your own figure is more important than evaluating it in relation to the "ideal" shape. Knowing your body, your face and its features and honestly recognizing its proportions and the way you carry yourself, helps you select the lines, the shapes, the silhouettes which enhance.

Use a hand-held mirror and turn slowly before the full length mirror to see yourself from every angle. This is how others see you. Note the way you hold your head. Is it straight, ears above shoulders or do you jut it forward? Observe your neck. Determine if it is long, short, thick, thin. Look at your chin from several angles. Step back and look at your eyes. Are they wide-set, close-set, deep-set; small, large, baggy? Your ears, do they lie flat or fan out? Is your hairline full, sparse, overgrown, or evenly shaped?

Are your shoulders wide, narrow, or sloping? Do you stand erect or do you slouch? Make a mental note of the rest of your body: breasts, upper arms, forearms, waist, stomach, hips, buttocks, thighs, calves, ankles, the length of your legs. Decide which are the most attractive features and which need camouflage.

Do you pass the pencil test? If your breasts are firm and high and will not hold a pencil beneath the bottom folds, you will look attractive in clothes without a brassiere. *Always wear a brassiere however while participating in active sports.*

If you have cellulite, diet and exercise will be beneficial, but in the meantime vow, *never to wear close fitting pants, particularly polyester which reveals cellulite right through the fabric!*

It is helpful to know if you are short-waisted, average, or long-waisted because this directly affects the way clothes fit. Turn your back to mirror. Visually note difference from waist to bottom of buttocks. If it looks *longer* than distance from waist to armpits, you are *short-waisted*. If the distance from waist to bottom looks *shorter,* you are *long-waisted*. If there is little visual difference you are *aver-*

age. If you are short-waisted, you probably have long legs. Long waisted people generally have shorter legs.

If what you see in the mirror displeases you, and if your measurements vary radically from the "ideal" do not be concerned, you are in the majority. Few women like the reflection they see, and high fashion photographic, showroom and runway models seldom measure up. Many have elongated bodies with narrow, sloping shoulders; infinitesimal bosoms; bony hips; flat rears and stringy arms and legs.

Thank goodness *our* success does not depend on our bodies!

HEMLINES AND BODY SHAPES

When the first edition of "I HAVEN'T A THING TO WEAR!" was published in 1968, I wrote . . . "It is never the length of the hemline one should be concerned with, but the total look one wishes to achieve, coupled with the length of one's leg." This was just prior to the miniskirt craze. How I hated to see miniskirts on "maximums!" Hemlines depend on body shape, legs, ankles, feet and shoes. Too long a skirt shortens a person. Too short a skirt makes a tall woman stilt-like. While current fashion is important, the key word concerning hemlines and fashion trends is *compromise.* Modify hemlines to suit your shape and still convey a sense of style.

To determine the best hemline for you, take the mirror test. While in front of the mirror observing your figure, drape a large towel, sheet, or length of fabric around your body. Tie or pin ends around neck. Put a belt on to hold drape in place. Choose three pair of shoes with varying heel heights and styles. Put each pair on and adjust drape to create a hemline which looks best with each heel height, *and the length of your lower leg.* This should be where you wear hemlines.

Those with specific problems such as knock-knees, fleshy knees or bowlegs, should wear hemlines longer. One of my relatives has badly bowed legs, and wears longer skirts, no matter what the current style. She seldom wears straight skirts, preferring the more flattering A-line and softly gathered dirndl-types. She is tall enough to carry the longer, fuller look. If she were shorter and heavier, her skirts could not be worn as long, despite the bowed legs. My admiration for her was boundless during the miniskirt era. She refused to wear skirts above the knee and she looked elegant while many others looked sadly out of place in miniskirts.

PROPER FIT AND BODY SHAPES

The way clothes fit is as important as color, texture, line and design. Clothes which fit handsomely, laying smoothly and neatly on the body, lend a look of quality. Well fitting, inexpensive clothes are more attractive than costly designs which droop. Many enjoy wearing casual clothes which wrinkle, slope, cinch, sag and bag, thinking it expresses a devil-may-care-attitude, but the effect more often is one of carelessness rather than chic.

Good fitting clothes are essential to a well turned out look, and for the less than perfect, unproportioned person, fit is *paramount!* Do not compromise on anything less than perfect fit.

If you are one of the 50 percent of women who require alterations, include this cost when planning purchases. If the outfit you like is too tight, buy the next size larger and have it fitted *down.* Opening seams on too-tight clothes places stress on fabrics and shortens wear. Needle and stitching marks show on certain fabrics and seams can split at inopportune times. In fitting down larger sizes, make sure shoulders fit.

Before you leave a dressing room with your new clothes, do FIT-TING ROOM CALISTHENICS. It prevents costly mistakes.

Swing arms wide. Lift arms overhead. See how the garment rides. Fold arms across chest. Look at *back* of outfit. If it shows every line of your bra, the top is too tight. Most importantly, *SIT DOWN* in the outfit, before you buy it. Many dressing rooms have chairs; if there are none, ask for one. Observe the look while seated and make sure fit is comfortable and not too tight.

Sandy Sprung, whose weight loss is the subject of "CANDY, CHOCOLATE, ICE CREAM 'N HOW TO LICK 'EM!" (Tandem Press, 1973), a book we co-authored, would treat herself at various plateaus to new outfits. She reached a size at which she felt attractive in a pants suit. A boutique near her Greenwich Village apartment featured a stunning grey silk pant suit in the window. Sandy bought it. The pants were tight, but she rationalized that since she planned to lose more weight, they would fit eventually and until then, the long tunic blouse was effective camouflage.

I was not with her when she bought the outfit, but I accompanied her to the party at which she first wore it. All of our friends complimented Sandy on her slimmer self and the lovely ensemble. After a while, giddy from the admiration and the drinks, Sandy plopped down on the sofa and everyone in the room heard the pants explode!

THE BODY SHAPES (sketch 1)

Physiologically, body types have been categorized into three shapes:

MESOMORPH—the classic, athletic figure with wide shoulders, broad chest, narrow hips, muscular arms and legs. Most mesomorphs are aggressive, competitive and domineering. Often they are champion athletes, enjoy physical exercise and action. They are adventurous and play to win.

ENDOMORPH—stocky, round body with short thick neck; short plump arms and legs. Most endomorphs are overweight with easy going, placid dispositions, and their reactions are generally slower.

ECTOMORPH—The figure extolled by high fashion; tall, thin, narrow angular body; slender arms, legs; long, stringy muscles. The true ectomorph is sensitive, tense and can be neurotic. Mentally they are alert, intelligent and generally are in the best health of the three body types.

Since there are many variables to these three basic body shapes and many have multiple characteristics of all three, I have formulated a group of six figure types which I have culled from observing thousands of women at my shows.

> *BIG AND BOUNTIFUL*
> *PETITE*
> *UMBRELLA*
> *KEEL-HEAVY*
> *TALL AND THIN*
> *LITTLE ORPHAN AVERAGE*   (sketch 2)

Amongst these six groups are those who are under 5′3″ and over 5′6″; short-waisted, long-waisted, small-waisted, thick-waisted. Those with heavy thighs, hips, buttocks; fleshy knees, thick ankles, bowed legs; short necks, long necks; sloping shoulders, narrow

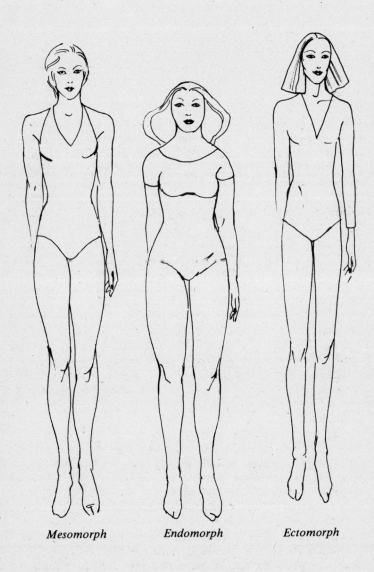

Mesomorph   *Endomorph*   *Ectomorph*

shoulders; skinny arms, heavy arms . . . and cellulite. *No matter, it is when we recognize our liabilities that we make assests of ourselves.*

A number of the suggestions listed for the various body shapes may seem to be repetitive, and in some instances, contradictory. This is because the advice on what to avoid, and what to choose relates to more than one body shape. Excessive contrasts in color, texture, line and design are as difficult to wear for one woman of a particular size and shape as another. There are infinite variables both in body shapes, and in design which relate to all.

To successfully camouflage an unproportioned figure requires a subtle touch and a sense of balance in choosing color, texture, line and design. One must create a harmonic symmetry with proportion and composition. The categories which follow lists ideas not only for the six figure shapes, but for specific parts of the face and body. Since these are generalizations meant for the majority, individual likes, dislikes and experiences with clothes and accessories will create exceptions to what is advised.

Do not be concerned. You either know your body better than anyone or you are preparing to do so with this book. Since your comfort and ease with clothes is what is most important, a compromise must be struck between what is suggested, what you enjoy and what you are used to wearing. If I have recommended avoiding items for your figure type that you wear and are comfortable with, reconsider them in the full length mirror. On the other hand if I have listed as a "good choice" an item which is anathema to you, why not give it a try? All you have to lose is the same old image!

BIG AND BOUNTIFUL

You were born either with a great many fat cells or you are a truly sensuous woman, enjoying every delicious dish you eat. If you would rather not diet, don't despair, *you can look beautiful* and many men prefer big, bountiful, loving women. Fashion would rather you disappeared, and it does little to help you. High fashion designers do not allow their clothes to be shown on heavier women and most also limit their dress sizes. Others however, are creating good designs which enhance the big and bountiful person. These clothes can be found in better specialty shops catering exclusively to the larger woman, or in special sections of better quality department stores.

Sketch 2

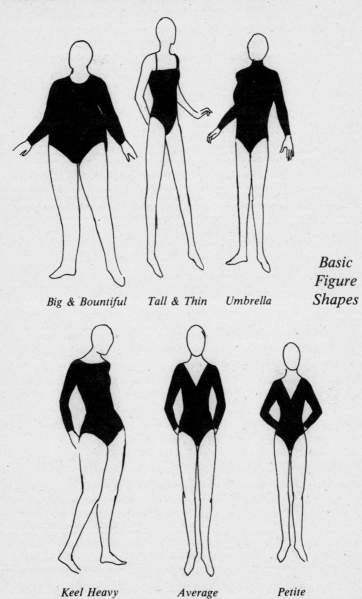

Big & Bountiful   Tall & Thin   Umbrella

Basic
Figure
Shapes

Keel Heavy   Average   Petite

17

AVOID: Anything tight! Nothing makes a woman look heavier than a garment which hugs! Beware of tight fitting sheaths and skirts which hug the hip and tuck in under buttocks. Too-tight pants which show cellulite. Vivid colors which screech, "Look how BIG I am!" Two-tone colors which cut your figure in half. Other choices which must be carefully considered are: bold plaids, patterns and horizontal lines which pattern you big. Heavy, bulky fabrics, body clinging knits, too-full skirts, big flares, boxy pleats and pockets, if not carefull proportioned will make you look heavier.

Be wary also of short, boxy, double-breasted jackets and wide lapels, (especially if you have an ample bosom) capes, flounces, showy belts, tucked-in shirts, sleeveless blouses and dresses. Dolman and full, deep-cut armholes can also be overwhelming. Do not be seen with long-haired furs except at the end of a leash! And . . . no Bermuda or short shorts unless you come equipped with a rear view mirror!

CHOOSE: Soft, flowing, fluid lines such as A-lines; eased or bias cuts; softly gathered, gored lines; knife-edge pleats. Slender, set-in sleeves in elbow or long lengths. Muted pretty colors as well as dramatic dark tones. The big woman need not limit herself to dark colors.

Large women can wear bright and bouncy colors *providing the texture of the fabric is understated and subdued.* For example, if you choose a beaded, sequined or patterned evening dress, avoid *HOT-PINK!* You could wear a beaded, sequined or patterned dress in dusky tones of grey, rose, blue, green or brown. To contrast colors, choose soft tones and wear them close to the face where they cast loving light and shadows. Do not contrast colors on waist and hips.

Flatly woven fabrics such as gabardines, fine wool, cotton and silk are flattering; as are flat furs such as broadtail, karacul, and persian lamb. Narrow belts will narrow the look. If you wear a skirt and blouse or a two-tone colored dress with belt, make the belt the color of the blouse rather than the skirt.

Long sleeves are kinder to heavy arms, and chiffon sleeves are an attractive accent for evening. Suit jackets should be below the hip; semi-fitted or slightly loose fitting. A single center vent at the back of a jacket is more slenderizing than side vents, which make hips look larger.

Accessories for the big and bountiful person should be scaled to size, with quality far more important than quantity. Slender people can wear outrageous, showy accents, but the big person needs elegant understatement. Select the *best* you can afford in jewelry, scarves, shoes, handbags, hats and belts.

AVOID: Round looks at the throat; choker type necklaces; Peter Pan collars; flouncy scarves; jewel necklines; small, round hats; scarves tied babushka style; tiny handbags or anything scaled too small for your size. If hands and arms are chubby, forego chunky bracelets. Compromise with accessories that are not too big, too small, too bright, too bold, too colorful.

CHOOSE: V- or U-shaped necklines; narrow, shawl type collars and lapels; jewelry and scarves in long lengths which elongate and slenderize. Hats of sufficient width and height to balance your overall shape. Nothing looks sillier on a big woman than a little pot sitting on top of her head! When choosing a hat, always make sure to look at yourself in a full length mirror. Most millinery departments have only table top mirrors. Take the hat and walk over to a full length mirror and check the balance and harmony of the line.

Clothes fitted for the big and bountiful woman should be eased: not too loose, not too tight. No need for a larger person to walk around in a tent. She can look handsome, elegant and feel attractive in well fitted suits, dresses, skirts, blouses and pants.

Big, bountiful people have to be careful of excessive contrast. For example, a large woman might have slender legs and beautiful, small feet, but if she chooses very high fashion shoes with spindly heels to highlight these lovely features, the contrast is too great, calling attention to the incongruity of her size. Compromise is kinder and she should choose a smart, classic pump or sandal shoe of excellent quality with a handsome heel; rather than a cloddy, "sensible" shoe or an ultra-high fashion spike. A slit skirt would be another way in which to call attention to lovely legs and pretty feet.

PETITE

The colors, shapes and designs which the small-boned person should avoid almost duplicates the list for the heavy woman, for scale and size are of utmost importance to both. Proportion and balance compliments the softer, rounder lines of a heavy figure, as well as the delicate stature of a petite person.

AVOID: Bright, contrasting colors and two-tone color combinations that slice you short. Wide belts, fully gathered skirts, horizontal patterns, huge prints; heavy, bulky fabrics, boxy jackets, shaggy coats and furs. Large handbags, giant-sized jewelry, big hats, hairdoes will overwhelm you; as will layering, *unless carefully coordinated with small-scaled items.* No cluttering scarves, bows or ruffles at the neckline.

CHOOSE: Fitted fashions, detailed delicately. Empire waistlines, princess lines, high necklines, light colors. Boleros, vests, toreador jackets, matador pants. Slim-legged pants lend a lengthening line. Wear short jackets to make your legs look longer. Match shoes and hats to draw the eye to your entire length. Uncluttered clothes and accessories, scaled small will make you look neat, trim and taller. Complement rather than conceal your fragile, feminine beauty with overpowering fashions.

Hemlines for the small woman should not be too short or too long. Balance and proportion is important. If leg is long from knee to ankle, the hemline can be longer. Most petite women look better in higher heeled, slenderly cut, strapless type shoes. Avoid clunky shoes and fancy, patterned hose which draw the eye down.

TALL AND THIN

In my happiest fantasy I awaken 5'10" tall, weighing 125 pounds, having just won the millionaire lottery! One is as unlikely as the other, but it is fun fantasizing.

My son Jonathan made his fantasy come true! He was determined to be tall and thin. The men in our family are of medium height, but Jonathan wanted to tower over his older brother, Jeff. As a baby Jonathan was round, ruddy, raucous. Later, as a small boy he was short, stocky and mischievous. He hung from a chinning bar, stretching, stretching, stretching. At school he took up wrestling. Suddenly and no one really remembers when, he was 6' 3" tall, weighing 160 pounds! His brother who was born lean and long is just 6 feet tall.

The tall, thin woman can wear almost everything in fashion, but even she must be selective, for neither is she perfectly proportioned. Her posture *MUST BE EXCELLENT!* A tall person who slouches accentuates her height and destroys the line of her clothes. Be proud of towering beauty and carry it gracefully!

AVOID: Slinky, clinging clothes; short, skimpy hemlines; pencil slim, unbroken one-color lines. Unbelted, tubular shapes; empire waistlines: lean coats; dark, somber colors; all make your angles acute!

CHOOSE: Lines that swing; fabrics that float, such as chiffons, gauzes, voiles; woolens with weight, in tweeds, mohair and bulky weaves; velvets; textures; all tailor the tall, thin lady more seductively. Plaids, prints, pockets, pleats, peplums; wear them plentifully and proudly. Belts, buckles, boots, bags; big accents add contour to an otherwise skinny shape. Scarves, bows, blousons fill you out. All colors, bright, blending or contrasting, are yours to enjoy. Black out black unless dramatized with contrast, either soft or vivid. Revel in all the rounded looks; layering; fabric upon fabric; line on line; the *new,* the *untried,* the *OUTRAGEOUS* that no one wears as well as you!

While tall, thin women have few problems with clothes, fitting is essential. Many have small hips and rears, and pants can look baggy. Eliminate extra fabric in the seat of trousers so they fit smoothly. Skirts are more flattering to a very thin woman than pants, because they lend a softer, more feminine line. Two-piece ensembles are also lovely, because they camouflage a flat rear better than a one-piece dress. This is especially true if the outfit is a knit. If pants are your passion however, wear them with flowing, loosely fitted tops.

UMBRELLA-SHAPE

Insisting on the very best fit in brassieres and being careful in choice of clothes, reproportions those who are full-bosomed. Generally short-waisted, with slimmer hips and thighs, the umbrella-shaped person looks best in subdued color with little accent above the waist.

AVOID: Tight tops and sheer or clinging fabrics which show bralines as well as round, square, cowl necklines and turtlenecks; princess and empire line dresses; frills, flounces, bows, and jewelry at the throat; pockets; tabs; embroidered or shirred blouses; dolman, puffy or full sleeves; double-breasted jackets; light-colored tops; tucked-in shirts; sweaters (unless they are cardigans worn open), wide belts, buckles, cinched waist-lines; horizontal stripes, bulky fabrics and layering.

CHOOSE: V-necklines, muted colors close to the face; small collars; darker tops over pants or skirts; longer, loosely structured, open jackets; unadorned bodices and dresses which move softly and gracefully. If you wear jewelry or scarves, select longer lengths.

Most large bosomed women require special fitting. Their tops need to be let out, and skirts taken in. Separates offer an easier solution than one-piece dresses. Since so many attractive choices are available in both casual and dressy separates, the umbrella shaped person can be easily suited.

KEEL-HEAVY

Most American women are smaller on top than at bottom, and again balance reproportions for an attractive look.

AVOID: Anything that cuts at the waist, accenting hips and bottom such as dark tops with light pants, or skirts. Short jackets; wide belts; fully gathered skirts; pleats; large patterns; bold plaids; princess lines; all widen hips. Forego clinging jersey, bulky wools, shiny taffetas, brocades, velvets or wide-wale corduroy below the waist. No back pockets, stitching or other accents either. And please, NO SHORTS, unless your legs are good and you wear a longer, loose flowing top.

CHOOSE: Smaller patterns in angular designs rather than circular, gored skirts, eased A-lines; empire lines; full cut, loose, unfitted clothes; gently gathered skirts; vests worn open, mid-length jackets if you are short (under 5'3") and longer jackets if you are taller; tunic tops; narrow belts worn loosely; all are flattering. Do not accent an hour-glass figure with a tightly drawn belt; it only emphasizes hips and bottom.

PANTS SUITS can be worn by heavy hipped women! If worn with a loose jacket, with another layer under the jacket or a tunic top, the pant suit will conceal big hips and rear end. Matching a hat to the blouse or combining color in hat and handbag, and keeping accessories coordinated to the top of the outfit, lift the eye away from hips and bottom.

Shoulder fit on small-busted, heavy-hipped women is important and separates are more functional and versatile. Most small-busted women have attractive shoulders; therefore accent this feature with shirring, yokes, tucking, smocking, gathers, embroidery, pockets, and tabs. These are all lovely details which lift the eye off hips and bottoms.

LITTLE ORPHAN AVERAGE

You would think the average sized woman, somewhere between 5'4" and 5'7" with proportions which present no particular problems would not be puzzled about what to wear. Not so. She can be more often typical than topical unless she skillfully establishes a unique fashion image. Since she can wear almost anything, her fashion identity could become confusing unless she ignites an individual look with creative coordinating.

Average sized women of moderate proportions have figure problems. For example, I am somewhat average size, but I have a thick waist and round stomach which makes me seem more short waisted than my measurements show. I try not to change color at the waist and I gave up my belts two inches ago. On the rare occasion when I wear a belt I push it below my natural waistline. I prefer overblouses and shirts atop skirts and pants, but sometimes there is the special shirt which looks best when tucked in. I then add a belt either the same color, or a color which blends softly with the shirt and hike the top up a bit to camouflage my waist. Sometimes I add a third layer shirt wearing it open so that the belt is seen only from the front. If I were small busted, I could wear a vest as the third layer, but my bra size precludes this. I match belts to my tops rather than to skirts or pants because it helps to slenderize the look of my waistline.

Additional variables in physical characteristics affect clothing choices. To narrow it down even more, the following offers specific guidelines.

Face and neck are to be considered in tandem when selecting line and color. One might have a round, squat face and a long neck; a strong jawline or a receding chin. Others a long, angular face and a short neck. Women with round faces should avoid necklines which emphasize that roundness such as the jewel, scoop or boat neck. V and square necklines are better. Women with angular, long faces should avoid V-necklines and severe colors. Square jawed women look best in necklines which add length such as the V, the square, the scoop. Women with thin faces look better in cowls, scoops, turtlenecks and bateau necklines.

ROUND FACE AND SHORT NECK

Lengthen the line with V-necklines and open collars. If bust is small, open shirt. You might be able to wear a scoop neckline if your neck is not heavy and you are slender overall. Avoid turtlenecks, high collars, jewel and Peter Pan collars; round-necked T-shirts; choker type jewelry, big earrings, full scarves and other full, round details. Forego flouncey, fancy hairdoes which frame the face. Hair is better brushed away and up from the neck. If you have a double chin, wear long jewelry accents or scarves tied low. Keep knot in scarf or pendant on jewelry below bustline.

ANGULAR FACE AND LONG NECK

Like the lucky person with a tall, thin figure, the woman with a long, swanlike neck can wear beautiful accents at the throat. Her only limitation is the shape of her face when choosing extreme lines. If she has a medium or roundish face, she can enhance a long neck with deep plunging V-necklines in soft, floating fabrics. If her face is narrow and angular, she would be better off in higher collars, ruffles, soft, rounded scarves. Most long-necked women look smashing in boat-necks, turtlenecks, cowl, mandarin and button-down collars. Exotic evening necklines are good unless one's shoulders are too broad, too narrow or sloping. Try one-shoulder dresses, halters and strapless tops. Hair is better worn longer and fuller. If choosing a severe, "small head" style, consider the shape of your face. Too long a face, or a heavy jaw requires soft hair accents.

SHOULDERS

Broad shoulders: avoid cape, dolman and puffy sleeves, padded shoulders, sleeveless dresses as well as bateau necklines and wide, horizontal designs. The look is softer if you narrow shoulders by illusion. Choose a smaller top or have the garment fitted so that the shoulder seam sits *inside* your true shoulder line. Soft fabric tops are kinder than stiff, ungiving materials which make shoulders look massive. Beware of square looks.

Narrow or sloping shoulders: Avoid raglan, and dolman sleeves; sleeveless and halter tops. You need the softness of set-in sleeves that have fullness such as puffs or gathers. Another good choice is cap sleeves. Turtlenecks, large coats and jackets, bulky fabrics and fully-cut big tops overpower narrow shoulders. Instead, wear small collars, boat necklines, padded shoulders. To create the illusion of a wider shoulder look, have the seam sit *outside* your shoulder line.

BOSOMS

Large or small bosomed women do not have insurmountable problems in choosing clothes because good brassiere construction solves most faults. Psychologically if your breasts are too much, or too little for you, consult a qualified and well-recommended plastic surgeon. There is no reason to be unhappy or uncomfortable. What you haven't got, you can get, and in this wonderful day and age, why not? If you do not have the desire or the means to surgically change your body, wear good fitting brassieres and have them custom made if necessary. Do not skimp on the cost. Find an experienced fitter and value her expertise. *The no-bra look is only for those who can pass the pencil test,* and even then not wearing a bra over a period of time — especially while running, jogging or participating in any sport — is unwise, because bosoms slacken sooner without needed support.

Natural, unseamed cups are more flattering than bras which give a super pointed look and are pulled too tightly.

If you are large bosomed, avoid tight tops (especially knits); clinging fabrics, wide belts, princess lines, pockets and other details on blouses and dress tops; puffy and dolman sleeves. You will look smaller in anything loose on top: V-necklines, open collars, blouses in soft fabrics such as silk.

Those who are tiny on top are wise to reject anything which reveals how flat chested they are. Avoid tight clinging knits and T-shirts. Choose instead full, loose, easy flowing tops in pretty prints and colors accented with shirring, yokes, smocking, gathers, tucks, embroidery and pockets. If you wear a padded bra make it *subtle.*

ARMS

Heavy or too-thin arms are best camouflaged with loose fitting sleeves. For both, the sleeveless look is unattractive, and tight fitting sleeves in clinging fabrics also underscore skinny or too-heavy arms. Choose instead, coverage in soft, sheer materials. Long sleeves; elbow length sleeves with bottoms turned up in casual folds, are attractive alternatives. Consider shoulders as well as arms when selecting garments with sleeves.

WAISTLINES

The uncorseted body is the most comfortable and how delightful that waists need not be cinched to Scarlett O'Hara's legendary 18 inch circlet. The natural look is acceptable, yet few women are satisfied with their waistlines. Since waistlines reveal weight gains and losses most readily, they are the easiest to control with diet and exercise. If you choose not to discipline yourself and you are content with your body, yet unhappy about your waistline, use contour to camouflage. Some waistline problems have nothing to do with weight. Those are: thick waists in proportion to the rest of your body; too small a waist in the hour-glass figure; the short-waisted; the long-waisted.

The thick- or short-waisted do best to avoid wide belts; wide waistbands; waist wraps; dirndl and fully gathered skirts. Short, fitted jackets; hip-hugger pants; two-tone or bright color combinations that break at the waist also accentuate girth.

Better choices are: overblouses; unbelted tunics; blouson style dresses, blouses and sportswear; loose jackets and jackets worn open. Two-color dressing is fine, if the colors are muted and blend softly. Vests and empire lines can be attractive if one has a small bosom. Wearing narrow belts the color of the top rather than the skirt or pants is also good camouflage.

Lucky, lucky is the long-waisted woman. Even if her waist is less than slender she looks slim. If she is truly reed-like she can wear wonderful wide accents. Separates and layered clothes look sensational on her as well. The one look she must beware of is a long, lean unbroken line in a tight fitting, knitted top.

STOMACHS

How well I know the problem of a round, protruding stomach! When I was ten I went to live with my Aunt Helen. My grandmother who had cared for me died, and my mother needed time to readjust. I was stringy and skinny. My aunt called me "Bean." Aunt Helen was a working woman, and to save time she would bathe my cousin June, then eight, and me together. One particular night as I stepped out of the tub Aunt Helen exclaimed, "My word, Bean, just look at that little pot, it's the only part of you that's round." We all laughed and I patted the "little pot." I thought it a mark of distinction, something June did not have.

How that pot has plagued me all my life! As I grew older and began to observe the bodies on other girls, I realized it was unnatural, particularly since I was athletic and exercised regularly. When I lose weight it becomes smaller, but my stomach has never been flat. It was not until I met Dr. Ralph Shaw of Hahnemann Hospital in Philadelphia, a leading expert in metabolic disorders, that I learned people who eat too much sugar and not enough protein develop pot-like stomachs and thick middles as part of the hyperinsulinism syndrome. drome.

My diet as a child undoubtedly contributed to this figure fault. My eating was unsupervised. My mother was at work, my grandmother too ill and unknowing to guide me. I ate what tasted best; what I could grab quickly; sugared foods, candy, cake, ice cream. It was only later when my interest in nutrition was sparked by working for Dr. Robert Anderson, one of the early nutritionists, that I realized how badly balanced my adolescent diet had been. Today I eat little sugar, salt or processed foods. On tour, however, I fly with a Hershey bar, because if the plane goes down, I do not want to die dieting!

To camouflage my round stomach I wear A-lines, eased and gored skirts as well as some skirts with sewn down pleats or stitching. If the stitching or pleat is short, it will not draw in under my stomach, accenting its roundness. Bias cuts are good for me as are side details, and side zippers. I prefer flat fabrics such as gabarines and fine wools. I avoid bulky, nubby materials, fully gathered skirts, wide belts, fly front and pleated pants. Sometimes I hike a dress up a bit with a narrow belt and blouse it, easing tightness over the stomach.

HIPS

Since hips can present a problem in all figure shapes, following is a quick and easy recap. If you are heavy hipped, avoid; tight, straight skirts and pants; fully gathered skirts and dirndls; pleated pants, horizontal stripes, brassy colors, clinging fabrics, front or rear patch pockets, back zippers, tucked-in shirts.

If you have a small waistline in relation to hip size do not cinch it with a tight, wide belt; choose a narrow, looser belt. The small waist is attractive, but you sacrifice the elegance a subdued, well proportioned look offers by blatantly highlighting an hour-glass figure. Your proportions are better in eased A-lines, lightly gathered skirts and pants suits, *provided the pants suit is worn with a loose fitting overblouse, tunic or jacket.*

My aunt Lil has instinctive good taste. She is less than five feet, three inches tall with an ample waistline and hips. She dislikes skirts and when wearing a suit, wears *only* pants. Skirts cut her in half, pants lengthen the line. The proportion of a jacket and skirt on a heavy hipped, short woman is delicate, with both the hemline of the skirt and that of the jacket to be considered. It is so subtle and so variable with each individual that mistakes in proportion can easily be made. Wearing pants solves this problem because of the overall linear look. But keep the jacket, tunic or vest on; otherwise the lengthening, slenderizing effect is gone.

Scarves, jewelry and color above the waist brings the eye up off the hips, as will monotone outfits and dark colored bottoms. Whatever you wear on the hips, it is best loose, unfitted. Check hemline diameter in a full length mirror when buying new clothes. See if it is in proportion to your hips. Narrow, skimpy hemlines accentuate the size of large hipped women.

If thighs and buttocks are heavy the same advice applies, with one additional caution: *Do not wear tight legged pants, or pants so tight in the buttocks that every indentation shows.* Buy larger size pants to accomodate heavy thighs and have them fitted *down.*

SHORT LEGS

Women under 5'3" and woman of average height who have short legs should keep lines longs, unbroken, using linear accents in both textures and color. Long sleeves, medium width belts, fitted jackets, short-hair furs, knife-edge pleated skirts worn over slim boots, pants worn over instep, vertical stripes; all lend a leaner, longer line from head to toe. Forego anything that brings the eye down such as a low-riding belt, pegged pants, horizontal stripes, hip-huggers, pedal pushers.

Being aware of your body makes you the best judge of what is most attractive and suitable for you. If you are uncertain about a particular line, a particular design, confide in someone you trust. Do *not* ask the salesperson trying to sell you the item, unless you know her well and your relationship is one of long standing.

Knowing your body breeds confidence. You will make the right decision! You need not be a slave to fashion's dictates. Set your own style. Create your own trends. Wear what you choose, when! If high fashion is very important to you and you enjoy adopting each new look as it hits the market, and you have the money to do so, it may be necessary for you to modify trendy new lines to suit your shape. Why not? Clever compromises often work better than total compliance.

Contouring and camouflage should be used only to compliment and flatter the *physical you.* It should not intrude on your personality, which enhances and strengthens *any* look you choose. Certainly the ensemble which pleases you most will spark your personality, creating facets which will bounce, sparkle and make you feel terrific!

The more sensational you feel, the more confident you become.

Suddenly you begin a new adventure, choosing clothes in designs, in colors, in textures you never thought you would wear. As simple a concept as COLOR, which we discuss next, takes on new meaning as you recognize how color compliments complexions, enhances moods and lends softness or clarity to body shapes. Suddenly you begin to use the full spectrum of color to cloak yourself in sensuality and you experiment more and more with color, shape and coordination, using clothes as canvases on which to imprint new personalities. Dressing now becomes a wonderfully creative experience, nourishing your psyche, and a well fed psyche improves anyone's look . . . no matter what the shape!

3

Color . . .
At No Cost!

"When you're pooped, wear pink" may sound frivolous, but it works! The entire range of pinks, from appealing pale pinks to rosy, healthy looking raspberry pinks, and sophisticated muted mauves, cast a warm glow, adding radiance to your face, making you look and feel lovelier.

Using color in clothes and makeup to create special effects is being fashion smart, for color creates mood, contour, composition and contrast. Color costs nothing extra and the right color can make the difference between success or failure, as color can jolt as well as tranquilize and knowing what to wear when and how is important. A good friend, a budding sales executive, came to me angry and frustrated. Her colorful, too-vivid appearance intimidated her supeior, a man unused to working with an attractive woman. On the other hand, as a young actress, I once lost a part because I looked too drab in the tailored grey suit I wore to the audition for the character they were casting.

Colors set the mood, the theme for any performance. On stage, color is carefully considered by directors. Many performers refuse to wear certain shades, insisting on special colors in clothes, special lighting and special backgrounds to compliment their natural coloring, their makeup and their body shapes.

When you set your own scene, the color in the clothes you are wearing, the makeup you are using and the lighting in which you will be seen, are integral parts of the overall fashion picture. Colors react differently in varying lights, and in varying seasons. Daylight, flourescents, incandescent lighting, muted evening lights, bright sunshine, winter, summer, fall, spring . . . all have special lighting effects which you can orchestrate for the roles you choose to play.

Become aware of the chemistry of color and what it does for the face and figure. Use color as the artist, the designer, to compliment, conceal, protect, exploit, excite, stimulate, de-tense. Combine color with color. Use one strong, intense color as a foundation and then accent with a contrasting or blending shade. Use neutrals, adding spicy color for cachet. Mute shades and shadows. Make Mondrian-like monochromatic effects. Play high color with high shine. Work color as a unit, a special effect, or as free wheeling contrast. Flash color like a kaleidescope. Create the excitement of sharp, graphic highlights. Try bi-color or tri-color dressing. Or just use the clean bareness of one color.

However you use it, your own coloring and shape sketch the best colors for you. Skin tones change from season to season and year to year. Few of us have the color we had at twenty. Even the color of eyes change subtly, becoming less bright as one matures. Hair colors change, so do body shapes. Being aware of these changes increases your sensitivity to the colors that do the most for you at different times in your life.

Colors should compliment the face and body as well as each other. Skin tones fall into three basic categories: light, medium, dark. Light skinned people look better in warm colors. Olive and dark skinned people look better in cooler colors. There is such great variation in skin tones and textures that even these simple rules do not apply in many instances.

To more accurately determine if the color compliments or washes you out, hold it up to your face. If you have pale skin, soft tones are more flattering. The darker your complexion, the stronger the color can be. If you have complexion problems, avoid vivid colors and strong patterns. Keep colors soft, patterns small, and textures smooth. Coordinate color with your natural coloring, with cosmetics, and the color of your hair. The more you experiment with color, the sharper your instincts become. Soon you begin to recognize and use the colors best for you.

The colors most basic for year round wear are: BLACK, WHITE, BROWN, BEIGE, BURGUNDY, MAHOGANY, GREY and NAVY BLUE.

BLACK is timelessly elegant and possesses beautiful fashion qualities. Black absorbs light rays and flatters the figure by diffusing bulk. It also drains color from the face, especially past forty, accentuating lines and wrinkles. Even though George Bernard Shaw gallantly stated to an aging Eleanora Duse that her face "bore the credentials of her humanity" there is no need to shout, "I HAVE LIVED" by wearing black, unadorned, close to the face.

Liven and lighten black with white, pastels or vivid colors in solids, prints and patterns. Wear the sharp contrast of black with white for a strong, dramatic look. Black as an accent on summer white is smashing! It is the most versatile color combination and makes an impression in any season, anywhere! Black with brown is beautiful, but beware if you are sallow-skinned, or at-the-moment-under-the-weather. Dark-toned color combinations are drab unless you have high color and good bones.

WHITE is the kindest color in the fashion spectrum, lending a shimmering quality to the face which softens the inevitable down-strokes of gravity. White reflects light rays and is cooler and more comfortable in warm climates, giving a crisp, clean freshness to the look. It also rounds out body shapes. To wear white overall, one need be fairly slender, but white worn as an accent is flattering to heavier women. If you are heavy-hipped, but smaller on top, wear loose-fitting white blouses, shirts and jackets. If you are smaller in the hip, but buxom on top, wear dark overblouses with white skirts or pants. As you ripen (you don't age, merely ripen, and the trick is not to look overripe) wear white as an accent close to the face: white shirts, blouses, collars, scarves, jewelry.

White can be worn in any season. If white in winter throws you off, think of being wrapped in ermine!

BROWN offers many creative possibilities. Warm and subtle, it combines beautifully with lighter shades and with pastels. Brown is an excellent counterpoint for prints and bright colored accessories. While black or brown are the easiest and most basic colors to accessorize, in coats they may not be the best, because shoe and handbag colors are limited. Dusky tones of taupe, wine, russet, blue, green and soft, multi-color tweeds are better choices for coats, allowing more varied and interesting interplay of colors in accessories.

BEIGE and CAMEL TONES are as versatile as black or white, and as warm and subtle as brown. A marvelous canvas color on which to splash others, beige tones can be worn in any season.

BURGUNDY and MAHOGANY are rich, interesting colors which lend punch and contrast to clothes. They are excellent colors for shoes, handbags and belts because they blend handsomely with other colors.

GREY is as changeable as *gray,* and its many variations afford muted tones from morning to midnight. A cold color, grey can look dismal unless accessorized deftly. Grey close to the face, like black, is too severe when the bloom is off the rose.

NAVY BLUE is brighter and more flattering to the face than black or grey, and kinder to the figure than white or beige. In its innumerable tones, navy blue is a great basic color for savvy accessorizing.

For warmer, brighter looks: try taupes, russets, plums, wines, medium blues, and shaded greens as basic colors. Fun to accessorize and flattering to the face and figure, these richer shades broaden your color image and offer a unique, unusual touch to an everyday wardrobe.

PARFAIT PASTELS such as lime, orange, lemon, raspberry, lavender, pale pinks and blues are perfectly lovely, provided you are figure perfect (well almost). If you are a dilettante dieter it might be best to use these colors as light, carefree accents rather than on the full shape.

CREAMY COLORS such as pink, mauve, beige, ivory and other muted pastels kindle a youthful glow, creating a feminine, fragile aura. Combining a pink, or pale aqua silk blouse with a grey or tweedy, tailored suit is an adroit touch for business.

BRIGHT, VIBRANT COLORS such as electric tones of red, orange, purple, yellow, blue and green are dynamic, strong, intense statements for special effects, as is silver worn as pure shine and gold as glitter. When buying electric colors, choose separates, because a supremely vivid, one-color outfit or a bi-color or tri-color dress can be easily outdated. Create your own kaleidescopes with solid color, bi-color or tri-color by using separates and layering with bold abandon.

I adore red and wear it often to heighten my color and my mood. My close friend and fellow ski instructor Anne suffered a nasty ligament tear when a student in her class barrelled into her. Anne is active, vivacious and a super tennis player and the weeks in a cast must have been wearing. When I visited, shortly after her release from the hospital, Anne was in a wheelchair wearing a bright red velour robe, her feet in shaggy red slippers and her cast decorated with greetings in red ink!

"Well Judith," she laughed, "you've always said, 'when you're blue, wear red!' "

Not only does red perk up your spirits, according to tests it also raises blood pressure and heart respiration rates. Grey on grey days is depressing and yellow and greens are a bad choice if you've had stomach trouble.

Combining colors with prints and patterns stimulates your untapped color talent for it challenges you to create unique, unexpected combinations. Highlight the colors in a print with accessories either in a coordinating solid color, or a blending second pattern. To bring new interest to an otherwise unchangeable pattern, either step down the color in the accessory by using a softer shade of the same color, or use a brighter tone to step it up.

For example: If you have a print dress containing black, brown, and beige, you could choose a solid color silk scarf in cinnamon and use gold jewelry. The next time around you might select a grey silk square and silver as the jewelry accent, or you could combine another pattern as the accent. If you choose a pattern, the *size, shape and texture* of that pattern is as important as the *colors.*

Combining prints and patterns with other prints and patterns requires skill, a good eye for balance and harmony, and good instincts. Work with solid colors first to strengthen your expertise and then experiment, keeping in mind that it is best to blend and contrast prints and patterns in the same tonal values. If you are using dark tones, then the accent print should be slightly lighter or slightly darker. If you are using a vivid color pattern, the accent pattern should be comparably bright.

To sharply contrast both pattern and tone is like skiing the High Rustler at Alta. You have to be *very sure* of your skills.

While the use of contemporary color bypasses old restrictions and transcends seasons, certain colors wear better in certain cities. Black is very fashionable in Latin countries and sophisticated northern cities, but less popular in Southern California, Hawaii, Florida and other warm climates where bright, sunny shades seem more at home.

Consider climate, ambience and purpose when choosing a personal palette; but feel free to experiment with all the lovely color options open to you. What works best for you is yours to enjoy! Your instincts and sensitivity for color, the mixing, matching, blending, and coordinating of it will sharpen the more you work with it. Color is the one commodity in fashion that costs nothing, so wrap yourself in radiance!

4

Classics . . .
As Time Resistant
As Chopin

If you want more from clothes, choose CLASSICS! If ease, versatility, economy and creativity are important to you, choose CLASSICS! Classics *work,* and they work simply because they offer a variety of options. When deftly accessorized, classics swing from trend to trend. They look chic and in step with style. Trendy things are fun, but following a trend too slavishly can trip you up. While today almost anything goes, do you feel attractive and comfortable in *anything?* No matter how much *"in"* a trend may be, if it is wrong for you, it should be *"out."*

CLASSICS assure you of versatility and value. Styles may change from one extreme to another, but CLASSICS provide a firm base on which to build a creative, always-on-the-ready wardrobe. With CLASSICS *you* are in *control,* for with a quick flip of a scarf, separates, a belt, jewelry and imagination, you can step into any hour of the day with style and éclat.

Fabric and color determines whether classics are casual, work-a-day or dressy. Buy the best fabrics you can afford for a wise fashion investment. Classic necklines are either jewel-type or V-shaped. Jewel-type necklines are the easiest to accessorize, their name signifying superb compatability with jewelry as well as with scarves, collars and other accents which frame the face lending softness, shape and color. V-shaped necklines are versatile and more flattering because they slenderize.

CLASSIC STYLE DRESSES   (sketch 3)

A-Line

Bias cut

Princess

Eased sheath

Sheath

Shirtwaist

CLASSIC STYLE SUITS AND SEPARATES   (sketch 4)

Box jacket, slim skirt

Blazer jacket, dirndl skirt

Fitted jacket, A-line skirt

Short jacket, pegged skirt

Silk shirt worn as belted jacket with skirt

Pant suit, straight leg trousers

Alternate jackets with skirts and dresses for a multitude of variations.

CLASSIC STYLE COATS   (sketch 5)

Polo coat

Trench coat

Single-breasted coat with notched collar

Double-breasted coat with notched collar

Princess coat with Peter Pan collar, full skirt

Collarless sweater coat

A very good classic coat makes you ready for any social encounter for it can be accessorized to look either casual or dressy. If you buy only one coat, choose a style which fits easily over suits. In cold, blustery climates, a coat with a large collar is more functional.

CLASSIC STYLE EVENING WEAR   (sketch 6)

Chiffon, Grecian style

One-shoulder sheath

Satin A-line with spaghetti straps and bias cut skirt

Silk shirt and full skirt separates

Classics in evening wear? By all means! Simple, elegant lines in beautiful fabrics are timeless.

CLASSIC STYLE TROUSERS   (sketch 7)

Side zipped pants, straight leg, no cuff

Fly-front pants, wider leg with cuff

Wider evening pants

Jeans

Comfortable, efficient and handsome, pants play an important role in the active person's wardrobe. As with other classics, fabric and color determine how and where pants fit into your life-style. Velvet or satin jeans offer a different dimension than denim. Finely tailored tweed trousers are terrific topside on the QE 2. Lissomely cut lame'evening pants are perfect for dinner by candlelight.

BUILDING A CLASSIC COLLECTION

If you have only unrelated, non-versatile, one-shot clothes in your closets, building a wardrobe of classics will require spending money, but in the long run, it is less costly, because classics enable you to coordinate and combine clothes more readily for social and business needs.

If you are a working woman on a tight budget, separates are your best buy. A winter and summer wardrobe will be needed even if you live in the sun belt, because in business it is necessary to wear clothes suitable for the season.

The following outlines an essential classic wardrobe. Translate the ideas for winter or summer by choice of fabrics and colors. Choosing transitional fabrics and colors enables you to wear some clothes year round. (See sketches 8 through 13)

These essential classics do not have to be purchased all at the same time. Buy conservatively. Since they are classic you can wait for out-of-season-sales. Add as you earn money. If you are a homemaker or student, you need less.

Women at home and at school dress more casually. They can easily get by with two skirts, two blouses, two sweaters and two short dresses. However, they need extra pants such as jeans.

To extend this wardrobe for summer, add classics in white or beige. Perhaps a white blazer, wrap skirt or trousers, a short voile dress in a summer print, or a strapless summer cotton which can double for evening when worn with a shawl. Two-piece cotton knits are wonderfully versatile and comfortable, affording numerous variations. Coordinate summer classics with the winter wardrobe using the blouses, shirts, sweaters, skirts and pants. If you cannot afford a summer coat, consider a taffeta or nylon raincoat in a bright color, when purchasing one of the two classic coats suggested.

As a young woman raising two sons, I could not afford expensive clothes, yet I needed to look well dressed in my job. I would add a good quality accessory to a simple dress or suit and the entire look was upgraded. I saved money on silk scarves by buying silk remnants in fabric stores and making my own. I browsed second hand stores for jewelry and other items. I scoured accessory departments during sales at fine shops such as Bergdorf's, Bendel's, Altman's and Sak's.

1 — Three short dresses of the softly structured type that can be worn from desk to dark. For example: a printed challis with a softly flared skirt; a solid color sheer wool sheath to be worn with a blazer and silk scarf; a free-flowing silk shirtwaist in a small print that is elegant and dressy, yet subdued enough for the office.

2 — Three skirts: two skirts either straight cut, bias cut or dirndl for daytime wear; one softly flared, full length skirt for evening.

3 — Two jackets of good-quality fabric and tailoring. Perhaps one velveteen blazer and one wool tweed. Lightweight wool can be worn year round. If you purchase a tweed suit with either a skirt or pants, or both, plus the velveteen blazer, you can wear the tweed jacket over winter skirts and the blazer for evening, both winter and summer.
4 — Three sweaters: V-neck, turtleneck, cowl or crew neck.

5 — Three blouses: two softly tailored blouses, one of which could be tunic style. Choose different necklines: bowed, drawstring, jewel-type or V-shaped. One filmy blouse for evening.

6 — Two shirts: trim, tailored, classic type shirts, solid color and patterned.

7 — One or two third layer accents such as a vest, jerkin, open, collarless jacket or cardigan sweater.

8 — Three pair pants: one wool to match jacket; another to accent jackets, a dressy pair for evening. Velveteen pants can be worn day or evening.

9 — Two coats: preferably one trench coat or polo coat in an all-weather fabric, plus a solid color, cloth coat. Each is suitable for casual daytimes or dressy evenings.

My particular ploy was to wear an expensive hat, which made my suit or dress look top notch.

Wearing quality touches close to the face focuses one's attention on your eyes and your personality. What you wear elsewhere becomes unimportant. Attractive accents near the face soften, add color and emphasize expressions.

Add elegance to an inexpensive blouse with a silk scarf; make a bargain dress look better with a simple piece of gold jewelry; camouflage a run-of-the-mill skirt with a well tailored jacket, and add élan to a low-cost coat with a smashing hat!

CLASSIC COLLECTIBLES

Accessories add variation and a personal touch to classics. These are discussed in detail in the chapters which follow, but listed herewith are suggestions on how to begin collecting classic essentials: scarves, belts, handbags, hats, shoes and hosiery. Brief mention is also given to hairdos, and makeup which are an integral part of a coordinated look.

BELTS: Ranging from simple ropes to leathers and metals which can cost hundreds of dollars, belts add proportion and interest to clothes. You can save money by making your own. Browse antique shops, garage sales and thrift shops for unusual and unique buckles. With an awl or hole punch, riveting tool and glue purchased in crafts supply shops, add leather, fabric or metal lengths to create your own belt designs. If this is inconvenient, take the length and buckle to the local shoe repair shop and they will stitch it for you at a reasonable cost.

Begin a belt wardrobe with:
1—A simple, small buckled leather belt ¾ to one inch wide in saddle, mahogany or cordovan. These colors blend best with most clothes.
2—A narrow chain or metallic belt for dress wear. Gold and silver metallic knits are most versatile.
3—A one inch white leather belt for summer.
4—A silk rope belt. Purchase it in the drapery department or trimming shop rather than in the belt section. It is less expensive and you

have a better choice of colors. Black is most versatile. Gunmetal, burgundy or bronze are other good choices.

Those who are long-waisted, or lean and long, wear wider belts handsomely, especially soft leather wraps in luscious colors which add new dimensions to dresses and pants.

HANDBAGS: Handbags are shoes no longer need be matched. Still a handsome look, it is not necessary. Handbags are more transitional now and can be blended with footwear for greater variation. Canvas, leathers and fabrics are fashionable year round.

The essential classics are:
1—Leather shoulder bag.
2—Leather pouch or clutch.
3—Fabric or beaded evening bag.

SHOES: While few women limit themselves to a simple shoe wardrobe, the soaring cost of leather shoes may make it necessary to buy less. The following assures that you will be well shod:
1—Medium heeled leather pumps to blend with skirts and pants. If you wear mainly tweeds and textures, choose grainy leather rather than smooth calfskin.
2—A pair of leather boots with a medium heel in a color which blends best with your suits and coat.
3—Closed toe, sling back shoes in suede or suede with a leather accent for desk to dark dresses.
4—Open toed, high heeled sandals for dressy daytime and evening needs.
5—Rainboots to protect shoes and feet in sloppy weather.

HOSIERY: Colors and textures in hosiery look best when they complement hemlines. For light colored chiffons, choose sheer hose in a natural shade. Textured, patterned hose is interesting with nubby tweeds. Too dark a color with a light outfit, or too light a tone with a dark ensemble jars the eye, focusing attention on the legs and disturbing the line. If legs are pale, select slightly darker shades. Tights and colorful patterns are fun when coordinated with sports clothes, and are functional in cold weather.

HATS: I am and always have been committed to hats, therefore I write this with cheerful bias. Hats are the ultimate accent! They turn a dress into an ensemble; a suit into a statement and a coat into a presence. There is an entire chapter devoted to hats in this book but every woman should have the following classics in her closet:

1—A small brimmed, medium crowned felt fedora in a color to blend with suits and coat, or a beret if under thirty-five.
2—A warm winter hat in wool; knitted wool; fur or fur felt. On cold days almost 65% of body heat is lost through the head. Wearing a winter hat not only adds chic to winter clothes, it keeps you healthy!
3—A medium or wide brimmed natural straw summer hat to protect the face from hot summer sun and add importance and style to casual summer clothes.

SCARVES: No classic wardrobe or accessory collection is complete without scarves. Since there is an extensively detailed "how-to" scarf chapter later on, the mention here is brief. If you do not wear scarves, begin now, because scarves more than any other accessory add diversity and distinction. Economical, no matter what their cost, scarves seldom wear out and are always in style.

Begin your collection with:
1—a 30" or 36" *silk square* in colors and patterns to blend or contrast with your wardrobe.
2—an *oblong silk* scarf in colors and patterns to *blend* with your classic collection.
3—a 24" *silk square,* either blending or contrasting.
4—A 48" or larger shawl in challis, or sheer wool.

   If you find it difficult to purchase 36" or larger squares make your own! You will save substantially by buying silk or sheer wool fabric and hand rolling the edges. One yard square of silk or sheer wool is far less costly than a manufactured scarf. Whenever you travel, be on the lookout for silks and wools in different textures and weights. You may find a perfect remnant from which to make a square or rectangular scarf. Handrolling edges is a pleasant sewing task and is ideal for evenings in front of TV or long, boring plane trips.

JEWELRY: While diamonds are desirable, in fashion it is *GOLD* which is a girl's best friend. A few, well chosen gold pieces upgrade an outfit pointing to a well turned out, polished woman. Gold blends beautifully with casual daytime clothes or after dark ensembles. Gold has more fashion status than silver and can be combined handsomely with pearls, jade, other precious stones, Venetian or antique glass beads.

Pearls are an important classic addition to any collection. They look lovely because pearls reflect light, creating an aura which flatters face and throat.

The classic jewelry essentials are:
Gold hoop or button earrings.
Gold chains in varying lengths and weights.
A gold pin or stick pin, plain or set with precious stones.
A gold ring set with precious stones.
A small gold watch
One or two pearl necklaces in varying lengths.
Pearl earrings.

THE FINISHING TOUCH for any wardrobe whether it be classic, eclectic, conservative, outrageous, custom-made or ready-to-wear is *YOU* . . . . your hair, makeup, hands, perfume and how they coordinate and complement the ensemble. Unkempt, straggly, out-of-date hairstyles destroy the effect. If your hair is unattractive and unmanageable like mine, wear a wig or a hat. If you are one of the lucky people whose hair can be arranged in a number of different styles, coordinate the styling with what you are wearing.

Makeup should blend in color and texture with the outfit. Heavy eye shadow and exotic cheeks are out of place in an office or sailing Nantucket Bay, nor would you want to look washed out and *au naturel* when dining by candlelight.

Highlight lovely hands and nails with colorful nail polish, rings, bracelets and other accents at the wrist such as ruffles, boa or trimming. If hands have aged (arthritis, liver spots, etc.) downplay them. Cash in rings and bracelets and wear polish in muted subtle tones.

PERFUME: The epilogue to any ensemble, perfume is such an individual choice, there can be few hard and fast rules. Not using perfume is neglecting a most indelible accent which evokes sensuality in the wearer and those around her. Many women are noted as much for their scent as their style.

It is not an absolute that one change perfume with a change of dress. Some change perfume when they change climates, others when they go from country to city. At home in the mountains in spring and summer, I wear little perfume because the bees believe I am a blossom.

Perfumed bath oil, especially in warm climates, can be more effective than perfume. Use it subtly, full strength. Pour a small amount of bath oil into a vial and carry it with you. A drop or two behind the ears, at the base of the throat and at the wrists absorb into the skin creating a luxuriously fragrant aura. Bath oil is less expensive than perfume and more lasting than cologne. Finding the fragrance that suits you best is a delightful shopping experience. How kind of perfume people to provide so many testers!

CLASSICS initiate an approach to fashion that not only takes you through the many needs of your days and nights, but enables you to cope with continuing style changes. To make CLASSICS super-attractive and individual requires an imaginative use of coordination and extra-interest accessory ornamentation, which is discussed at length in the following section dealing with our fifth concept. . . . COORDINATION.

5

Coordination . . .
The Talented Touch

Coordination is the fun part of fashion, and putting it all together is the fullest expression of your creative instinct. Considering clothes in the way we discuss, as canvases on which to imprint new personalities, the manner in which you coordinate colors, shapes and accessories are the finishing strokes, the talented touch.

You are the sum total of many moods, interests and imagination and the way you wear clothes highlights your dramatic ability to be whatever you want to be. At one time coordinating clothes was structured, sterile, with rigid rules for what was "proper". Many remember white gloves, pillbox hat and pearls with basic black. While it is easier to follow blueprints of what to wear when and how, it is more creative and relaxing to allow our tastes free rein, to experiment with new ideas!

Before we explore ways in which to build individuality with accessories, let us recognize the *essentials,* those necessities we cannot do without. They are *underwear, lingerie* and *hosiery.*

THE NECESSITIES

The terms, "underwear" and "lingerie" are not redundant because underneath it all, they express different concepts. *Underwear* is work-a-day; bras, panties, foundations and slips. *Lingerie* represents the luxurious options that lend sensuality to whatever is worn on top. Wearing cotton panties under jogging shorts and a cotton sports bra makes one feel totally different than when wearing lace trimmed satin briefs and bandeau. The latter is *lingerie;* the former, *underwear.*

Some women spend very little on lingerie, thinking that since it cannot be seen, why buy expensive, fancy underclothes.

Feeling lovely all over is important to the final look, for this feeling is reflected in attitudes and the expression of femininity. Even those on spartan budgets ought to indulge occasionally in exquisite lingerie, or at least trim what they have with lace and satin. Lace trimmings and satin ribbons by the yard are still one of the best buys in stores. Panties, bras, slips, camisoles can be trimmed by hand as one watches television, or whenever there is free time. Rather than buy tennis panties in sports shops, buy terry or cotton briefs in bargain basements and trim them yourself to save money.

Lovely lingerie can be collected by shopping sales, or by using Christmas gift certificates after the holidays. If you let friends and family know that the gift you enjoy most is lingerie, the lushest, laciest, least practical possible, you will soon have enviable ensembles.

Lingerie departments have become fashion sections with attractive multiple displays of color coordinated brassieres, panties, slips and camisoles for you to peruse. No longer tucked away in glass cases or behind counters, lingerie merchandising now affords you the freedom of self-selection and browsing.

The type of lingerie you choose can be limited by your size. Larger women require non-transparent brassieres and panties as well as figure control briefs and control top panty hose. Slimmer women can indulge their fantasies in a wider range of bras, and panties in more lightweight fabrics.

Some fashions, especially those for summer, can be so lightweight and sheer that underclothes are as much an accessory as a necessity, and should be selected to coordinate with what is worn on top.

Your first instinct might be to choose white underpants when wearing white slacks, but the right choice is a tone closest to your own skin such as the natural, nude shades. Beige-toned lingerie is the most practical because it blends with your skin. With all the lovely lace and satin trimmed camisoles available, there is no need for a brassiere to show through when wearing a sheer or lightweight blouse. There is nothing glamorous about a see-through blouse and brassiere. Camisoles offer a more provocative feminine touch, especially if the blouse is worn open as a third layer with a lacy, ribbon-trimmed camisole peeking through.

Pantyhose and panty combinations which offer an unbroken line are preferable to bikini or other panty lines showing through tight fitting trousers and skirts.

Slips, half-slips and camisoles are not only necessary liners for sheer or clinging fabrics, they are *accessory coordinates* which add color and interest to their outer layers.

A woman at the Broadmoor in Colorado Springs one balmy June evening caught my attention. She wore a sheer, silk organza dress in soft silver grey. Underneath, a slip of pink and grey silk showed through the plunging bodice. The cocktail party was crowded and as we converged on the buffet, I complimented the woman on the dress. She recognized me from my show that morning and confided:

"This dress is one of those collectibles you talked about. When I first bought it years ago, it had three layers of turquoise taffeta slips which made the skirt very full. I tired of that, and needed a slimmer line, because I've gained some weight. I bought the pink and grey silk print and made the slip and camisole, which incidentally I can wear alone, if I want a lean, bare look."

The creative possibilities with lingerie are unlimited. Many of the new coordinated ensembles can be worn as loungewear or for at-home-entertaining. Others, more lush, can be worn out for evening and dance wear, especially when accessorized with feather boas, third layer silk blouses, and exotic jackets in sheer or fancy fabrics.

As with most other fashions, you are completely free to choose what looks best on your figure and what works best with your personality and lifestyle.

Unless you are a tiny A-cup or the smallest of B's, a good fitting brassiere is your most *essential* undergarment. Many young women growing up in the sixties and seventies opted to go bra-less as an expression of new found freedom. Many of these women, depending on the size and weight of their breasts, have begun to sag prematurely. Our breasts are muscleless, fibrous skin tissue which is unattached to the muscle layer of our body and stretches easily. Without support, breasts give in to gravity.

Not wearing a brassiere sets a woman up for a downfall later in life. If the woman is involved in sports the damage is greater! More women are physically active than ever, enjoying a wide range of activities that may slim and tighten thighs, hips, waist and buttocks but play havoc with breasts. If you participate in sports regularly, wear a specially designed sports bra. They are comfortable and practical and a wide variety of choices are available with new designs and improved products being constantly introduced.

Your shape, rather than your age, determines how you look braless in clothes. There are young women whose breasts are not fit, and mature women who can still pass the pencil test. Generally it is safest if you limit going bra-less to particular clothes such as: halter tops, strapless and sun-dresses, bathing suits and other sports clothes which have built-in bra tops.

Even if you know exactly which brassiere style you prefer and you have purchased it time and time again, it is best to try a new brassiere on for fit, *each time you shop.* Designs change constantly, but more to the point, so do you! Changes occur in your breasts due to menses, childbirth, oral contraceptives, weight loss, (or gain), and hormonal increases and decreases.

Buying the right size brassiere for your figure assures a smooth look. How well I remember the first time I was fitted for a brassiere! I was a teenager and painfully shy. I hugged my blouse to me, until the salesclerk insisted I drop it. I was so surprised when she measured the area *under my bust* I lost my inhibition about standing there topless. Before going to the store I had measured myself at home, placing the tape around my body, directly over the nipples.

"Aren't you going to measure my bust?" I asked.

"Of course," she laughed, "this is all part of it. I do this first to determine your body size. I measure the ribcage and then add five inches to find out what size you should wear."

"What am I?" I asked, curious. I had never measured anything other than my waist, bust and hips before.

"Thirty inches, that means you would wear a size 36."

"I thought you said, five inches."

"I did," she replied, "but if you fall in between, we go up to the next larger size so that the band won't be too tight."

She then measured across the nipples of my breasts to determine my cup size. If this measurement is one inch more than the ribcage measurement you wear an A-cup; two inches more, B; three inches, C; four, D.

I have been grateful to her all these years for her teachings. I remeasure myself occasionally since my weight fluctuates. When measuring, the tape should be snug, but not tight.

I took my mother shopping after she had recovered from an illness. Since she had lost weight she needed new underclothes, and particularly a good brassiere. I was amazed to discover that she had never learned how to put on a brassiere properly. Mother has a large bosom and she attempted to squeeze her breasts into the cups, while standing straight.

The proper way to put on a brassiere is to slip the straps over your shoulders so that they sit squarely in the little hollow. Then, *bend over,* holding the sides of the brassiere *up* so that you ease your breasts fully into the cups. Straighten up and still holding onto the fabric, hook it in back. Make sure the band of the bra sits low and is not raised high across your back. Adjust the straps so that the cups are smooth. Do not attempt to wear the straps super short to give you a better uplift. If the brassiere is your proper size, it should fit well, be totally comfortable, and you should move easily with it.

TO TEST FOR PROPER FIT

a) Slide your finger under the band. If you can do so easily the size is correct. If the band curls or cuts, the bra is too tight.

b) Drop one strap. If you sag badly, the style or size is wrong for you.

c) If the back rides up you lose support.

d) Wrinkled cups mean the bra is too big; it can also mean the cup is too *small.* If too small, the breasts will be pushed against the body and not fill out the cups. If you overflow the cup, the design or the size is not for you.

e) Bulges and gapping indicate incorrect size and style.

A wardrobe of brassieres is needed to complement different kinds of clothes one wears; brassieres in colors to coordinate with ensembles and brassieres of different designs and fabrics to suit specific clothes. For example: sports bras for active needs; bras with good lift and support for clothes that cling; a bra with natural, unseamed cups and smooth, non-adjustable straps (no buckles) to wear under sweaters, clinging tops and lightweight fabrics. For dressy occasions an underwire strapless bra; a convertible for backless, strapless and halter tops; a plunge bra for deeply cut V-necklines and lacy bras to wear under sheers.

The fabrics available in brassieres are as wide ranging as the designs. In addition to Lycras and Helencas made of spandex, and nylons such as Qiana, Antron, Antron III, knitted tricots, laces, we now have brassieres in luxury fabrics such as silk, chiffon, charmeuse, satin and crepe de Chine. For the lady that likes to be well dressed underneath there are unlimited choices.

A word to those who still insist on wearing "foundation garments." While there are wispy, sexy one piece spandex undergarments and lightweight briefs which give a soft, natural control to the body, wearing tight-fitting, structured foundations makes a woman look ungiving, unnatural and unattractive. If one is large or certain parts of the body flabby, it is better to wear softly flowing separates and dresses in a size that does not bind rather than to encase oneself in a corset and figure revealing clothes. It is not only more comfortable to wear loose fitting designs that give the body graceful movement, it looks more natural. Figure concealing third layers such as long open tunics make one look slimmer than figure restricting foundations.

Try control-top panty hose or spandex briefs as alternatives to foundation garments, and if you are really motivated, diet and exercise do wonders!

HOSIERY

Fashions in stockings, panty hose, tights, socks and knee-hi's fluctuate with the times and design as do other ready-to-wear. Pantyhose in all its variations, its weights, textures and sizes have freed women from foundation garments and garter belts. While garter belts and stockings are sexy, the freedom and ease of panty hose are enjoyed by most.

Mature women with leg problems such as varicose veins or other discolorations find comfort and camouflage in support panty hose in varying weights. Younger women bouncing through busy days ease tired legs in sheerer support hose. Larger women whose stomachs are less than flat and whose rears bounce, will find control-top panty hose a comfortable way to look trimmer. All-in-one, unseamed panty and hose combinations erase lines, keeping one's look smooth in tight pants and skirts.

Coordinate hosiery with outer garments and with skin tones just as you coordinate other accessories, keeping in mind: color, texture and purpose.

Hosiery in slightly darker tones looks better with brown, black or navy blue. When wearing beiges, light greys, reds, medium-blues and lighter shades, hosiery in slightly darker than natural skin tones is best. Pale legs look prettier in warm tan shades. Excessive contrast such as dark hose with light colors; or light hose with dark shades is unsettling, and not an elegant look. It can be very effective, however, when one wants an outrageous appearance such as at Halloween.

Textured hose and tights in blending or contrasting colors perk up winter wear and keep you warm and toasty. The young can add colorful patterned knee socks for layered looks with winter sports clothes. Combine hosiery weights with fabrics and shoes. Heavier weights and textures look splendid with tweeds, nubby wools, walking shoes or boots. Wear sheers with chiffons, other filmy fabrics and sandals. Avoid reinforced backs or toes with bareback or open-toed shoes.

Since saving money is important, this idea passed on to me by students who also work as waitresses might be of interest to you. These young women cut the ripped legs off pantyhose and combine unripped legs and panties. It means wearing two pairs of panties, but the girls do not mind when they save such substantial amounts. And for those who have maverick toes which constantly rip sheer sandal feet, why not mend the ripped toes and wear the mended hose with closed-toe shoes and boots?

As I write, hosiery with clockings, beading and sequins is back in style. If you have exquisite sheer hose that have ripped, try gluing sequins onto the rip with Sebo glue. It will look like a sparkling clocking and you can wear them out dancing! You can also mend hosiery with embroidery floss and fancy stitches. Try a chain or feather stitch in a colorful thread. You will be right in style and will have saved money!

CONVERSATION PIECES

Accessories are the alternative to looking like everyone else in a ready-to-wear world, and the way you combine and coordinate colors, textures and accents bespeaks your sense of style and how you feel about yourself. A good accessory is one of a kind, special, memorable.

Accessories are only as important as the *total look,* and that is your aim, a finished, polished appearance that underscores your individuality and identity.

As with any other art, accessorizing requires an adroit blending of balance, harmony, composition and proportion. To develop an eye and sensitivity in how to coordinate for the clothes you wear, your figure, face and the occasion, scan fashion magazines, people-watch, attend store fashion shows, and try on new ideas in stores whenever you browse or shop.

Do not be timid about trying new ideas with clothes and coordination. All that can happen is that you will make a mistake. So what? Mistakes are no more than a learning process. One person's mistake can be another's good fortune. A well known designer years back brought out the smoke ring scarf and it bombed because no one knew how to wear it. I experimented and found that it was lovely when I brought the smoke ring through the brassiere strap, up and over the neckline to lay as a silky puff on the shoulder of the dress. It gave me many other ideas for ways to wear smoke rings (see scarf chapter) and they are still an important addition to my show, amusing audiences to this day. Her mistake was a definite plus for me.

If in doubt, do not overdo. For example, if you wear a scarf, earrings and a hat, downplay further accents; a small belt in a color and texture that blends with the dress is alright, but a contrasting leather wrap at the waist is too much.

Accessories can contrast or coordinate, and should complement each other in color, theme, texture, as well as what you are wearing, the image you wish to project, and the occasion. An attractive accessory makes all the difference in the world to an outfit. Gold chains or other jewelry dress up a daytime basic for evening. A scarf adds softness and drape to a simple blouse. A belt creates new proportions and shape to a sheath. Honey toned leather boots, shoulder pouch and a smashing Stetson add elegance and dash to faded denim. A mink or lambskin vest upgrades and updates an old jumpsuit. Sometimes one strong hit of color is a special effect accessory.

Boring one-dimensional clothes become conversation pieces with accessories. Following are suggestions to sharpen and stimulate your accessorizing wit.

JEWELRY

Misplacing jewelry on clothes offers opportunities for unconventional dressing. Try jewelry in non-traditional places such as: on the *backline* of a dress; at the waist; on a pocket, shoulder, collar;

assymetrically rather than centered. Gold chain necklaces can be wrapped around wrists and ankles and worn as bracelets. (sketch 14)

At a recent show at the Contemporary Resort Hotel in Orlando for the women attending the Heavy Specialized Carrier's Conference, I admired an unusual necklace worn by a woman in the audience. The necklace, which was wrapped several times around her neck, extended to the waist. It was a series of taupe colored, rolled satin ribbons accented with a large and beautiful pearl-like shell. Shirley explained that it was a belt she tired of wearing and much preferred as a necklace.

Jewelry takes on new dimensions when it underscores and accents other accessories such as scarves, hats, sashes and handbags. I had my ears pierced a few years ago, and they closed soon after because they became infected. I had purchased two pair of gold earrings and was dismayed when I could no longer wear them. Playing around one day, trying to find another use for them I discovered one pair made beautiful studs to pierce through my scarves; the other longer pair, in an antique Florentine design set with garnets, looked great set onto the rolled up sleeves of a coffee colored silk shirt. It held them in place and made an interesting new accent!

Combine gold chains with silver; pearls with other necklaces. Blend chains and necklaces with pins. If you plan a busy day at the office to be followed by dinner and theatre, without a chance to change, wear dressy, precious jewelry *inside your dress* during the day. Carrying fine jewelry in your purse or hiding it in your desk is risky. Whenever you travel keep precious jewelry *on you* or inside your clothes. When you leave a theatre, restaurant or club late at night, put necklaces *inside* your dress, obscure bracelets up your sleeves and turn rings so that precious stones are hidden in your hand. I am not a nervous Nellie, only realistic about what the problems are.

A woman's taste in jewelry is so individual, no one can suggest what is suitable for any one person. For some women, jewelry becomes a trademark and they wear one or two identifying pieces constantly. Others see jewelry as an investment and are avid collectors, but wear little, keeping precious pieces in a vault. Still others delight in wearing the latest trends in non-valuable costume pieces, changing their collections as the styles change. Some women never wear jewelry at all.

Design changes in jewelry occur as frequently as in other fashions and one can out-date up-to-date ensembles by wearing styles in

jewelry that are passé. Costume jewelry tends to become dated. Unless you are very clever at redoing it, or you wish to stash costume pieces away in hopes that styles will change, it might be best to sell it at flea markets or give it away and take a tax deduction. On the other hand, if you collect precious jewelry it pays to have fine pieces remade into contemporary designs.

As in clothes, proportions in jewelry as they relate to your face and figure are to be considered. Round, chunky chokers, pins and earrings accentuate round faces; rings and bracelets call attention to pudgy hands and wrists; tiny pins scattered about do not compliment the image of a big-boned person. If one is large and round, matinee and long length necklaces, and drop earrings, elongate. Jewelry coordinated with one's size, the textures and shapes one is wearing will create a mood, an ambience that adds extra depth to the ensemble.

At the Las Vegas Hilton last year, I noticed a young woman amongst many bikini-clad beauties. Her suit was no more than two black slashes on a bronze body. What made her stand out from the others who were equally as beautiful was a snake bracelet in heavy, brushed gold which entwined her upper arm almost to the shoulder. Ordinarily that bracelet would have been suitable only with the most starkly exotic evening dress, but it was enormously effective on her in this instance, because it was Las Vegas and she not only played it against the lean simplicity of her barely clad body, she stalked the pool as if it were her own private Garden of Eden.

Another memory emerges which is not quite as pleasant. At one of my shows in Chicago, a lady approached wearing a print dress, a three strand necklace of garishly colored stones (it was only noon), matching earrings and an armful of bracelets in different colors! Baubles, bangles and beads; so lovely in song, but so dreadful on . . . especially in matched sets.

Forage through your jewelry collection to discover new uses for precious and costume pieces. For example: bracelets can be worn as buckles for scarf belts; rings become scarf holders; pins replace missing buttons; gold cufflinks can be made into new earrings, or vice versa, or a single earring left from a pair becomes a lovely pendant. Recycling jewelry you are tired of, or have not used in years, is fun, offering many creative possibilities.

Jewelry should not overpower you or your look. For daytime, jewelry is best when it is simple and understated. Nothing is more distracting in an office than jangling bracelets and fingers flashing with rings. After five, indulge whatever jewelry fantasies you have.

Pearls add an incredibly lovely luster to bare skin, and making love in nothing but a strand or two is a real turn on!

SHOES

Comfort comes first when it comes to shoes! They must fit, then flatter. No matter how stylish, unique or daring the design may be, if the shoe fits poorly, pinches, slips, or gaps, forget it.

If your feet are less than lovely, simple, understated shoes call less attention to them. Wide straps, ankle straps and two-tone shoes do not flatter heavy legs and wide feet. T-straps, sling-back sandals, and pumps with a V-vamp are more slimming and better choices. While straps of most types look lovely on slender feet, if your feet are long and narrow, avoid high T and V-cuts. Square, round and off-center lines are more complimentary to elongated feet.

Select shoes with utmost care, choosing heels that are well shaped and suitable for your needs. We have come full circle with stiletto heels and narrow toes once again high style. How sad for aching feet! If you insist on wearing these high heeled monsters to the office, keep a more comfortable pair in your desk and wear them when you are seated, changing whenever you need to be visible. When choosing dressy shoes, remember it takes stamina and guts to dance till dawn in slender straps and sky-high heels, so be practical about your feet.

Consider the following when purchasing shoes:
a) Choose shoes with leather welt and uppers. Leather allows feet to breathe and is a more comfortable choice as well as being more elegant.
b) Look at the welt which holds uppers and sole together. A well-made welt keeps the shoe in shape.
c) Check the counter. A counter is the back of the shoe above the heel. Notice how a shoe salesperson bends this part of the shoe before placing it on your foot. Good counters snap back when pressed, test them. A counter that fits properly, snug against the heel, prevents gaping. The counter should not fit too tightly, nor be too loose, otherwise the shoe will rub and cause a blister.
d) Run your hand inside the shoe, down to the toe. If your fingers feel stitching or ridges, you can be sure your feet will feel it too!

One's feet need daily tender loving care! Perhaps if feet could smile we would pay as much attention to them as we do our teeth! The fact is that our faces do reflect our feet. Feet are one of the most critical parts of the body. Dr. Louis Newman, a friend and Philadelphia foot surgeon, tells me that the foot has four arches: two metatarsals, the more important one running across the ball of the foot; and the other at the junction where the metatarsal bones, coming from the toe, join the ankle. The other two arches run lengthwise along the bottom of the foot and are known as inner and outer longitudinals. Supporting all this is tissue at the ball and heel of our feet and fibrous layers interconnecting throughout which act as shock absorbers.

High heels force the weight of the body from the heels (which are designed to carry this weight) forward to the metatarsal arch. If worn continually, high heels will cause the tendons in the back of the foot to shrink. To prevent tendon shrinkage, alternate wearing high and low heels. Narrow, cramped shoes cause corns, calluses and bunions, which are inflammations of the first joint of the big toe. Bunions, fallen arches and other foot faults can be genetic, and contrary to what you might think, flat feet function as well if not better than high arched feet. If however you have flat feet and experience pain and other problems you will need supportive, well fitting shoes with arch inserts. It is wise to institute a consistent program of foot care and have your feet checked regularly by a foot doctor.

Thicker soles cushion feet on hard pavements and platform soles are more comfortable and healthier for feet because in addition to the cushioning effect, platforms lessen heel heights and its affect on the metatarsals.

If you participate actively in running, walking, tennis, golf, skiing and other sports, do not skimp on the best specialized sports shoes you can buy. They make a tremendous difference in your performance and the health of your feet. We see a dramatic difference in skiing ability amongst beginners who wear good boots and those who do not.

The best exercise for feet is walking. Running can trigger hidden weaknesses. Walking briskly stimulates circulation and is good not only for the feet but for the heart as well. Walking barefoot on grass, and sand is not only a wonderfully sensual experience it is good for the feet! To strengthen feet, walk first on toes, then heels, outside of soles, inside of soles. Exercising individual sections increases foot flexibility. You can do these exercises at home on a carpeted surface. Try them while getting dressed in the morning before you go to work or start a busy day.

Flat feet can also be strengthened by exercise. As a child I had flat feet and wore shoes with steel arches. My first summer at a health camp when I saw my wet, barefoot imprint I was shocked. It was totally flat. I was advised to go barefoot and to practice picking up pebbles with my toes. I did this and other foot exercises all summer and in the fall my wet imprint showed a well defined curve which exists to this day.

Wash feet frequently and dust with powder or cornstarch. Encased in synthetic hosiery and often cramped tightly into shoes, feet are in a dark, damp environment all day and need to be aired and washed to prevent fungus. Good foot care and good dental care go hand in hand, they both lead to happy smiles!

HANDBAGS

To counter the clobbering I have received on my travels by women wielding heavy handbags, two suggestions on the proper way to carry purses so they do not slug others unintentionally.

If the handbag has a handle, place arm through handle from the *outside in* (sketch 15). This keeps palm to the waist and elbow close to the body, steadying the handbag, and making it more resistant to purse snatching. When carrying a shoulder bag, do not let it swing carelessly. It bumps others as you go by and any miscreant can easily make off with it. Hold onto the strap of the shoulder bag with your hand, keeping it close to the body.

A handbag is a somewhat permanent addition to the waist, shoulder and hipline of your clothes, for that is where it is usually carried. Handbag proportions are important because the correct shape and size can complement your outfit, and a poor choice can wreck an otherwise lovely line. Long, narrow bags make you look taller; a squat, short, straight-across-cut, cuts your height. When purchasing a handbag, check the overall look. Mirrors in handbag departments are like those in hat sections, table height. Take the handbag to a full length mirror and take a look at the total effect. Your instincts have been honed and you will be able to tell if the shape and size are right for your figure, the kinds of clothes you wear and your needs.

Classic shapes are best and last longest, and if you are investing in good leather handbags this is a consideration not to be lightly dismissed. I have a collection of simple leather clutches which I stored when styles changed to larger shapes. Now that clutches are

Sketch 15

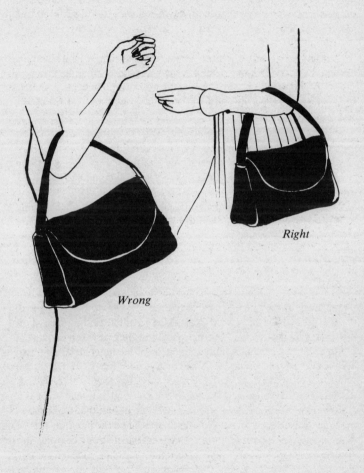

Wrong

Right

back, my leathers are right in style. Fine leathers or fabrics are a good investment. They add éclat to an ensemble, upgrading less than costly suits and separates. The flat handled bag, the clutch, the envelope, the soft pouch are all lines which are timeless. If you avoid handbag gimmicks, what you have should last. Colors are fun, so do not select only drab shades. A vivid accent or two is a very useful addition to a handbag collection. A handbag is an accessory as well as a necessity and should be used to add interest to an outfit.

Leathers of all kinds, simply sewn, are best for suits and coats. Larger shapes with more detailing such as saddle stitching, brass or silver fastenings and buckles, pockets and other details in cowhides, suedes, canvas, tapestries and leather with canvas are fun for sports and country wear.

Small clutches or pretty poufs in fabrics, beading, embroidery, jeweled, gold, silver, satin, velvet or kids are lovely for evening. For sheer enjoyment and practicality how about the little containers on chains and silk cords? What a terrific idea for dancing and nights on the town!

Check clasps, handles, chains, frames and zippers when buying bags to see if they will take the kind of wear you intend to give them.

GLOVES

At one time no woman was considered well dressed without a pair of gloves. Our freer, easier, more eclectic lifestyle now makes gloves mandatory only to keep hands warm. Fine leathers; kids and pigskins however still add elan to clothes. My son Jeff gave me a pair of Isotoners last Christmas, and I liked them so much I bought two additional pairs in colors to blend with other outfits. I find them sensational for driving, and I particularly like them for traveling, because they fit so easily over rings.

Fond and funny memories of gloves as conversation pieces in by-gone days come to mind. When I first began to perform in 1958, I was engaged to appear at a major convention in San Francisco, and invited to a cocktail party which opened the meeting. I knew no one and the party was huge. Since San Francisco is an elegant city and in 1958 one dressed more formally, I went to the party in a simple black dress, feathered black toque (same as is being worn today), one *white* kid glove, and one *black* kid glove. I no sooner entered the packed ballroom than a striking looking man approached me smiling.

"Do you always do that?" he asked.

"Do what?" I fenced.

With an amused, inviting look he continued, "Don't you know you're wearing two different gloves?"

"The only thing I know for sure, is that I have another pair at home just like these," I replied easily.

He burst out laughing and said, "Marvelous, I've always wanted to meet a woman who wouldn't let her right hand know what her left hand's doing!"

The next two days in San Francisco were divine.

Gloves like hats add distinction, a finished touch, giving one a special *soignée* feeling. Lovely leathers with a new coat make you itch to carry tiny, gold wrapped packages from Cartier's. White kid, especially in long, 16 button length turn an old turkey of a dress into a splendid creation. You stand elegantly, fully expecting a Rolls to draw up and whisk you to the ball! And pigskins with tweeds or denim make a walk through the woods feel as though you are tramping the moors of Balmoral with Prince Charles.

Gloves are great! Wear them not only for warmth, but for dash!

FURS

Fur is fabulous for sure, and as long as you do not wear furs from endangered species, they are a useful, flattering addition to an accessory collection. Whether you choose a hat, collar, ascot, vest, jacket, shawl or coat; furs add a look of luxury to the plainest outfit. A fur should be the best you can afford. A fine lambskin is preferable to cheap mink, and a good fur trim is better than a full coat of a lifeless, dull, shedding bargain. Furs are a luxury item only as long as they look luxurious. When they've aged noticeably, turn them into linings or fur throws for après ski. Since wearing qualities differ, select a fur which leads the life you lead. Perishable chinchilla or sheared beaver is a poor choice for an on-the-move-woman. This lady needs a fur that is as hardy as she. Whichever fur you choose, allow it to envelope you with its sensual softness, but do not allow it to totally hide you . . . check its proportions with your shape and height.

Furs fall into two categories: the long haired furs which have sleek outer hairs and thick, soft underfur; the short, flat furs such as calfskin or curly-like Persian lamb. These have only one layer of fur.

Both types can be bleached. The long haired furs can be plucked and sheared to plush, velvet like textures such as sheared beaver.

Neither fur is better than the other, they all have excellent qualities, and depending on how, where and when you choose to wear furs you may prefer one kind to the other. Try on a variety of furs in both types to get the feel of what you like best. The sheared furs may mat when wet, the long hairs sometimes shed. It is important that you be aware of these various qualities with furs and the source from which you buy your furs should specialize in them, for only a specialist can tell you what to expect.

A specialist can also advise and help you with matting; but nothing helps shedding. This happens when the skins have dried out. Buying furs in a store or fur salon that has an established reputation, or has been recommended by someone you know who is satisfied with previous purchases and service, is safest. Comparison shop before you buy and try several stores before you make a decision, because a very good fur is expensive and maybe a one time purchase for you.

Look at the labels when you browse for furs, because any fur product costing more than $5.00 must bear a label which lists: the make of the fur, the country of origin and the processing. The true name of the fur is indicated. For example if the fur is a mink-dyed muskrat, it will appear as "dyed muskrat." The country of origin is important in determining the value and quality because Russian sable is more opulent and lustrous than a similar coat made from Canadian sable. The processing which changes the natural texture and color through shearing, tip dyeing, or dyeing informs you of how the fur has been treated. Furs, even second-hand furs, must be labelled by law, but second-hand furs may not contain the country of origin, since it may not be known.

Fine furs have a lustrous, shiny look and the fur is thick or lush depending on whether it is long haired or flat fur. Cheap furs look dull and as lifeless as hair that needs washing. Good quality furs are matched expertly, with the color, depth and texture even. Fur should be thick and heavy on hard-wear areas such as collars, cuffs, front edges, sleeves and pockets. Make sure fur coats fit comfortably, if they are too tight, the pelted seams may split; too large a coat makes you look mountainous.

Some furs do not span generation gaps kindly. Lynx, red fox, raccoon or wolf coats look sensational on tall, slender, youngish women, but less attractive on mature women. Nothing ages a woman more than dressing too young. And, conversely, a mink or persian lamb coat in too severe a line may not have enough pizzazz for a younger woman. Therefore if you do not want to fall flat on your fashion face, respect the age you are at the moment and choose a fur which adds glamour, warmth and comfort.

HOW TO CARE FOR FURS

a) Furs need room in closets. Do not bunch or crush them against other clothes. Hang on well padded, wide-shouldered hangers.

b) Do not hang in a brighly lit room or closet. Bright light can change the fur's color through oxidation. If you must hang fur in a bright light, cover it with a cloth cover.

c) Never cover fur with a plastic bag! Plastic prevents air circulation and will dry out skins. If you wish to cover fur, use a dark colored cloth.

d) Furs can take some wet or snowy weather. After all, doesn't the animal? But if the fur becomes soaked through, it is best to take it to a furrier to be treated. Should fur become slightly wet, do not place it near heat. Shake it and hang to dry where air circulates freely. Do not comb or brush wet fur. Like human hair, combing or brushing fur while wet stretches it and causes splitting.

f) Having furs professionally cleaned once a year prolongs their life by removing grit, dirt and air pollution chemicals. Professional care also keeps leather supple and restores luster. Make sure to mend all rips or tears promptly.

g) Jewelry, perfume and furs seem to go hand in hand, but not together! Be careful of heavy jewelry such as bracelets rubbing against fur and causing wear. Jewelry or flowers pinned to furs cause punctures which can lead to rips and tears. Perfume contains alcohol which stiffens hair and dries leather. It should never be applied directly to fur.

h) Store furs in professional vaults which are temperature and humidity controlled during warm weather. Do not treat them yourself with chemicals or sprays with which you have no expertise. Furs are a costly and valuable investment. Treating them kindly insures not only the investment you've made, but your enjoyment of this most luxurious and sensual accessory.

EYEGLASSES

Despite Dorothy Parker and her famous (or infamous) quote . . . "Men don't make passes at girls who wear glasses," eyeglasses have become superb fashion accessories, certainly more glamorous than tired looking eyes straining to see.

No woman need be upset over myopia, astigmatism or far-sightedness. Since the designer influence on frames, glasses can actually enhance one's looks, and with all the incredible advances in contact lenses, those who detest wearing glasses have more options than ever. Even surgery to reshape corneas in near-sighted people is being perfected! My son Jonathan has had special contacts fitted which he seldom removes. A new development, not yet available in the United States, they were prescribed in Canada and he wears them while sleeping, showering and swimming!

Know the shape of your face, your features and their characteristics when you select eyeglasses. Is your nose short, wide, long, small or prominent? Are your eyes wide-apart or close together? Are your features regular, irregular, delicate or strong? Know also your skin tone and the colors you wear most and coordinate the color, as well as the shape of the frame to your face.

For example: mature people and those with pale skins look better in frames whose color is warm and rosy rather than grey, light, brown or amber, which may make them seem washed out. Warm tones such as plum, rust, rich brown are better for those with sallow or olive skins. If you have high, vivid coloring, then the cooler shades; blues, greens and greys are best. Stark, black frames are good only on young, unlined faces with good color and skin.

The lens, bridge and temple determine the overall shape of eyeglasses, and the color and shape can do much to camouflage. Frames with darker colors on the outside edge and no color at the bridge make close-set eyes seem wider; a dark bridge makes wide set eyes seem close, and a darker, heavier bridge shortens the look of a long, prominent nose.

Follow natural browline with frames at the level or slightly above

Round

Heart Shape

Square

Rectangular

Diamond

the brow. Too far above or too far below lends an eerie, strange look to the face.

The following suggestions should be of help when you choose new glasses: (sketch 16)

ROUND FACE. Angular lines break up the round look. Avoid Granny, Ben Franklin, and other too-small frames which emphasize roundness.

RECTANGULAR FACE. Width at the brow is needed to counter-balance a large jaw. Frames which widen out on top and narrow towards the cheek are flattering.

SQUARE FACE. Curves and rounded shapes soften the severity of a square face.

HEART-SHAPED FACE, NARROW CHIN. Squarish type frames fill out narrow chins and equalize width of brow.

DIAMOND-SHAPED, OR LONG FACE. Larger, roundish style cut the length of a long, narrow face. A frame that is wider on top creates the illusion of a wider brow.

ETHNIC CLOTHES

The penny-pinching will find natural fibers and interesting jewelry in ethnic stores for less money: cotton shirts, blouses and skirts from Mexico; wool jackets, ponchos, vests, shirts and skirts from Peru, Ecuador and Columbia; silk saris, silk by the yard, cotton madras and mirror trimmed cottons from India; cotton caftans, dashikis, and bolts of hand printed cotton cloth from Africa; embroidered silk robes, jackets, shawls, scarves and satin slippers from China and Japan.

The more adventurous might wish to try an embroidered silk Oriental robe with a large obi sash or a Chinese jacket sold in karate shops over pants with cloth or straw Coolie slippers for at home entertaining or a special party. One of the more popular current looks is the Oriental type hair-do accented with bamboo, bone or enamelled Japanese and Chinese hair sticks, which sell for upwards of $10.00 each in fine stores. It is a lovely, exotic look and you can easily make all the hair sticks you want simply by enamelling and varnishing *chopsticks* . . . especially those used in the Benihana Restaurants which are not round, but square, tapering gracefully, closely simulating the shape of the expensive hair ornaments sold in stores.

Shop ethnic stores for tons of different kinds of jewelry: Colombian emeralds; South African diamonds; Indian rubies . . . did we say penny pinching? More realistically; Mexican silver and turquoise are less expensive than authentic American Indian jewelry. Large, rough-cut stones of amber and coral, ebony and ivory bracelets and pendants found in African shops cost less than their polished counterparts in department and jewelry stores. Greek donkey beads, which you can string yourself to make handsome necklaces, are less costly than good costume jewelry. East Indian mosaics which lend a delicate touch to tailored clothes are sound jewelry investments, as are the fairly inexpensive jade, ivory and enamelled pieces found in Oriental shops.

Handbags from foreign countries are interesting and functional. Little Greek string tote bags are fun. Just the other night, I bought a tiny, beautifully printed red satin disco bag on a long string to give as a gift. It was only $1.75 in an Oriental shop.

Consider also the exotic perfumes found in these shops to coordinate ethnics scents with your outfits . . . I do not, however, advise wearing sheep oil with Greek skirts or Turkish coats.

When you travel, shop the native stores and invest in: hand knits, wools and laces from Ireland, Scotland, England, Belgium, Norway, Iceland, Sweden and Finland; leathers from Spain, Italy and Morrocco; fox hats, fur coats and vests, amber jewelry from Russia; cotton gauzes from Greece and sheepskin from Turkey; bolts of silk and other exotic fabrics from India and the Orient. Every country has its special treasures for your home and wardrobe. Ethnic treasures are fashion investments which give you years of wear and enjoyment. They are classic and timeless and are out of style only when they wear out!

LAYERING

Layering is the easiest way to climate control wardrobes as well as add new dimensions to ensembles. You can be warmer or cooler simply by the way you choose to layer clothes. And save money by mixing synthetics and natural fibers, keeping the natural fiber closest to the skin for the most efficient warmth or coolness. Skiers and others outdoors in cold weather wear a number of lightweight layers rather than one or two heavy articles, because air trapped inside layers adds to insulation.

There is a definite duality in fashion between older and younger, heavier and slimmer. To look best, vary the clothes you wear to suit your age and size. People of *any age* can layer clothes and accessories to complement the look and suit the need, *but the way you do it differs.* For example: leg warmers, *over* jeans *look* great on young women; leg warmers *under* jeans *feel* great on the more mature person. Boots in outrageous colors *over* pants look smashing on the slimly youthful; the same boots, *under* pants add color and warmth for those less slim and less young.

Layering can also dress down or dress up clothes. My creative friend Anne (she of the red-decorated leg cast) toned down a dressy evening gown for a late afternoon wedding reception by coordinating it with a simple wool sweater and belt.

Layering also camouflages. A woman took me aside after a show in Portland, Oregon to confide in a whisper that the outfit she was wearing was a spur-of-the-moment creation. When she dressed that morning, she found the "few pounds" she had gained would not permit the top of her shirtwaist dress to close properly.

"It puckered, and I was due to be picked up shortly, so I quickly grabbed a sleeveless blouse and wore it underneath."

She was wearing the shirtwaist dress open to the waist, revealing a jewel neckline blouse in soft pink which coordinated handsomely with the deep mauve print of the dress.

Vests in all their variations add interest through layering. Down vests in clear, bright colors worn over jackets and pants, sweaters and skirts, light cloth coats, short ski jackets spice up cool weather dressing. Reversible vests lined in re-cycled furs, wools, leathers, suedes, look great with business or sports clothes. Dressy vests in velvets, brocades, satins, felts, wools, plaids, stripes, solids, plain or embroidered, beaded or sequined, create fabulous accents for after-five.

Shirts on shirts; shirts worn as jackets; tunics, overblouses; scarves, shawls; stockings; shorts on tights; skirts over leotards and short shorts; drawstring harem pants over a body suit; petticoats and camisoles worn over and under clothes, accessorized with colorful cummerbunds or stretch belts; belts on belts . . . the opportunities for fanciful layering and accessorizing is unlimited!

Even jewelry can be layered for an unpredictable look. I met a beautiful blonde young woman with one of those marvelously bony faces we all yearn for at the Marco Beach Hotel in Florida. I had noticed her in the audience because she was wearing two pairs of gold hoop earrings in each ear. Jill had two piercings in each ear, just above and to the side of each other and she told me that she layered her earrings for special effects. This time she wore a small gold hoop inside a larger circle; other times she mixed studs with hoops and precious stones with gold.

Add interest to outdated jewelry by combining it with contemporary pieces; layer chains and beads; beads and pearls; chains, beads, and pearls; necklaces with other necklaces and charms or pins; bracelets in different colors or metals. Let your imagination take over as you twist, twirl and tally your jewelry collection into new looks!

Remember when you were a little girl and played "dress-up?" Playing that game now with all that you have collected in your closet and dresser drawers can save you a bundle on new clothes and give you outfits that are different, individual and fun to wear!

THE MULTI

A dress as an accessory? If all the accessorizing and coordinating skills you are developing are not enough for a complete and total change, the MULTI surely is. When I designed it years ago as a gimmick for the Mike Douglas, Phil Donahue, and Dinah Shore shows, I had no idea that it would be so functional. I intended it initially as a one-time TV visual that would create conversation. It has become the mainstay of my show and the instructions for the MULTI have sold and continue to sell in the thousands. Others must be finding it as convenient as I have.

THE MULTI is the ultimate accessory dress because it becomes so many different outfits. The idea for THE MULTI actually began many years previously when I designed my first show dress. A convertible sheath in sheer black wool, that dress had a drop-down hem which made it full length for evening. The inside of the hem was lined in lace so that when lowered, the hemline mark of the short length was not visible. In those days, in addition to a heavy lecture schedule I had a busy public relations business and I needed a dress that would

Sketch 17

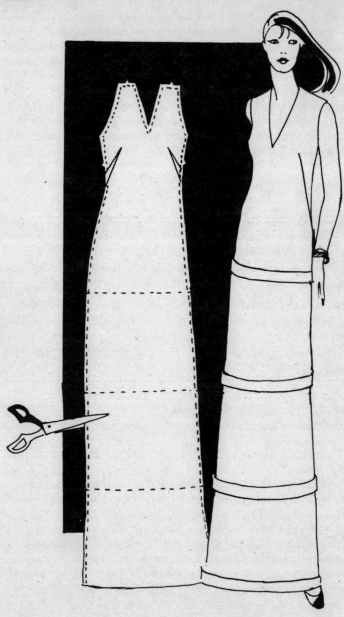

work instantly, if I had to go from day to dark without a chance to change. One rainy, miserable night it paid me back for the hours I spent developing it. I was to attend a formal, fund-raising ball with Isaiah Roossine, a dear friend and lighting designer, who waited impatiently and resplendent in evening dress at the airport while my plane from Chicago circled, unable to land because of bad weather. When it finally taxied to the gate, it was too late for me to go home to change.

Cy was grim . . . "It's black tie, Judith!"

"I know, don't worry," I soothed, "I have my black tie on underneath."

"What?"

"Just wait a moment," I said, scurrying to the ladies room, where I quickly undid the hem to the amazement of a lady standing at the sink.

When I walked out in a full length gown, Cy gasped:

"I'll be damned, a drop-down, drop-dead dress!"

THE MULTI is a more sophisticated and functional idea than that first dress and you will enjoy its versatility, for it is a *SNAP!* Quick as your nimble fingers, the MULTI is ready for action . . . from daytime, datetime looks right on through to the dressiest evening affairs. THE MULTI is for women who wish to own an easily varied and fashionable alternative to packing a lot of clothes. All you need are its few pieces for many days of traveling, yet you'll always be able to appear in one different look after another.

Here's how to add . . . or subtract to create the MULTI.

Buy any pattern which offers a simple, classic, uncluttered straight line dress. The MULTI can be made with either round, turtleneck or V-necklines; either sleeveless or with bracelet-length sleeves. (sketch 17)

Cut pattern to tunic-length. If you are 5'4" and under, tunic should be wrist-length. If you are over 5'4", tunic should be cut to fingertip-length. It is important for you to add 3½" when cutting tunic to make a 1½" cuffed hem. If you prefer a wider cuffed hem, cut 4" for a 2" cuff, etc. If there is no right side to the fabric, fold fabric up and blind-stitch. If there is a distinct difference in either the weave, pattern or color of both sides of the fabric, fold hem under, then up for cuff and blind-stitch. (sketch 18)

To make the additional tiers for your MULTI measure the dis-

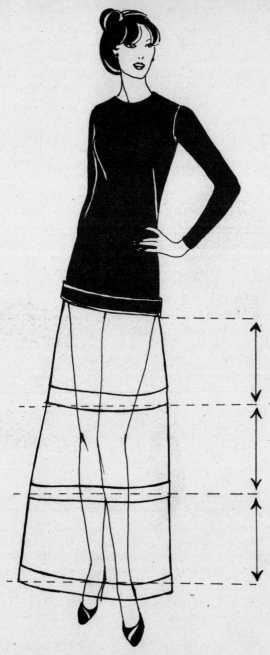

Sketch 18

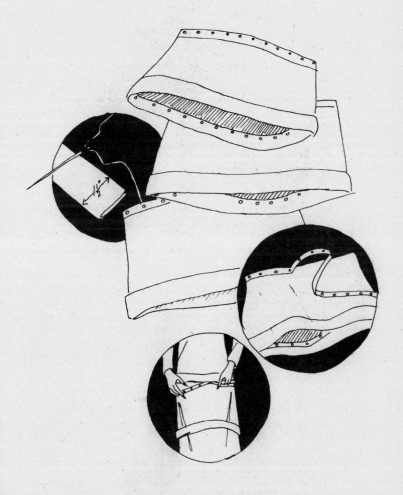

$1\frac{1}{2}''$

87

tance between your fingertips or wrist to your ankle or heel, depending on how low you prefer your hemline.

Divide by three . . . Cut the fabric into three equal tiers, making sure to add 3½" to each tier, so that it can be hemmed to match the tunic cuff. To attach tiers for various lengths, sew on snaps. Snaps are the easiest way in which to attach the tiers to each other. Snaps can be purchased on tape and sewn directly to the underside of the hem, and the corresponding tape to the outside top of the next attaching tier. Certain synthetic fabrics are not compatible with the tape sewn snaps. Therefore, it may be necessary to sew each snap on by hand. Tedious, yes, but do it while watching television and it won't seem to take any time at all.

To insure that you will not confuse your different tiers, sew one or two snaps on each hem with different bright colored threads. Do this with the corresponding snaps on the attaching tiers. (sketch 18)

Sew the snaps approximately 2" apart. There is no problem in sitting. You will find that the snaps do not come apart. Just be careful when sliding across the seat of a car.

The cuffs add a finished look to the MULTI and provide the means by which the separate tiers are attached. For very light-weight fabrics you may need a heavier banded cuff to hold the attaching tiers. Cut longer lengths on tunic and tiers, and fold cuffed hems to two or three or four thicknesses.

The second tier offers you the choice of wearing a mid-calf length. It is important to maintain this tier for the overall proportion of the long-line dress. (sketch 18)

Two tunic tops are preferable. Sleeved tunics afford a more tailored look and are handsome with street-length skirts or slacks. Sleeveless tunics are dressier with mid-calf and full-lengths. (sketch 19)

THE MULTI—VARIATIONS

Add pants to the tunic, either in matching or contrasting fabrics. Make them yourself or choose any compatible pair from your closet.

Add one, two, or three skirt tiers. Go from street to mid-calf to full lengths, as your needs vary. Create original looks for a variety of skirts to be worn with your basic tunic top. Perhaps, a plaid in a bias swirl . . . or a bright, colorful chiffon in an exotic print. Add a matching chiffon scarf at the waist or on the head for evening accents.

Part 2

Doing It!

6

Scarves—
How To Tie One On

Silky, feminine, soft, colorful, flattering, scarves more than any other accessory stimulate your creative expression, adding cachet, character, and proportion to outfits otherwise anonymous.

Wind them handsomely around every part of you! Wear them on your neck, your head, your hips, your wrists, even your legs . . . for the way to use scarves is as varied as their shapes and colors.

Use scarves for camouflage: to mask an unattractive neck or surgical scar; to soften a skimpy hairline; to cover a shoulder sling; to wrap around a knee brace while skiing. Scarves are protective as well, to keep you warm on icy days and to make you look chic in stormy weather.

A joyful and playful experience, mastering these easy ways to wear scarves will stimulate your own imagination for ideas we haven't even thought of!

Many women ask me how they can keep their scarves from sliding around. Scarves will slip unless anchored. While a costume pin or hidden safety pin will hold a scarf in place, a fabric loop, sewn into the neckline of clothes, is even better. The loop becomes an integral part of the garment and affords opportunities for creative variations with scarves and other accents not possible with pins. Loops can be made of matching or contrasting fabrics. Experiment with the fol-

The
Loop

Pin from inside ⟋

Using the loop

Petal Flounce

*Add
pin to
hold in
place*

Flower Flounce

lowing suggestions and you will find wearing scarves and other neckline accents a carefree experience!

THE LOOP   (sketch 20)

Fold 2 inch square of fabric into double thickness. (To match a ready-to-wear garment, snip fabric from under hem or inside facing.) Stitch one end; turn inside out. Sew or pin unstitched end to *inside* facing of neckline. Bring *stitched* end up and over neckline. Secure to *outside* by pinning from *inside.* Since fabric is doubled, pin will not show. Ideas for using loop appear throughout this chapter.

For contrast, loops can be made of grosgrain, velvet, taffeta or satin ribbon as well as soft leathers, suede or felt. If you wish to add versatility to prints, plaids, checks, tweeds and textures, make loops either of matching cloth or contrasting solids.

Place loops at any angle: at shoulder; apex of V-necklines; assymetrically or centered. Loops not only anchor scarves, they work well with bows; big and little, fussy or tailored; organdy ruffles; eyelet embroidery; glittery net; jewelry, and flowers.   (sketch 21)

Sew two different colored bows together. Stitch a sheer plaid organza bow to a solid color silk. Make a three-layered bow (print in center between two sheer solids). Thread chains through loop. Use a stickpin or other favored jewelry . . . many variations are possible. Let your imagination create your own designs.

When not needed, unpin the loop, tuck it back inside neckline and top can be used for other types of accessorizing.

Loops on sleeves anchor lace, ruffles, embroidered edgings, fringe, fabric, scarves, boa, updating outfits with which you have become bored. These ideas are to get you started on your own. They are a take off point for imaginative use of trimming to change clothes still functional but which you are tired of emotionally.

Another way to hold scarves in place are your brassiere straps! (And you thought they were only for holding up two things?) Brassiere straps are super to prevent scarf slippage!

PETAL FLOUNCE   (sketch 22)
Pick up 24 or 30 inch square scarf in center.
Pull through brassiere strap at shoulder and out over neckline.

Tuck end under flounce.
Secure with jewelry or hidden safety pin.

FLOWER FLOUNCE   (sketch 22)
Follow same directions for the Petal Flounce.
Bring end of scarf *out over flounce*. Widen into well.
Place small pin in center for flower effect.

BASIC SCARF FOLD   (sketch 23)
Square scarves are more versatile than oblongs and are better buys
if your budget is limited. Every square can be made into an oblong
with the basic scarf fold, and the folded square has a fullness which
is particularly attractive when draped. The basic fold is necessary for
many of the scarf variations in this chapter and for head wraps. It
is easy to learn:
Lay square scarf flat. Fold ends into center, overlap. Double again
for narrower effect. Scarf will lay neatly, flat on the neck.

VARIATIONS WITH BASIC SCARF FOLD   (sketch 23)
Tie into square knot. Wear knot centered, at the shoulder, or back
of neck. To make square knot: cross one end over the other and loop;
cross opposite end over, and knot.

BRA-CROSS   (sketch 24)
24 or 30 inch square, basic fold. Drape around neck; cross ends in
front; secure around bra straps. A lovely look for difficult to accessorize cowl, ring or stand-up collars, the bra-cross keeps you warm on
wintry days.

PUSSYCAT BOW   (sketch 25)
Flattering and feminine, Pussycat Bows are good contrast for tailored outfits. A 24 inch scarf becomes a smaller, tighter bow; a 30 inch
square a larger, softer bow. Make basic fold. Pull each end part way
through loop. Widen to create fullness. Silk crepes and twills make
firmer bows, chiffons wispier ones.

CASUAL TIE   (sketch 25)
24 or 30 inch scarf, basic fold. Pull through loop.

CASUAL FLOUNCE   (sketch 25)
24 or 30 inch scarf, basic fold. Bring round neck, make one end
longer; pull longer end over shorter as illustrated.

TWISTED CHOKER (sketch 26)
18 or 24 inch square, basic fold. Tie knot in center; tie ends in back, tuck in; or twist scarf into thin rope, tie and wear ends loose, or tucked in.

DOG COLLAR (sketch 26)
24 or 30 inch square, basic fold. Drape around neck, ends in back. Cross ends, bring to front and tie into square knot. Widen ends so they stand out.

DOG COLLAR ASCOT (sketch 26)
Same as above, but after you bring ends to front, flip one end over the other and widen into ascot. These two dog collar ties look great on T-shirts, sweat shirts and jogging suits. They add a little extra touch which might catch the eye of that other early morning jogger!

FLOUNCE FOLD (sketch 27)
The accordian pleated flounce fold adds a soft, feminine touch to the most severely tailored clothes. Hold 30 inch square taut in both hands. Accordian pleat by folding scarf back and forth. Drape around neck, pull through loop (or circle pin). Separate folds, creating a fluted fall.

RING FLOUNCE (sketch 27)
Pleat flounce as above. Pull through loop, then pull scarf up slightly at shoulder creating a shorter flare and a standup collar effect.

JABOT FLOUNCE (sketch 27)
Pleat flounce. Shorten one end, pulling short end over long. Widen and anchor with stickpin.

SHORT FLOUNCE (sketch 27)
Pleat 24 or 30 inch square. Tie around neck and fan out. Or wear on your handbag or as a pony-tail flounce. Pony-tail flounces fill out skimpy hair and when used in a color which blends with hair, make it seem thicker. When worn on shoulder handbag it helps to prevent straps from slipping off shoulder.
Note: When using flounce folds through the loop you may find that loop will have to be either longer or shorter to accommodate thickness of fabric. Simply adjust the pinning.

Basic
Scarf
Fold

1.

2.

3.

4.

Bra Cross

The Pussycat Bow

The Casual Tie

The Casual Flounce

Twisted Collar

Tuck ends
under

Dog Collar

Dog Collar Ascot

Flounce Fold

Pick up

1.   2.

Ring Flounce

Jabot Flounce

Ponytail Flounce

Handbag Flounce

Turn knotted
scarf inside out

The Knotted Ascot

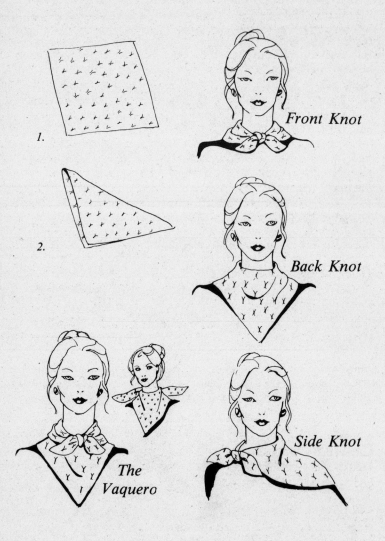

1.

2.

Front Knot

Back Knot

The
Vaquero

Side Knot

KNOTTED ASCOT   (sketch 28)

Foldover, oblong ascots are a pain in the ascot because they slip and require constant adjustment. The knotted ascot stays in place and it fills in widely cut necklines. Lift 24 or 30 inch square directly in center. Tie a tight knot. Flip square over so that knot is inside. Pull ends taut, tie in back, tuck under collar and pin. Tuck triangular end of ascot into bra and secure. If scarf drapes to one side, knot is not centered. Redo.

Wear knotted ascot with: cardigan sweaters (open the first three buttons), shirts, shirtwaist dresses and V-necklines of any kind. The lushest ascots are of silk, but interesting variations can be made with sheer wools, and other fabrics. Ascots of velvets, satins, laces and sequined or jewel-studded fabrics are stunning evening accents, especially when worn with velvet or satin blazers.

TRIANGULAR FOLD   (sketch 29)

Fold 24 or 30 inch square into triangle. Tie ends into square knot. Wear centered, at shoulder or in back.

THE VAQUERO   (sketch 29)

Make triangular fold. With point in front, bring ends around neck, cross over, bring to front, tie in square knot.

OBLONG SCARVES

Long, rectangular scarves, while not as versatile as the square should be included in any sophisticated scarf wardrobe. Their longer length is particuarly useful when tying scarves for V-necklines, which are more flattering, especially for the heavier person.

OBLONG FOLD   (sketch 30)

Lay scarf out. Fold one side ⅓ up. Fold opposite side to overlap. Fold once more. If you do not want too narrow a scarf, eliminate last fold.

OBLONG KNOT   (sketch 30)

Make oblong fold. Bring scarf around neck, with one end longer. Loop an open knot with this longer end. Pull shorter end through loop. Even out ends. (Fantastic camouflage for front-buttoned, too-tight blouses.)

Oblong Fold

Fold up bottom 1/3

Fold top over

Blithe Spirit

Single scarf pulled through loop

CRISS-CROSS   (sketch 30)
Make oblong fold. Bring around neck. Criss-cross under bosom. Secure to bra.

V-LOOP   (sketch 30)
Make oblong fold. Pull scarf through loop sewn into bottom of V-neckline. A lady once wrote to tell me that after she had seen me perform, she went home and sewed loops on her *brassiere* to wear with V-neckline scarves!

V-BOWS   (sketch 30)
Make oblong fold. Pull through loop, tie into flowing bow.

BLITHE SPIRIT   (sketch 31)
Long, rectangular panels also make for a delightful, floating look. A silky or sheer gossamer fall that follows you as you move lends fluidity and grace to short or long evening dresses; or turns daytime dresses into after-five ensembles with the twist of a knot! Handy for traveling or for those special times when you must go from day to dark with no time to go home and change; the Blithe Spirit is the answer! Tie two long silk or chiffon lengths into a square knot. Fling over shoulders. Secure to neckline with jewelry or a hidden pin. Or take one very long length, pull it through loop and toss backwards. Add a jeweled pin to loop. Fabrics that float, silk that swings, all add drama and a deliciously fragile feeling.

The Blithe Spirit is excellent camouflage if you have gained weight and the extra pounds show in back along the brassiere and panty line. Tossed over the shoulder, these lengths conceal telltale bulges. Choose silks and chiffons in solids or prints; or combine light and dark tone chiffons. Double the lengths for a Salome effect. If you cannot find long lengths in manufactured scarves, buy fabric; cut to desired length and hand roll the edges. You will save substantially by making your own lengths out of yard goods.

CIRCLE SCARVES

The circular, cowl-type scarf known as a "smoke ring" was bought by thousands of women several years ago, who stuck them into dresser drawers because they found them difficult to wear. If you see any silk smoke rings at yard sales and flea markets, grab them up.

Sketch 32

4. Dropped bow

7. V-neck with flower

6. Smoke ring epaulet

1. Through bra strap around neck

5. Jabot

2. Through bra strap on shoulder

3. Side sweep through loop

111

If you've saved those you bought, haul them out and wear them. The following illustrates how circle scarves can be valuable additions to an accessory wardrobe.

Circle scarves create new necklines, updating clothes with which you have become bored. If you have a skimpy or stretched-out turtleneck, a smoke rings fills it out and makes it more interesting. For a voluptuous feeling, add a velvet circle scarf to a crew-neck sweater; combine it with a long skirt and you have an evening ensemble. If a tweedy dress itches at the neck, a silk smoke ring adds comfort and éclat. Change colors you've tired of, colors which need to be muted, sharpened or livened, with cowl scarf overlays . . . vary textures. A circle scarf tucked into a coat creates not only warmth at the throat, but eliminates the bulkiness of a square or oblong scarf while it maintains a voluminous, contemporary look!

If you have no smoke rings and cannot find one, they are easy to make. You won't even need a sewing machine if you can do a small handstitch. Buy silk, velvet, jersey, wool, or whatever fabric you like best. Cut a piece approximately 14 by 30 inches. Double 14 inch width into 7 inches, stitch. Cut ends of 30 inch length on bias and sew together. You now have a circle scarf 7 × 15 inches which you slip over your head. Since it is a bias cut, it stretches and can also be used as a headband or hatband.

CIRCLE SHOULDER FLOUNCE (sketch 32)
The brassiere strap holds these variations in place.
#1 Drape circle scarf around neck, pull through brassiere strap, up and out over shoulder of top.
#2 Pull circle scarf through bra strap and out over shoulder. (Do not drape around neck.)

CIRCLE SIDE-SWEEP   (sketch 32)
#3 Drop over head, pull through loop.

CIRCLE BOW   (sketch 32)
#4 Pull through loop for a dropped bow effect.

CIRCLE JABOT   (sketch 32)
#5 Pull through loop. Bring short end over longer, pin.

CIRCLE EPAULET (sketch 32)

#6 Attach circle or bar pin to shoulder of garment. Pull scarf through.

V-NECK CIRCLE (sketch 32)
#7 Add color and drape to V-necks with circle scarves. Drape around neckline, tucking end into bra. Secure with pin; or wear scarf outside of V, accented with flower or jewelry as illustrated.

SCARF BLOUSES (sketches 33 & 34)

When you need a silk blouse in a hurry, scarf blouses made of 30 *inch* or 36 *inch* squares are the answer! Worn for day or evening, silk scarf blouses are also cooler and more comfortable under suit jackets on hot days then sleeved shirts or blouses. Scarf blouses pack easily for traveling. They save room in your suitcase and double as shawls, cocoon capes, beach coverups, head and hip wraps. You can add finishing touches to scarf blouses with jewelry, belts, or another small scarf tied around the throat. Try a scarf blouse under an old shirt worn open.

With the cost of silk shirts soaring, silk scarf blouses are economical. In addition, colors and patterns in scarves and silk yard goods are more vivid and varied than those found in blouses and shirts. Make your own squares by buying one yard of silk fabric 36 inches wide. Use full 36 inches or cut square to 30 inches. Hand roll the edges. Without a jacket, the 36 inch scarf blouse is a handsome halter and looks sensational atop evening skirts or satin pants. Even if you are not small and firm-bosomed, the halters made of 36 inch squares afford numerous folds which kindly camouflage mature breasts. Do not wear the 30 inch scarf blouse without the jacket unless you have a young looking bosom.

TRIANGLE TOP (sketch 33)
Fold 30 or 36 inch square into triangle. Sew snaps into top ends of *30 inch* triangle. Drop over head. Close snaps at back of neck. Tie other two ends around waist. Tie *36 inch* triangle around neck. Fan out or tuck ends in. Fold bottom of triangle over one or two times to create a belt effect and tie in back.

DRAPED COWL (sketch 34)
Tie two top ends of 36 inch square around neck. Fan ends out or tuck

Snap

Snap

Snaps

Tie on scarf

Triangle Top

Draped Cowl

Take two top corners

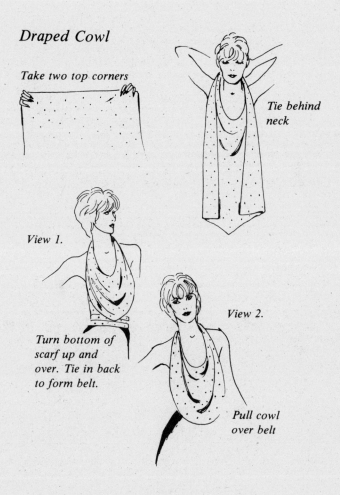

*Tie behind
neck*

View 1.

*Turn bottom of
scarf up and
over. Tie in back
to form belt.*

View 2.

*Pull cowl
over belt*

The
Scarf
Dickey

Cocoon Cape

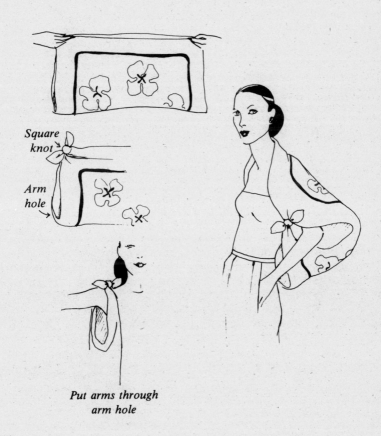

Square knot

Arm hole

Put arms through
arm hole

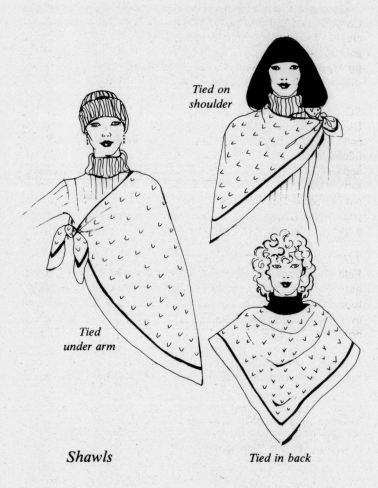

*Tied on
shoulder*

*Tied
under arm*

Shawls

Tied in back

in. Fold bottom up as belt or wear bloused over top of waistband. Tie in back.

Experiment with fabrics other than silk for interesting effects. Combine two layers of silk chiffon in varying colors. Try paisleys, challis, fine combed cottons, sequined or jewel-studded nets, lace, gold and silver threaded silks. Bead or sequin the pattern in the lace for super sparkle. Imagine how sequined lace and jewel-studded nets shimmer atop slinky pants or under velvet blazers!

SCARF DICKEY (sketch 35)
Use oblong scarf or fabric 48 inches or longer. Criss-cross. Overlap ends. Stitch to ribbon or belt made of same fabric. Gather top in soft folds and stitch so that dickey lays neatly on back of neck. Blend light and dark color chiffons for variations. Make reversibles, perhaps satin on one side, velvet on the other. Make slinky evening dickeys out of sequined, jeweled, lacy and brocaded fabrics. Seek out lush, penny-pinching remnants in fabric shops. Wear the scarf dickey as a halter or topped with a jacket.

THE COCOON CAPE (sketch 36)
Fold 36 inch silk square in half. Tie square knots at each end. Fan out evenly. Put arms through and you have a billowing topper for tube and other strapless tops (some made of scarves.) When worn over a solid color, long sleeved sheath, the COCOON CAPE in a brightly colored, silk print is smashing!

SHAWLS (sketch 37)
Large sized shawls are great for creative accessorizing. Over a turtle-neck, a shawl is more versatile, flattering and comfortable than a poncho. Around the shoulders, or the hips it adds a new dimension. Traveling with a wool or challis shawl is handier than taking a coat, because of the many different ways in which it can be worn . . . and shawls are attractive alternatives to sweaters in spring and fall.

SCARF HALTERS

Bare and beautifully convenient, scarf halters are best on those who can afford to bare it. If you are slender and taut on top, try them. They are comfortable and easy to make.

1.

3.

2.

4.

Halter Ties

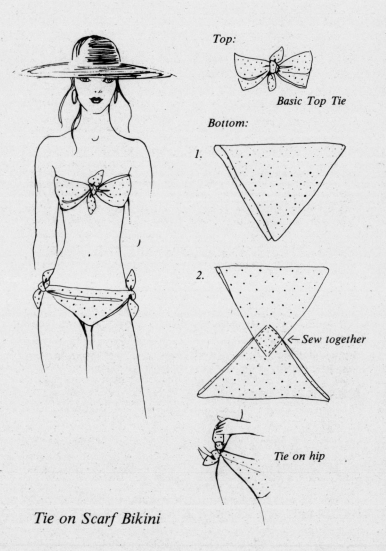

Top:

Basic Top Tie

Bottom:

1.

2.

← Sew together

Tie on hip

Tie on Scarf Bikini

BASIC HALTER TIE   (sketch 38)
#1 Tie two oblong scarves or fabric at least 30 inches long together with square knot. Place knot in center of bosom, tie ends behind back. Use cotton because silk tends to slip.

CROSS-MY-HEART-TIE   (sketch 38)
#2 Drape scarf around neck, cross over bosom, tie in back.

SHOULDER HALTER   (sketch 38)
#3 A three yard rectangular length is needed. Drape around neck, bringing fabric to the back under arms. Criss-cross in back. Bring fabric to front and tie with square knot, tucking ends in.

TWIST HALTER   (sketch 38)
#4 Use two 36 inch squares. Make basic scarf folds. Drape one folded square around bosom and tie in back. Roll other folded square tightly; loop through center of fabric tied around bosom. Tie in back of neck. Place tied end under fabric between breasts so that line at back of neck is smooth; or tie a knot in center of bosom for accent and tie again at back of neck.

SCARF BIKINI   (sketch 39)
Fold two square 36 inch scarves or fabric into two triangles. Double stitch pointed ends of triangles securely. Tie around hip. Yard square cotton remnants are ideal for these bikini wraps and less expensive than manufactured bikinis. Remnants are even less expensive than yard goods cut from bolts!

SKIRT WRAPS   (sketch 40)
A bikini coverup; the skirt wrap is made with two 36 inch scarves or one piece of fabric, 36 × 72 inches. When crafted of cotton or terry, the skirt wrap is delightful beach wear, and when opened, can be used as a sand mat. Made of silk or exotic fabrics, the skirt wrap provides endless variety for late day and evening wear. For short, short skirt wraps, fold fabric in half lengthwise.
1—Drape 36 × 72 inch fabric around waist. Center fabric with longer length in right hand, shorter in left. (Reverse if you are left-handed.)
2—Grasp center of fabric (marked middle on sketch). Tie securely to end of fabric in *left* hand.
3—Make a small neat knot, smoothing out ends so that knot lays as flat as possible.

4—Fold remaining fabric in *right* hand in *half,* tuck behind knot. Finished skirt wrap flows gracefully to ankle and your choice of fabric sets the theme.

GRECIAN WRAP (sketch 41)
Fabric required is 36 × 72 inches, or you can sew two scarves together to obtain a 72 inch length. Hold material in front of you with one corner at right shoulder. (Reverse if you are left-handed.) Pull fabric under left arm and around back. Make sure it is taut. Wrap fabric under bust and under left arm again. Tie tightly on right shoulder. Wear it short for the beach, long for evening.

HALTER WRAP (sketch 42)
Wrap scarf or fabric behind back, bring ends to front. Hold fabric taut and out. Cross two ends twisting the fabric of each end tightly into rope. Tie behind neck. This wrap is especially lovely when done with fabric that has a soft, silky-type "hand" such as cotton sheers, jersey, Qiana or Trevira.

SCARF SKIRTS (sketch 43)
Two 36 inch scarves or fabric are needed, plus ribbon or tape for drawstring. Print scarves and border printed fabric make colorful, comfortable and economical skirts. Fabric stores also sell border printed lengths which require only simple stitching to make a short or full length skirt. Fabric choice will determine how and where you use the scarf skirt. Cottons, terrys, velours are for casual and sports occasions. Silks, satins, laces and other fancy fabrics create dressy skirts.

Sew right sides of two 36 inch scarves or fabric together. Allow ½ inch or more seam allowance. (If you are more than size 12, use 45 or 48 inch width.) Pink and press seams open. Make one inch hem at top for drawstring casing. Stitch both top and bottom of casing hem; thread ribbon or tape through casing for drawstring.

Accent with gypsy hip wrap or a scarf belt wrapped double around waist. If you are larger than size 12 forego the waist wraps and wear an overblouse loose or belted, with a narrow belt which matches the blouse.

TRIANGLE TOGA (sketch 44)
Take two 46 inch squares; seam sides ½ inch from edge, leaving 10 inches open at sides for armholes. Join triangles at shoulders, turning

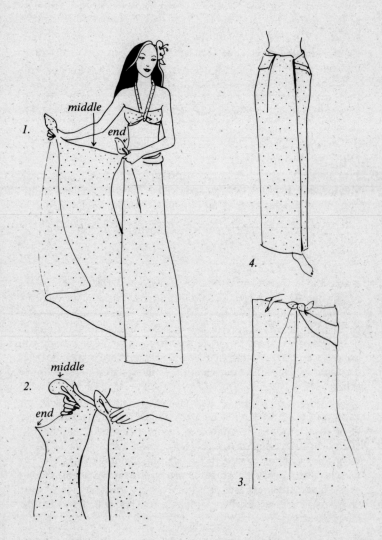

1.

middle

end

2.

middle

end

3.

4.

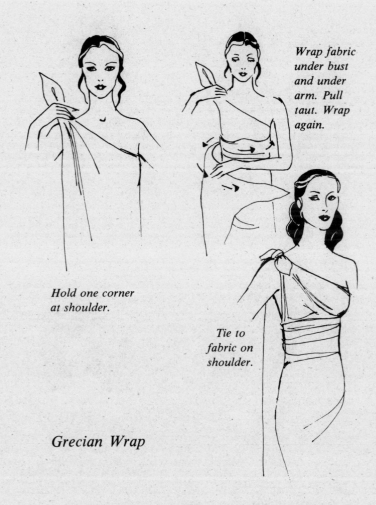

Wrap fabric
under bust
and under
arm. Pull
taut. Wrap
again.

Hold one corner
at shoulder.

Tie to
fabric on
shoulder.

Grecian Wrap

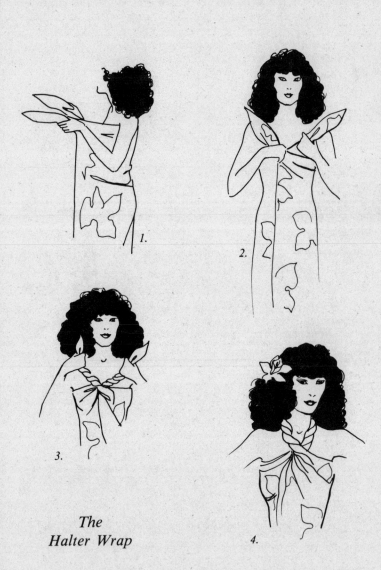

1.

2.

3.

*The
Halter Wrap*

4.

Scarf Skirt

Stitch wrong sides together ½″ seam.

Fold. Stitch ½″ seam.

Fold over top 1″ to inside, stitch to form casing.

Hem bottom. Pull ribbon through casing.

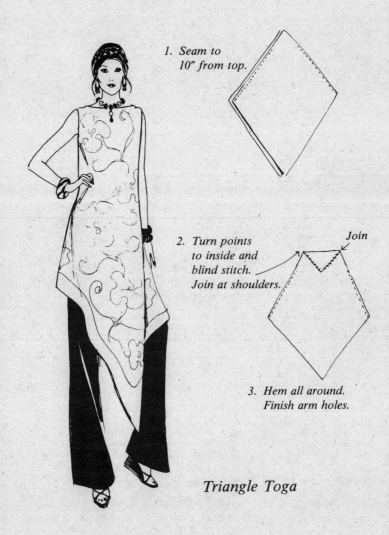

1. Seam to 10″ from top.

2. Turn points to inside and blind stitch. Join at shoulders.

Join

3. Hem all around. Finish arm holes.

Triangle Toga

Gypsy Wrap

Hip Wrap

Empire
Sash

Stole

Twisted
Belt

triangle tops under to form bateau neckline. Top or blind stitch neckline and armhole openings. Hem all around. Slip over head and allow to fall gracefully.

Color and fabric make the Triangle Toga casual or excitingly dressy. An ideal design for bold, bi-color dressing, the Triangle Toga made in vivid cottons or terry is ideal as a coverup for bathing suits, shorts and pants. When made in lustrous silks or synthetics and worn with a colorful headwrap and massive jewelry it makes a striking evening ensemble.

GYPSY WRAP (sketch 45)
Fold a print scarf (36 or 48 inches) into triangle. Tie at hip. The Gypsy wrap can also be worn toreador style over one shoulder, and under the other. Try it with a stunning beach hat and a rose in your hair!

HIP, WAIST SASHES AND STOLES (sketch 45)
Centered or side-swept, loosely hung or tied tightly, empire style, or at the waist, sashes and stoles add contrast and character to pants, skirts and dresses. Choose long lengths in exotic colors and cloth. Heavier textures sit better. Fine, silky fabrics slip.

TWISTED BELT (sketch 45)
Twist different color scarves into a rope belt, or plait chiffon and other soft fabrics into a braided belt. Scarves should be long enough so that ends fan out into soft folds.

Silky scarf accents in patterns, prints and solids create softness and drape. In muted, shaded, or bold toned colors, scarves add a distinctive and individual touch to clothes. Many other accents can be combined with scarves to fully express your coordinating talents.

Rummage through drawers, sewing baskets and attic trunks for collectibles which when used with purpose, become design. Trek to trimming stores, explore boutiques, bazaars, yard sales, antique shops. Seek out the unique, the extra special accent that you will wear with stunning effect. Collect fabrics, beading, embroideries and fancy trims. Look for remnants of costly designer fabrics which are too small, or too expensive for dresses or suits but create sensational scarf blouses, bows, ties, dickeys, wrap skirts and sashes.

With your accessorizing antennae sensitized to the potential of putting it all together you will create many unique, unusual images, expressing your talented touch!

7

Hats To Take You Everywhere

Late for a show one day, I hurried into a taxi exclaiming, "Would you please take me to the Plaza as quickly as possible?"

"Lady, with that hat, I'd take you anywhere!" the cabbie grinned. And he did, faster than any cab ride I've known. When we arrived at the Plaza Hotel, it was noon, and terribly crowded. The doorman was busy, and the cabbie got out of the car, walked around, opened the door and helped me out, show luggage and all.

A man waiting for a taxi said, "That's one for the books, when did you ever see a New York cabbie do that before?"

My driver, smiling, tipped his hat as I paid him and winked at the man . . . "With that hat, how could I help it?"

In a recent interview, Yves St. Laurant is quoted as saying, "The world of fashion is total illusion."

Wearing a hat creates an illusion of beauty and class that no other accessory can match. Fashion creates beauty, not only in what we wear, but in our manners and attitude, and in the attitude which others express to us. The well-groomed, handsomely dressed, self-confident person moves with ease and efficiency in an everchanging and increasingly demanding society.

While it is no longer an absolute that one must wear a hat as it was years ago, and many woman elect to go hatless, the fact is that an ordinary looking woman takes on charisma with the right kind of hat! Men open doors for her, and other doors open as well, for

132

when a hat compliments a woman's face, and completes her costume, it lends an indefinable magnetism that draws people. The woman not only looks elegant, distinctive, important, she looks *special.*

A hat that is truly a *hat,* worn with confidence and flair, not only makes a woman look years younger, it makes her more interesting, and creates in her a sensuous, feminine feeling. She becomes the kind of woman who turns heads, and how they turn!

How many times has your head turned in an airport or on a city street when a man wearing a dashing snapbrim strides by, when a vibrant young woman, hair flying under a perky beret, runs to greet friends, or when a chic, stylish lady in a slouch hat, trenchcoat and attaché case steps smartly with business companions?

I have watched with amusement for 22 years scene after scene and it is always the same . . . people with hats are looked at, which is what scares many out of wearing a hat! They are concerned about being conspicuous. And yet, many strive for attention and shock value with open-to-the-waist-shirts, see-through blouses, slit-to-the-thigh skirts and postage stamp bikinis. Why not hats? If you do not feel conspicuous in a stunning ensemble, why should you be wary of wearing a stunning hat? Hats do not create problems, more often they compensate for them. Some women have the confidence to wear the most outlandish outfits, yet do not have the courage to wear a hat!

One spring, my walk-in-show hat was a beautiful Frank Olive design, very much like his current line. It was a wide-brimmed shocking pink silk. Its softly shaped contours and warm color were kind to my face. A very large woman came up after the performance and gushed, "I just love your hat, *I wish I had the nerve to wear it.* "

She was wearing a *shocking pink shirtwaist dress belted at the waist!* All 250 pounds of her! *I would not have had the nerve to wear that!* If only she had worn a subdued, beltless dress and accessorized it with the hat I was wearing, she would have looked magnificent instead of mountainous. The accent would have been on her friendly face, rather than on her full blown frame.

Hats do for women (and men) what they cannot do for themselves, creating an aura of contour and color which softens lines, bringing radiance to the face and a finished, confident touch to the total look. Designers, fashion editors and photographers know how hats enhance ensembles and include headwear in fashion shows, press showings, photographic layouts and advertising to punctuate a costume's dramatic appeal.

Hats are especially complimentary to today's more natural, loosely structured hairstyles. Short, shaggy cuts, little-head-pulled-back looks, long, flowing hair and short, sculpted cuts look smashing with hats. And the hats themselves are so comfortable and easy to wear. Choosing a hat is not difficult; you've become aware of which lines are best for you and the following guidelines for hats add to this awareness.

HOW TO CHOOSE A HAT

In addition to checking the look both *coming* and *going* in a table-top mirror and hand mirror; check the *overall look in a full-length mirror.* A hat that fits your face may be all wrong for the total look. Wear an outfit you plan to wear with the hat, or if the hat is intended to fit almost everything you have, in your mind's eye have a clear picture of the shapes it will coordinate with. Hats should enhance, not overwhelm.

Despite design changes, hats fall into the basic shapes illustrated. Crown heights and brim widths will vary from year to year, but essentially the shapes sketched remain classic.   (sketch 46)

Small brims and higher crowns look best on petite women, lengthening their silhouette.

Berets and flat crowned hats look better on the young. They compliment long hairdoes and shorten an elongated face. Those with short necks and round faces should avoid berets and flat crowns.

Softly contoured brims; upturned brims and profile hats flatter those who wear glasses. Tilt hats slightly when wearing glasses. (I wear my hats tilted so that people do not notice my teeth tilt too. I have an uncorrected bite and wearing hats to the side tricks the eye.)

Turbans have been timeless since the days of the old Arab Sheiks or was it chic Arabs? If a turban does not fit you properly, stuff it with tissue or hose so that it sits full and high. (Hosiery in your hat is great insurance if you *run* into trouble. An extra pair may get a snag in your bag, but they'll never run in your bun.) For those with good skin and even features, turbans are terrific for travel and marvelous camouflage. Want to have a frizzy, fuzzy look for a night on the town?

Set your hair in tight, tight pin curls, and wear a turban to the office. Going to an important meeting on the coast or overseas? Wash and set your hair, put the turban on, travel elegantly and arrive with a hairdo that is fresh and shining. If you have a widow's peak, the turban is for you! A beautiful woman I know pencils in a widow's peak with eyebrow crayon whenever she wears a turban.

Rounded crowns in Bowler, Derby, Toques and Pillbox styles are best on those with long, slender faces and swan like necks.

Chin-straps, helmet-type hats and Western Stetsons are most attractive on those with youthful faces and figures, although the Stetson worn with Western clothes and jeans looks great on more mature women with slender bodies.

Big, floppy shapes look beautiful on most women no matter what their age! The hat should dominate. Do not fight it with other accents. Keep all else a mere whisper. Allow nothing to detract from the lovely shape on your head.

Flowered hats, unless they are exceptional as to design, shape and quality, seldom wear well, and become outdated quickly. However, a hat with a singular flower detail on a shape whose mass and color spell good design and craftsmanship is a good investment. You can always remove the flower if the style has faded.

Balance and harmony of line and color are essential when you choose a hat. The shape of your face, body and hairstyle determines the kinds of hats you wear best. Small, short women should avoid large hats with floppy or wide brims, and flat crown. Yet small women can wear stunning, brimmed hats, providing the rest of their ensembles are muted and do not break the longer lines they need.

The bigger the women, the bigger the hat should be! Nothing looks sillier on a big, bountiful person than a little "pot" atop her head. This rule however does not preclude big women from wearing small cocktail and evening hats, provided they have feathers, boa or other details which lend width and height, creating an illusion of fuller proportions.

Color in hats is to be considered as carefully as shape. The colors which blend best with winter wardrobes are: camel, grey, rust, burgundy, medium blue, winter white and a rich, true red.

The colors most useful for spring and summer are: beige, bone, toast, white, off-white and soft pastels.

Black, brown, or navy hats, because they do little for the skin, are best in straws, shiny straws, silks, textured fabrics, woven ribbons, velvets or furs. Texture, light play and volume enhance dark hats. Unless the shape is a knockout, or your hair light and skin *young,* a little dark hat does nothing for you.

Simple, unadorned hats are timeless and allow you to change the look with imaginative accessorizing. The wide-brimmed hat is wonderfully versatile. (sketch 47) Shapes change from time to time from high crowns to flat, but even this is manageable. When the style changed recently from a high-crown sailor to a flatter-crowned cartwheel, I tucked in and stitched the high crown of my soft straw to create a low-crowned cartwheel at no extra cost. When the style reverts, I will simply snip the stitches, pop the crown up and steam it.

While the wide-brimmed hat is the easiest to accessorize, different and interesting effects can be achieved with smaller shapes, by adding scarves, stickpins, grosgrain or velvet ribbons, a flower, or jewelry accent.

Beach hats in natural straws are delightful changelings for summer city and travel wear with the flick of a scarf, belt or jewelry. For the beach, nothing makes one look more glamorous than a wide-brimmed beach hat, scarf and sunglasses. Slipcover a beach hat for a special effect. (sketch 48)

Create additional and unique special effects by wearing hats backwards and sideways as well as forward! I do this frequently and no one knows whether I am coming or going! The secret to successful double-takes, to getting two and three looks for the price of one, lies in the shape. Two-faced hats should have fairly uniform brims and crowns with details that lend easily to reversing such as bands, buckles or bows, although my favorite, which is sketched, has none of these features. Hats sometimes look better backwards, as this does on me. Can you tell back from front? (sketch 49)

I even had a hat I turned inside out! It was soft, white leather with a flexible crown lined in black taffeta. When the leather crown became worn and shabby, I turned the hat inside out, removed the label, cleaned the glued area with dry cleaning fluid, restitched the inner band and wore it with the brim turned up, revealing an attractive slash of white leather. While there are few hats you can turn inside out, you might someday come across one that works!

If you own no other hat, you should have one . . . *for the day after the night before.* Every woman, no matter what her age, needs a hat to shadow her face at those times when she'd rather stay in bed. Never let them wonder *how you are . . . just who you are!* Besides, getting dressed and going out beats giving into fatigue, boredom and the I-don't-care-who-sees-me-anyway blues.

Some people tell shaggy dog stories. I have a shaggy hat story. I also have a shaggy hat, a lamb's wool toque I've owned for 22 years which still keeps me warm and comfortable on wet, snowy days. Every time the hat gets wet, it gets curly. Isn't it ironic that the only thing to curl up on my head would be a hat? On a trip to Fargo, North Dakota last January to speak for the North Dakota Grain Dealers, I was caught in a heavy snowstorm and my hat curled wetly and tightly! I went to the ladies room before my show and began to comb the hat out, when I noticed a woman looking at me strangely:

"Pardon me," she said, "are you really combing your *hat?*"

"Certainly," I smiled, "doesn't everyone?"

Good looking rain and storm hats are so much more attractive and functional than babushkas or plastic wraps tied around the head. Babushkas and plastic wraps flatten hairdos and fracture egos! What man would open a storm-tossed door for you? He thinks you can plow up a whole field, what do you need him for! Buy a dashing, smashing, rain or storm hat and plow into blustery, blowy, stormy weather with a conquering spirit, knowing you are challenging nature head on, looking sensational!

HEAD WRAPS

Scarves are lovely in unfriendly weather, or worn on the head in general, but not as babushkas . . . as headwraps, coordinated with the total look to add shape, interest and color to your face and figure.

THE STORM WRAP   (sketch 49)
Whenever it is too breezy or stormy for a hat or hairdo, fold scarf into triangle, place on head like a babushka, but instead of tying ends under chin, cross them, bring to back and tie. Pick scarf up slightly in back and drape over tie so that it forms a snood effect. Turn up collar, put on a pair of dark glasses, belt a polo coat and hop into a low-slung Jaguar. That's coordination!

Safari Sash

Tailored Tuck

Organdy Ruffle

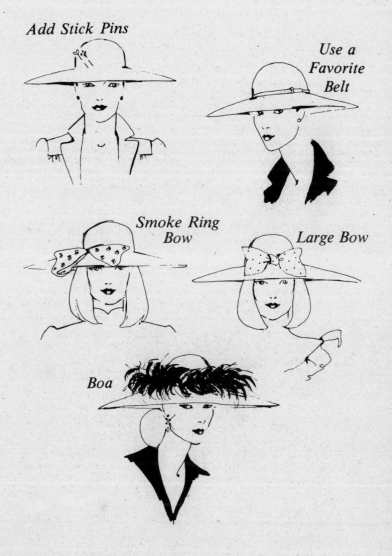

Add Stick Pins

Use a
Favorite
Belt

Smoke Ring
Bow

Large Bow

Boa

Drape triangular ↗
scarf over crown.

Criss cross ends.
Tie in back.
Tuck ends under.

Storm Wrap

Twisted Turban

1. Cross in front.

2. Cross again
   to form knot.

3. Cross in back.
   Tuck ends.

Tube Twist

1.

2.

3. Center on forehead.

4. Tie in back.

5. Tuck ends under.

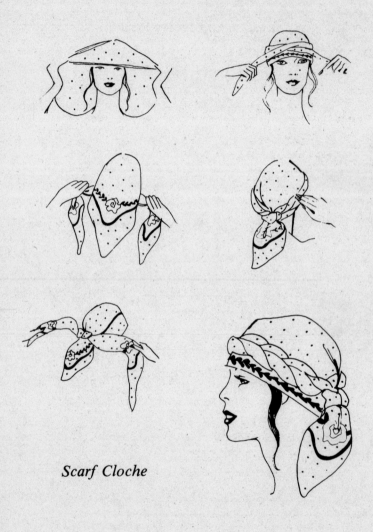

Scarf Cloche

Variations on Small Scarf Head Wraps

Basic "small-scarf" head wrap.

Tie and tuck ends under towards front.

Add twisted tube folded scarf. Center on forehead.

Tie in back. Tuck in ends.

Add long scarf tube-folded and twisted into rope.

Criss-cross.

Bring ends toward front.

Tie bow in front.

TWISTED SCARF TURBAN (sketch 50)
In dressy or casual fabric, the twisted scarf turban can be worn after-five or on the beach. Alter the size and shape of the turban by using either square or rectangular scarves or fabric in varying sizes. If the scarf is smaller, the turban will not be as full. If you use a square, bring corners together to make a triangle. Place center fold low on forehead, cross ends in back twisting them into tightly rolled ropes, bringing them up in front, tucking them into each other. Tuck the end of the triangle in back over the crossed ropes. If you use rectangular fabric or scarf, you will have a turban effect with an open crown.

THE TUBE TWIST (sketch 51)
Take two cotton squares. Silk and silk blends are dressier, but will slip unless anchored with a hat pin. Do basic scarf fold (see sketch 23 in scarf chapter). Roll cylinder effect. Twist rolled scarfs. Place low on forehead. Tie in back. Tuck ends in.

SCARF CLOCHES (sketches 52 and 53)
The two versions sketched show the effects achieved when using smaller and larger scarves. Sketch number 52: Center a square scarf folded into a triangle low on forehead. Tie in back. Let tails hang loose or tuck them in. Add an additional twisted scarf rope for accent if desired. Sketch number 53: Do the same with a smaller square. Achieve different looks with the added tie-on by placing the tied ends up front, to the side, off-center, or in back.

Hats or the delightfully fey headwraps add elegance, dignity and prestige to your image. Do not wear a hat out of a sense of social obligation or duty, or a scarf to keep your hair in place. Make headgear a statement, part of your overall, totally coordinated look, even if it is only a man's visor cap with baggy pants. Also do not make the mistake of choosing a too-dressy daytime hat or an evening hat that is not dressy enough. Satins, rhinestones and coq feathers are for after five. Exciting head dressing is a fashion experience, sure to spark your look . . . and your outlook . . . as well as the man in your life. *MEN LOVE HATS* . . . and with that hat lady, he'll take you everywhere!

8

Clothes . . . For Special Times In Your Life

In 1952 I was perhaps the youngest and one of very few women advertising managers of a major national company. Even though I was responsible for a $7,000,000 advertising budget, my salary was half that paid to my male predecessor. I had left the theater two years before because I needed a steady income to support my two young sons. I was dating a possessive, authoritative commercial artist. He invited me one evening to attend an opening at New York's famed Copacabana night club. We were to join two other couples. The men were art directors at major agencies. My friend cautioned me to wear "something quiet and subdued," because, and I quote, "they are important clients, and the women are older and less attractive than you. If they feel uncomfortable because you're younger it won't go well for me."

I acquiesced because even as a young woman I felt it important that the person I was with be comfortable. Although I longed to wear my dressiest ensemble for what was a gala event, I chose instead a simple wool suit, soft white blouse and pearls. My makeup was just a touch of lipstick and eyeshadow. I was so understated I could just as well have been home, and when we met our companions I wished I were. I also cried in silent rage for an airbrush and paint pots to spray my date back to his studio.

The "two older, less attractive" women were stunning! Older yes, but better! They totally eclipsed and made dowdy a skinny-haired,

149

pale-faced young woman dressed in a suit more suitable to the office than to a glamorous evening at the Copa. One woman had a mane of white hair which swept back off her forehead in a series of sculptured waves. Her enormous blue eyes were ringed in purple eyeshadow which matched the dress plunging to her navel. Her false eyelashes were so long and thick that when she leaned towards her husband, they dusted the lint from his jacket. The other woman had blue-black hair to her bare shoulders. She towered over her rotund companion and wore a strapless red satin sheath which had been sprayed on her voluptuous body. Her heaving breasts threatened to split the bodice at any moment. As my date bent to pick his eyeballs up from the floor, he whispered to me meekly, "I'm sorry!"

There are moments in everyone's life when wearing the wrong clothes makes you feel incompetent, insecure and wrathful. Special occasions require clothes of a particular nature, for the way you dress reveals more about you than an autobiography. When it is a very special time in your life, wear clothes that not only compliment you best, but are utterly perfect for the occasion. Referring to the concepts that are the basis of this book — COMFORT . . . CONTOUR . . . COLOR . . . CLASSICS . . . COORDINATION — will enhance your selection and prevent you crying . . . "I HAVEN'T A THING TO WEAR!"

WEDDINGS

For the lady about to be married, whether it is the first time or the tenth, the occasion is the most exciting in her life, and she should dress from the skin out in the loveliest, most luxurious, most appropriate ensemble she can afford. Despite the tendency by many to forego marriage, and the incredible increase in divorce, people of all ages say "I DO" every day, and weddings, formal, informal or offbeat, are a delight!

Before you even contemplate buying a wedding dress or accessories, determine what kind of wedding you want, when and where. If it is to be formal or semi-formal with attendents and a number of guests, don't go it alone. Consult the experts. Browse through bridal magazines and bridal shops. The more research you do, the less likely you are to make costly mistakes. I'm a romantic about weddings as I think is any woman planning to marry, otherwise why would she?

If you plan to be married in a simple ceremony, perhaps in a judge's office, choose a silk suit or soft flowing short silk dress in white, pastels or a rich color (depending on season). Underneath wear satiny, sensual lingerie, the prettiest you can find. Keep accessories to a minimum; no brash jewelry. You want nothing to conflict with that lovely band on your third finger, left hand. Good quality pearls, antique cameos or gold chains may be worn. For a truly elegant touch, wear a small, silky hat to blend with the suit or dress. Shoes and handbag should be understated and softly feminine.

When attending such a ceremony, wear a simple suit and silk blouse in a subdued shade. Do not wear the same color, or a color similar in tone, to that chosen by the bride. If she is wearing a hat, you should too, but keep it small and understated. A guest at a wedding should never compete with the lady being married.

Gardens and other outdoor weddings are traditionally romantic. Dress to complement the setting in a wedding dress spun fairy like of chiffon, organdy, voile, batiste, peau de soie or gauze. If you are a young bride, wear ribbons or flowers in your hair, or a wide brimmed hat trimmed with streamers and a flower accent. If you are a more mature bride, the softly shaped, wide brim hat without flowers or ribbons is flattering and appropriate.

Attendants at a garden wedding do not necessarily have to wear matching colors. While the design of the dress should be soft and similar, solid colors can be varied, giving a foggy rainbow effect. A hazy, Monet-like print can also be used. While white is traditional with first-time brides, many are opting for pastels and other soft shades. Women who have been married previously often select white. Except for super formal weddings there is a much freer attitude about color. White has so many tonal variations, one can have a white wedding without using crisp, pristine, virgin white.

If you are a guest at an outdoor wedding, avoid stiff, structured clothes. Choose a soft, flowing dress or suit in light colors or prints. The dress can be short or long. A summer type hat, small clutch bag and sandals would complete this airy, lissome look. If you decide to wear pants (poor choice) make sure they are loose and silky rather than tailored.

The formal wedding requires planning and lucky ladies selecting church or temple ceremonies, followed by a catered dinner or buffet, have many choices open to them, and many fine bridal shops and consultants from whom to seek advice. Whatever season you choose; wherever you plan the formal ceremony, your first consideration is cost. Establish a budget immediately and try to stick with it. If costs must be trimmed, cut down on the number of attendants. Rather have two less bridesmaids than skimp on your wedding gown and accessories. Cut out the hors d'ouevres before you cut back on your trousseau. A trousseau bought wisely becomes the backbone of a new bride's wardrobe and may represent the only clothes she will be able to afford that year! In selecting a trousseau, except for the lingerie, do not allow your fantasies to sway you from the concepts. COMFORT . . . CONTOUR . . . COLOR . . . CLASSICS . . . and COORDINATION are more important than ever. What you buy now will indelibly establish your fashion image with your husband.

When invited to a formal wedding, reflect the privilege of your invitation by wearing an elegant, dressy ensemble. No matter what time of day a formal wedding is held, it is sure to be a dressy occasion so wear your best. If you are invited to the reception, a long gown is preferable. If you attend only the ceremony, a short, dressy suit or dress is appropriate.

The best advice for a mother-of-the-bride is to consult with her daughter to affect a warm, loving compromise between what she might want to wear and what the bride prefers. It is *her* wedding, *her* day and if the mother-of-the-bride should choose an outfit her daughter is unhappy with, there can be no joy for either. Low cut, body-revealing clothes and bold colors should be avoided by the mothers of the bride and groom. An elegant, regal look highlights the prestige of a parent making a dignified, tasteful backdrop for those getting married. The clothes should reflect the season, time and place, but should not be too stiff or uncomfortable looking. All too often I have seen mothers-of-the-bride (and groom) look as if they have been poured into heavy, brocaded corsets. Chose soft colors, soft fabrics and float around like a blithe spirit. Your child is getting married, enjoy every moment!

SPECIAL CELEBRATIONS

Award dinners, banquets, bar and bas mitzvahs, christenings, communions, graduations, reunions, are all very special occasions at which you want to look glamorous, elegant and feminine.

If you are to receive an award at a black-tie affair, wear a dressy, dramatic long gown that signifies your stature. If it is not black-tie, wear the prettiest, softest dinner dress or suit you have. When accepting or presenting awards wear a warm, rich color enhancing to your face, for you will be making a speech, and dais lights can be glaring. Harsh, dark colors give faces a drawn look. Formal or informal, presenter or recipient, make sure your dress is not too tight and moves freely, so that when you rise and step to the podium, it does not ride up, wrinkle or bind. If you are presenting an award, wear a subtle, understated garment so as not to detract from the person being honored. If your outfit is too blatant or bold in color, the audience will look at you rather than the recipient.

Banquets, charity balls, opera openings and other black-tie affairs are when you pull out all the stops! Wear the most opulent outfits in your closet. If your social calendar is heavily laced with functions requiring formal dress, and your budget is limited, remember that simple, uncluttered, full-length sheaths can become dramatic changelings. Accessorize with feather boa, satin sashes, silk scarf wraps, organdy or silk ruffles, eyelet embroidery, beading, sequins, little satin jackets, cocoon capes and all kinds of jewelry. Haul out your ingenuity to create a variety of smashing evening clothes.

Religious celebrations such as bar mitzvahs, bas mitzvahs, christenings and communions require joyous colors to suit the happy occasion. Silk suits and dresses, pretty hats and lacy mantillas are lovely and appropriate for church and temple services. If the religious ceremony is followed later in the day or evening by a formal function, you may wish to change to more formal clothes to enjoy the fun you are sure to have.

Graduations at all levels are a time to rejoice and to bolster the graduate with your loving presence looking simply splendid. Whether the graduate is your child, the man you love, or a parent, they are proud of you and the support you have given them. Your pride in their accomplishment enhances their sense of achievement and your attendance in the loveliest outfit you can put together makes the event memorable.

My son Jeff still speaks of his high school graduation in 1964. He did not attend his college commencement in 1968 because he graduated in January and was off to the West Coast before the ceremonies. It seems that his high school graduation fills him with the most nostalgia. The setting and our presence, dressed for the lovely June day, and the graceful gardens that graced the campus undoubtedly contribute to this memory.

He attended a Quaker school in Philadelphia and the ceremony was traditional with a procession of young women wearing white, red sashed dresses and carrying red roses, young men in navy blue blazers with the school crest, white trousers, silk ties and red carnations in their lapels. Bright sunshine highlighted them as music swelled and they made their way past the stone-turreted school, through the gardens and up onto the platform.

If my daughter's graduation from Yale is as formal and traditional as its opening convocation, it will be another special moment, and I will discuss with her what she prefers I wear. When the graduate is your daughter, the decision is more delicate. Daughters do not enjoy being upstaged by mothers and prefer them in subtle, understated clothes.

When *you* are the graduate, what you wear reflects the way you feel about yourself, your school and how you relate to your peers. Wear what makes you the most comfortable; what makes you feel the most attractive, and what makes you happiest. Graduation is indeed a celebration, enjoy every moment, it never comes again.

Reunions are a time when everyone eyes each other closely to see how well they have handled the years and its changes. Therefore look as young, vibrant and pretty as you can. Reunions are not necessarily easy times. Memories tend to be bittersweet. Be relaxed, gay, charming and enjoy the *now.* Longing for the past may be romantic, but *now* is the best time of your life!

Wear easy going clothes in happy colors that make you look youthful, clothes with soft, graceful movement. Avoid tight, straight lines that hug your body and emphasize the years. If you have maintained the leanness of youth, show off your figure in form fitting designs. When attending a reunion with your mate, either his reunion or yours, you and he will be considered as one, and your combined appearance speaks for both of you. Dress to complement each other.

INFANTICIPATING

Except for getting married, no time is more special than the nine months one awaits the birth of their first child. Nor does any time seem as interminably long. Yet no period in a woman's life fades faster, and it is as nature intended. If we remembered the discomforts, the bulge of our bodies better, we would probably be less eager to try it again. I remember my pregnancies only with joy, and I cherish three healthy, intelligent children who are loving, caring adults.

While she may not think so, the pregnant woman is more beautiful

when carrying her child than at any other time. There is a luminosity about her that writers have recognized and artists have illustrated. Yet many pregnant women are insecure about their looks and go through frustrating decisions about what to wear, especially if it is an important social function.

We *have* come a long way, and how wonderful it is to see pregnant women hosting television programs and active in careers. Pregnant women are no longer "ladies in waiting" but active participants, even in sports! Today's pregnant woman need clothes which focus on her freedom, versatility and practicality; transitional fashions which will be useful not only while pregnant, but later on.

Do the unexpected while expecting. Do not buy maternity clothes until you can't possibly get away with it any longer, and even then, you can sew up drawstring separates to see you through. The drawstring pants, skirts and tunics sketched are easy to make. Later on wear them to take care of the baby or for sports clothes. When accessorized with contemporary accents they can also be worn post-maternity as part of every day wardrobes. (sketch 54)

Pattern companies have detailed directions for making drawstring clothes and their patterns are easy to follow. Buy fabric for these separates in cotton, challis, silk, synthetic blends, soft wools, in pretty colors, prints and paisleys. Terry cloth and flannel are wonderfully comfortable and can be used after the baby is born for jogging and beach wear. When you tire of them, drawstring pants will fit your husband. Wear your husband's old shirts with the sleeves rolled up over the drawstring pants or shorts. After your child has arrived, wear the drawstring tops belted over skirts and pants.

Full length elastic waist skirts are super as maternity wear! Pull them up over your breasts and wear as a midi! For example: in summer, a long, light fabric skirt pulled up over your breasts becomes a strapless sundress. In cold weather, a long, heavier fabric skirt worn under a tunic with boots is a fashionable alternative. The larger you become the shorter the skirt becomes. (sketch 55)

No matter where hemlines are at the time you become pregnant, wear them longer. Longer hemline dresses are more flattering and preferable to tight pants and short, flared maternity tops. If you prefer pants and tops, choose soft fabrics and loose fitting tunics which come to at least your fingertips and better yet, the knee. As you come closer to due date, shorter blouses tend to flare out and shorten at a most unattractive angle.

Artists smocks bought in art supply stores are another way to save

spending on more costly and limited maternity clothes. While pregnant, wear them with a flowing tie. Once your figure has returned those smocks look striking worn with a sash or belt over pants, skirts, bathing suits or around the house.

Ethnic clothes which are cut full and have a yoke are more functional than maternity clothes, because they have a fashion life long after nine months. Caftans and caftan type shirts from East Indian shops; dashikis from Africa, and djellabas are not only comfortable while pregnant, they are handsome post-maternity dressing. Headwraps worn with dashikis, caftans and other clothes look fantastic. They bring the eye up from the body. Any accessory which focuses on a mother-to-be's radiant face and eyes makes for a beautiful look.

Soft flowing cotton gauze gowns are ideal during summer pregnancies. They are lovely later on when worn with wide Obi sashes or belted with drapery rope.

Caftans, ethnic clothes and drawstring clothes spun from supple spool silk can, with the adroit use of color, texture and accessories, make exciting evening wear that does not shout "maternity dress."

Lee Wydra, the talented artist whose sketches illustrate this book, is also a well known designer of onstage clothes for entertainers, especially rock groups. I have asked Lee to include some of the dressy designs she creates for women who perform while pregnant. Perhaps you would like to adapt these ideas for your own use. (sketch 56)

There are certain maternity essentials pregnant women must have. These are: sturdy, supportive shoes with low to medium heels. Too low or too high a heel can cause backaches. You will want to do a good deal of walking while pregnant, and whatever you spend on good leather shoes is an important investment. Since your feet will swell it may be necessary for you to buy another pair in a larger size later on. Avoid man-made materials as they tend to make the feet perspire.

Hosiery which does not bind or constrict your circulation is essential, and support panty hose may be your answer during the early months. As you grow, switch to support stockings and a well made undergarment. If your back begins to ache, buy a well fitting and comfortable maternity foundation. Better to have the support and comfort of what you might think is an unattractive garment than to have pain and discomfort distort your face and movements.

Do not skimp on well made, supportive brassieres. Your breasts will swell and become painful, and a good fitting brassiere will not only relieve discomfort, it will shape your breasts more attractively under clothes. When you are pregnant do not go bra-less even if you can. Breasts need support particularly at this time. Choose a wider shoulder strap if you are full bosomed, and select one or two bras that are trimmed with lace to give you a sensuous, feminine feeling. Buy two nursing brassieres as you come closer to delivery, so that you can take them to the hospital. I hope you plan on nursing your child, because, a good start is your second greatest gift. Breast feeding is not only the healthiest way to raise a child, it is healthy for the mother. Nursing returns your uterus to normal more quickly and fulfills the natural function of the breasts. Even if you can nurse for only a short time, it will be beneficial to the baby and to you. Hopefully you will continue to breast feed for a year or more.

Another necessity while pregnant is a liquid, lissome nightgown and robe, the laciest you can afford. Feeling desireable soothes the pregnant woman and slipping into bed scented and silkened fills her with a warm, wonderful feeling that gentles the child within.

When you pack your suitcase for the hospital do not take a form fitting dress. I know how anxious you are to see your waistline again, but your body will not return to normal that quickly. Choose something that is eased, loose and pretty, with a bodice that opens from the front so that it will be easy for you to nurse. Along with your toiletries, cosmetics, and other personal belongings, take an extravagent, maribou trimmed satin bed jacket for the utter, complete, sheer sensual enjoyment of seeing a flat tummy again!

CLOTHES AND DIETS

How do you dress during the countdown between the beginning of a diet and its ultimate end! *What do you do in the meantime?* Strategy is needed to help keep you on the diet and fun to be with at the same time.

Nothing lifts one's spirits more and musters emotional support than *new clothes.* Therefore do not limit buying clothes while dieting. Instead, go all out! Buy something smashing, something splendid, expensive . . . and *smaller in size.* To be realistic, do not buy anything which you may be stuck with if your discipline disappears. Instead buy separates!

The best diets take time. Your weight, like the fog in Carl Sandburg's poem, "creeps up on little cat feet." Like fog, weight needs to be burned off slowly, with a consistent eating program that is safe and sensible. Handsome, easy to care for, economical separates will work with you over the weeks and months it takes to get into shape.

Select transitional, loosely cut styles in casual and dressy fabrics such as: A-line or lightly gathered skirts which can easily be altered later on to fit a smaller waistline; jackets which can be worn open while you are heavier and buttoned when you become slim.

During the "takeoff," wear new skirts and pants that may be snug, slightly open under overblouses and jackets. No one knows the top is unbuttoned and you can breathe with ease, anticipating the day when it can be secured and you run your fingers around the waistband. Skirts and pants with elastic tops are figure-wise, expanding as needed. Wear them belted when you become slender enough to tuck shirts inside. Loose jackets can also be belted when you reach your goal.

Dress up while dieting! Try on new makeup, new hairstyles! Feeling attractive helps you sustain momentum towards a lovelier you! Accessories are the answer during this transitory period. Add excitement to the clothes you have with new silk scarves, shawls, vests, jewelry, a rakish hat, a splendid handbag, sexy shoes, and a handsome belt. Yes, a *belt,* the accessory which shouts . . . *SLIMNESS!* Later on, these wise purchases add spice to the new clothes your smaller size demands.

If you plan to lose a great deal of weight, choose shoes knowing that foot sizes become smaller with weight loss. Sandals are best because straps can be adjusted for a slimmer foot, and the openness will better accommodate your new size.

Color too, enhances the slimdown period. Use soft tones of brighter colors when dieting rather than dark, somber shades. Dusky, muted, pretty colors are kinder and psychologically soothing. Lighter shades also give you more honest readings of weight loss and your changing shape than darker, slimming colors.

Every day is a special time in your life. A time when *anything* can happen! Be ready for it! Enjoy its ever changing rhythms, its opportunities, by creating looks that keep pace with new experiences, with new outlooks.

9

The Quality Touch

Can you imagine what it must feel like to make love on royal blue, silk velvet sheets? That's what fabric is all about. The feel, the touch, the "hand," the way it sits on your skin. Fabric and color create a mood influencing the way you feel about yourself. The variety of fabrics and colors in clothes enables you to be many different people, enjoying the eclecticism of today's varying lifestyles.

The equestrian in nattily tailored whipcords performs differently than the casual rider in chaps. If you disco in denim you swing differently than if you were in satin.

Unfair though it may be, when you walk into a room, the quality of the clothes you wear indelibly establishes your status. Like it or not, you are judged by what you wear and the impression you create results in the way you are treated.

The woman waltzing into the opera in an emerald green silk velvet cape cascading from her shoulders could probably hold up the box office and the guard at the door would open it for her, tipping his hat as she leaves with the loot. On the other hand, even a Vanderbilt in jeans is *persona non grata* at River House.

Quality in fabrics and tailoring establishes "a touch of class" which instills confidence in you and the people with whom you communicate. When I went apartment hunting in Miami to find a hideaway so that I could finish this book, I happened to be wearing a favorite outfit suitable for the balmy December weather, a navy blue wool Stanley Blacker blazer, white cotton pants, white silk shirt and a silk scarf in tones of grey, orange and blue. I had seen a complex I thought would be ideal. It was small, quiet, secluded, on the water, and well maintained. While other buildings on the Island had vacancy signs, this did not. I traipsed the Island from one end to the other and could not find anything I liked. At 5:30 I was about to give up, when I decided to inquire at the building I wanted. As I emerged from my car, a man approached me.

"Could you please tell me who the manager might be?" I asked.

"I am," he replied, carefully looking me up and down.

"Would you have a vacancy," I smiled.

"For whom?" he continued, his steely eyes penetrating.

"For me," I laughed.

Then began a series of interrogations . . . "Do you have animals, children, how many people, how long" etc. etc.

The upshot was that he did indeed have an available apartment, and because the complex was small and he was selective, he never advertised. He rented me a lovely, furnished apartment, at a rent lower than others I had investigated that day. I am certain that had I been dressed in jeans and T-shirts, I would have gotten nowhere with this man who takes pride in the meticulous manner in which he manages the property entrusted to him.

You *know* how confident you are when your clothes are "right" for the occasion; when they make you feel vital, beautiful, on top of it all! It is a warm, comforting sensation and is reflected in the pleasing smiles and glances that come your way. No matter what you are doing, you do it better when what you wear makes you feel good about yourself.

And yet, inflation and escalating costs makes it unrealistic to expect that the average woman can afford to always buy the best, but with a little knowledge, *she can buy the very best she can afford* and make it look smashing on her! Balancing your needs with your checkbook is going to require resourcefulness, discipline and the determination to forego clothes that cry, CHEAP! CHEAP!

Ready-to-wear manufacturers, as everyone else caught in the inflation spiral, have taken to shortcuts; subtle ways in which to save by cutting back on quality in fabrics and tailoring. Sometimes almost invisible, sometimes blatant, these quality shortcuts have become prevalent and unless you do your own sewing, it is difficult to be assured of top notch quality at a price you can afford. While you may be adept with the needle, treadling your home and career may leave little time for the Singer and you need clothes that are fashionable and worth their cost.

That is why I wish to awaken your sensitivity to the sorcery of fabric, and those little tailoring touches which help determine if you are getting good value for your money.

First off, forget about fussiness and cluttery clothes that become easily outdated. If you want the ruffled look, take the Priscillas off your kitchen window and resew the ruffles into collars and cuffs. Simple, elegant lines in good quality fabrics and tailoring transcend design changes and keep you looking in tune with current trends.

And, for those with a true spirit of adventure, shopping in nontraditional areas such as second hand stores, thrift shops, auctions, garage sales and factory outlets may yield exciting buys at low cost. No matter where you shop, however, know what to look for in tailoring, fit, and fabrics!

TAILORING

Quality touches are:

GENEROUS SEAMS AND HEMS: If seams and hems are tacky, scant and fraying, it's a bad buy. Choose something else. Skimpy seams are a ripoff. I turn garments inside out and check stitching, especially in armholes. Armhole seams should be slashed to prevent puckering and ripping.

MATCHED SEAMS: Patterns, plaids and stripes should look like Marines on Dress Parade! Every line perfect. If seams at shoulders, back, sides and inseams do not match, it might as well rain on your parade.

STITCHING: If the article is top-stitched or stitching is a finished detail, it should be even, unbroken, especially on pockets, cuffs, collars and lapels.

DARTS: If your bosom is above or below the bodice dart, someone's aim is off! Make sure darts are in the right place for your figure and are sewn evenly and neatly.

SHOULDERS: Lips can pucker, but never shoulders (as can happen in cheap polyester construction). Natural or padded shoulders should sit smoothly right on your bones. If they do not, alteration is necessary and since re-fitting shoulders is complicated and expensive, give ill-fitting tops the cold shoulder.

SLEEVES: Set-in, fitted armholes should be comfortable, not too tight or tense under arms. Dolman and raglan sleeves are special. Check fit from *back* as well as front and examine inside stitching. On elbow length sleeves see if inside hems have sufficient fabric so that you can turn it up a bit if you wish. Full length sleeves are to end at wrist. Too short or too long a full length sleeve ruins the line.

HEMLINES: Skimpy hemlines leave little room for a change of pace or a change of mind. Fabric also alters hemlines by creating an optical illusion. Heavy, dark color hems look longer, therefore wear them shorter. Fabrics that float, such as chiffons, organzas and other light colored lightweights look shorter. Wear them longer. Don't let Sam who made the pants too long (or too short) do you in. Make certain that full-length pants cover your instep and beware of short pantlegs. The back can be slightly longer. If a particular pant is *slightly* shorter when you wear a higher heel, wearing the same color hose and shoes as the pants is perfect camouflage. Wear shoes with the type of heel you wear most frequently when you shop for pants. If you intend to wear dress pants with ultra high heels, take the shoes along when shopping.

LININGS: The purpose of a lining is to assure a smooth fit and to take stress off the outer garment so that it lasts longer. Lined skirts and jackets are a plus factor, especially with synthetic fabrics, for synthetics do not hold their shape as well as natural fibers. Linings should fit with ease, particularly in sleeves and shoulders. If the skirt is half-lined, check rear to see if half lining can be seen through fabric.

ZIPPERS: Beware of cheap zippers, they will do you out! If you like the garment and it is otherwise a good buy, replace a poor zipper with one that is stronger and more secure. I recently purchased white cotton slacks made in India. They were on sale at a 50% discount. I was suprised at the incongruity of the construction. The seams were all smartly finished; the pockets roomy and well made with piping at points of stress, but the zipper came apart as I was trying on the pants. The saleslady curtly said, "That's why we've marked these down, none of the zippers are any good." I did not argue, the pants were 100% cotton and cut in a classic, timeless design. I bought them and replaced the zipper.

BUTTONHOLES: Should be strong and evenly stitched. If bound, check seaming. Make sure it is even.

BUTTONS on coats and suits made of heavier fabrics should have round stems. Better quality clothes will have buttons made of bone, wood or mother-of-pearl and often extra buttons will be sewn into a seam or attached in a plastic packet. Remove any loose buttons before the garment is wrapped. Less expensive clothes have plastic buttons and changing buttons on a low cost garment upgrades its look.

While a high school student at Burke Mountain Academy in Vermont, training to be a ski racer, my daughter saved money on clothes by shopping at a fantastic thrift shop called, "The Whippletree." Her most amazing find was a beautiful burgundy wool coat which she bought for 25¢, that's right, *twenty-five-cents!*. The coat was soiled but it had lovely classic lines; Princess style with set-in sleeves and a Peter Pan collar. It was lined in burgundy satin and the stitching, lining, seams and fabric all reflected the coat's past glory. We sent it to the best cleaner in town and bought natural wood buttons in a warm brown shade. When finished the coat had cost a total of $10.25! It still looks as good as new and this past fall I clipped a Lord and Taylor ad and sent it to my daughter at Yale. The coat in the ad duplicated her find, line for line. It was on *sale* for $248.00!

If you want the most for your money, keep it simple. This does not mean you have to always buy "sensible," somber clothes that offer little excitement. On the contrary if you select exciting, good quality fabrics, you can have a wonderfully put together look, because fabrics add sensuality, shape, color and texture, making you *feel* lovely!

FABRICS

I am a pack rat, collecting, stashing for "someday" projects. The little weekend ski cabin I now live in permanently is an accordian, ever expanding to contain my "finds." One day, my middle son, Jonathan, a sculptor and artist and a collector of wood, marble and metal for his own needs, yelped as he waded through a pile of books, magazines and manuscripts, "Mom, if I asked you for an elephant tusk you'd say . . . 'what size, four foot or eight?' "

Some collect glass, others antiques. My passions are books, bottles, paintings and fabrics. Over the years I have built an eclectic collection of fabrics, all of which I will use "someday." Buying fabric is a wise investment. Many of my purchases made years ago, especially the wools, silks, 100% cottons and the silk embroideries are more valuable today than when I first bought them, many as remnants. Even if you do not sew you can have your clothes custom-made. I find in my travels many young women who have set up shop in their homes and have become skillful couturiers offering fine craftsmanship and sometimes original designs for very little more than what you pay for ready-to-wear.

There's been no time these past few years to make my show dresses and the last two were sewn by young women in small, out-of-the-way communities in rural Pennsylvania. When you travel, browse for fabrics in off-the-beaten-track-shops, as well as the big, elegant houses. Head for the sale and remnant counters first. You will find unique patterns, blends and textures in foreign countries and in various sectors of the United States where more and more, young people are weaving, hand-painting and designing fabrics as an art form.

The touch, the feel, the "hand" of a fabric and the way it moves on your body is what should determine your choice. No matter the design, the price, if it does not *feel comfortable,* pass. Caress fabric between your fingers and hold it to your face. You can actually *feel* cheap fabric.

While synthetics work best for me onstage, offstage I prefer natural fibers. The warmth of wool, the comfort of cotton and the slinking softness of silk on my skin are sensations that are delightful. Besides, natural fibers look more luxurious and hold their shape better.

It takes time to learn about fabrics; their construction, quality, characteristics and wearing ability. Let labels guide you as you learn, for labels spell out the fiber contents, the dry-cleanables and how to wash the washables. Good quality fabric houses guard their reputations and a well known label is your best assurance. Read all labels and follow instructions for care.

THE NATURAL FIBERS

COTTON: Just as I LOVE NEW YORK . . . I LOVE COTTON! Hardy, versatile, it is the most comfortable of all fabrics. Marvelously absorbent, it feels sensational against the skin and with new technology it can be color-fast, pre-shrunk, wrinkle-resistant and wash and wear. Look for 100% cotton and also enjoy the many cotton blends. Strong, pliable and lustrous, cotton is fashionable all year round. It is not relegated to summer and resort wear. There are almost as many varieties of cottons as there are colors. Some cottons are so handsomely finished, they are used for evening wear. Familiarize yourself with all that is available and check labels for care.

LINEN: Produced from flax (Belgium has the finest flax plants), most fine quality linens come from Ireland where it has been manufactured since the 8th century! Linen goes back even further, dating to prehistoric times. Egyptian linen is legendary and proof of its amazing durability are the linen burial shrouds found on mummified remains. Linen actually improves with age and is wonderfully washable, cool and absorbent. It does have drawbacks as well as being very expensive.

The expense can be amortized however, as linen outlasts most other fabrics and in table linens particularly, linen represents an investment and heritage which can be passed on to succeeding generations. Its tendency to wrinkle is another matter, and despite crease-resistent treatment, linen wrinkles and requires ironing which can present a problem when traveling. While I have seen others carry off the rumpled, wrinkled look with aplomb and elegance, I personally am uncomfortable in the unpressed look. I prefer my linen on the table, crisply ironed and shining.

Linen is labeled as to content and anything sold as "linen" must contain at least 50% pure linen with all other fibers listed in order of weight. If the other contents are less than 5%, they are listed as "other fibers" or "miscellaneous fibers." Fabric technology is so advanced, many fabrics can look like linen and not contain any linen. It might have a linen finish, but is not linen, therefore check labels to make sure you are getting what you are paying for!

SILK: Those crafty little earthworms industriously spinning silken threads have no idea of how ensnared I am by their spun magic! How I *adore* silk! It is a passion with me, and represents my most extravagent clothing expenditures. In its many exquisite variations, silk has so many fantastic qualities that whatever you spend, it is worth it!

One splendid silk shirt or dress is worth dozens of synthetics. The colors in silk are pure, vivid, memorable, for silk takes dye better than any other fabric. As a skier who has often been out in wind chill factors of 38 degrees below zero, I know how well closely woven silk generates heat against the body. I have been telling audiences for years of the way I keep my hands and feet warm while skiing. I tie a silk square *doubling* it around the *back of my neck* and wear it *under* my turtleneck cotton shirt. The back of the neck is the region through which nerves transmit messages to the brain, and when my neck is warm, my hands and feet stay warm. I have experimented enough to know that it works for me . . . try it for yourself.

Silk is also cool in summer. There are lightweight, loosely woven silks that are comfortably cool, so much better than wearing synthetics on a hot day. Silk is absorbent and no matter the heat or the humidity, you will feel dry. Although it looks fragile, incandescent and incredibly delicate, silk, like a woman, is STRONG and wears wonderfully.

The many textures available in silk stem from the way the different yarns are manufactured and the two different types of earthworms who produce their sorcery. Wild silkworms spin a coarser thread and the fabric is know as tussah. Wild silk has a hard, rough, nubby texture, a different color and is less lustrous than cultivated, finely reeled silk, which is shiny smooth. Since raw silk does not go through as many refining processes as reeled silk, it is less expensive. It has a particularly good quality for suits. In silk manufacturing every conceivable part is used, including the tangled fibers from outside the cocoon which is made into *spun silk.* More like cotton than silk, *spun silk* has a fuzzy quality and is not as strong or shiny, but it is less expensive.

Pure silk on a label means there is no artificial weighting, which is a manufacturing process that makes silk feel heavier, but lessens its wearing abilities.

Silk garments should not fit too snugly, because if let out, stitches will show. While I have a friend who regularly hand washes his silk shirts, and I wash all of my silk scarves, it is best to have silk professionally dry cleaned, and silk labels state, "dry clean only."

I was in a dressing room recently and overheard the woman in the next cubicle. "I love this dress," she exclaimed, "but I am paying four dollars to clean my silk shirts now, and this will probably cost me ten."

The cost of caring for silk cannot be denied. I am more careful when I wear silk and I grimace when I pay the cleaning bills, but when I feel its silken warmth or coolness, its sensualness against my skin, cost and care foolishly fade.

WOOL: How amazing wool is. Warm, water repellent and versatile, wool comes in many varieties such as: alpaca, cashmere, mohair and vicuna, which are sheared from various species of goats. Camel's hair, another fine wool product, is from the hardy desert beast. Obtained through a process of bleaching, spinning and weaving, wool is resilient and holds its shape beautifully. "Reprocessed wool" is made of used wools which have been cleaned and rewoven into new cloth. It is less expensive, somewhat less resilient and less warm than virgin wool.

Wool content and the precentages of wool in blends are clearly labeled. Since there are many different weights and textures, check labels. Acquaint yourself with wool manufacturers by noting their ads and reading the fashion pages.

Weights and textures in wool give them special qualities for specific garments: sheer wool crepe is more suitable for dresses than suits; heavy tweeds are better for jackets and coats. Sheer wool can be worn year round, while the heavier weights would be too warm for summer. Knitted wools drape beautifully, offering versatility and comfort at a lower cost than woven wool. Knits too, come in different weights and quality. Fold knitted wools over a well padded hanger or in a drawer rather than hang them from the shoulder.

Worsteds and gabardines are stout, long wearing wools which never "seat-out" and seldom wear out; that is why most uniforms are made of gabardines and worsteds. Their only drawback is their tendency to shine after extensive wear.

Tweeds, too, come in many weights and even the loosely woven kind have a rock-ribbed strength that wears as well as the hardy Scots and Irish who weave them. A tweed stormcoat I purchased in Dublin more than seven years ago is still the handiest and most handsome bad weather coat in my wardrobe. I doubt that it will ever wear out, and its classic line has weathered hemline and design changes.

RAYON AND ACETATE: Fabrics of special quality which are being used extensively in fashion, rayons, rayon blends, and acetates were considered the first "synthetics." They are not true synthetics because they are vegetable in origin, manufactured from cellulose fibers which come from wood pulp and cotton. Thus they have many advantages of the natural fibers such as breatheability, soft texture, good "hand" as well as easy care and maintenance. Rayon breathes better than acetate because it is derived only from a vegetable base. Acetate which has been combined with acetic acid still breathes better than purely chemical based, synthetic fabrics. Rayons and acetates are more comfortable to wear than true synthetics.

SYNTHETICS: Man's incredible contribution to fashion, testtube fabrics simulate the best qualities of natural fibers at the lowest possible cost and with an ease of maintenance which offers advantages such as wash and wear, permanent press, soil, shrinkage and fading resistance.

Synthetics have drawbacks in that they do not breathe, which makes them uncomfortable. They also create static electricity and pull. Some synthetics lose their shape, sagging eventually at knees, elbows and seats. For practicality's sake, synthetics are a boon to those who travel, to those on a budget and to those who refuse to plug in an iron.

The almost limitless variety of synthetics and synthetic-natural fiber blends, in their many grades and qualities may confuse you, especially with so many manufacturers who have individual processes and labels. Remembering the three major synthetics by their generic names will make it easier for you to know what the fabric is intended to do:

ACRYLIC resembles wool
NYLON resembles silk
POLYESTER resembles cotton

Both the generic term and the manufacturer's trade name for the particular fiber or blend will appear on the label as well as instructions for its care. Synthetics are no longer confined to tacky type outfits. Well known designers are creating costly, opulent clothes from synthetic fabrics.

This brief introduction into the complex field of tailoring, fit and fabrics is intended only as a cursory glance, to give you an idea of what goes into the making of the clothes you wear and what to look for when buying.

While line and design are important, fabric establishes the quality touch. Entering a room in a pure silk, wool or linen ensemble makes a different statement than entering in polyester, but to save money, you can combine the best of low cost fabric with natural fibers, and still look elegant. For comfort, wear natural fibers close to the skin and use synthetics as toppers. Blends are best for office and travel clothes because they are less costly than the naturals and do not require special care.

Being aware of fabric, fit and tailoring gives your clothes a subtle touch of class, creating a fashion image of which you will be proud. Even an ordinary person becomes someone special in an ensemble which makes them feel splendid!

10

The Finishing Touch

I was in Las Vegas appearing for the National Automobile Dealers Association. After my show, I meandered through the vast convention hall in which hundreds of brightly lit and colorful booths offered products and services for the automotive industry. As I passed an exhibit of computers the young woman on duty beckoned to me.

"Hi," she smiled. "I just wanted to tell you how much I enjoyed your show, and how helpful it has been to me. As you can see I am imprisoned in the corporate uniform." She indicated the grey blazer and skirt she was wearing. "Tomorrow I intend to spice it up and change my makeup too."

We chatted animatedly and I was pleased to learn that her company had arranged schedules so that the women executives attending the meeting would have time to catch my show.

This particular young woman looked as drab as a computer read-out. While her suit was handsomely tailored; she wore the face she woke up with, and her hair looked as if she hated it. What she needed desperately was a *finishing touch,* a hairdo and makeup which would add the pizzazz that sparks a warm-colorful-got-it-all-together-look.

There is nothing wrong with wearing no makeup provided one has exquisite skin, vivid coloring with well defined eyebrows and thick eyelashes which lend contrast and shape to the face. If one is pale with a less than perfect skin, and eyebrows and lashes so bland as to be non-existent, then wearing no makeup in public is like not wearing clothes. You look naked. There is a great deal of difference between a natural look, artfully conceived through deft makeup magic, and unknowing, uncaring paleness.

To feel utterly feminine, beautiful and fashionable, know what is new in makeup and hairdo trends and translate them as you do clothes into your own personal language. Many women are so aware of what the latest styles are in clothes, yet so chained by habit to outdated faces and hairstyles, they downgrade the splendid new outfits they have bought. I know a woman who still makes up and wears her hair like Bette Davis did in her early movies. If Bette Davis no longer looks like Bette Davis did in 1938, why should anyone else?

Cosmetics and hairstyles change as often as clothes. When new collections are shown, designers check the *total look* on the models introducing their line and carefully coordinate hairstyles, makeup colors and textures.

Today's hairstyles and makeup are eclectic, realistic and natural looking. They suit our action lives. There is no longer one "face" to be worn at all times. There are many "faces" for the many faceted lives we live, our moods and our clothes. If we do not wear one outfit, why should we wear one "face?" My country face is well scrubbed with little makeup other than moisturizer; barely brown brows, eye-shadow and light lip gloss. My in-town face is more carefully sculpted with color and shadow. My show face is more vivid, with dramatic, defined highlights that become diffused under stage lights and play against the colors I use, enabling audiences to see my expressions even at great distance.

Dress your face and hair as you do your body; to suit the color and textures of your clothes, the time and place in which you wear them, and the mood you wish to create. To put your best face forward, begin with the skin.

THE SKIN

Dermatologists and beauty experts all agree that a consistent program of cleansing, toning and moisturizing is essential in an environment of chemicals, pollutants, central heat and air conditioning. To be a fresh-faced, clear-skinned soap and water beauty is increasingly difficult in our complicated world.

Step one is to identify your skin type:

Ideal skin: smooth, generally poreless and flawless.

Dry skin: feels tight, is flaky, somewhat ashy, but poreless.

Oily skin: enlarged pores, prone to blemishes and eruptions.

Combination skin: the most common with a "T-zone" of oily areas on forehead, nose and chin.

The type of skin to strive for is an ideal complexion which looks healthy, rosy, and has just the right amount of oil and a poreless appearance. Your genes and hormonal makeup establish the skin you have, but good nutrition and health habits improve it immeasurably. Even if you have been lucky enough to have inherited beautiful skin, a diet of junk foods, smoking, alcohol, drugs, excessive stress, and emotional upsets will soon etch your face with lines and discolorations. We discuss a health program in the WINNING part of this book which will help build a healthy complexion from the *inside.* In this chapter we deal with the best ways to care for your skin from the *outside,* and how to use makeup techniques.

The ideal skin is in a state of equilibrium. It is neither too dry nor too oily. It looks fantastic and if you have such a skin you have many options. You can wear all different kinds of makeup, or you can be totally natural. Anything goes. The rest have to be content with trying to achieve the look of an ideal skin.

The rules are simple:
To have beautiful skin; keep it *bright, tight* and *clean!*
To keep skin *bright* is as basic as the three "R's" . . . really good foods, rest and relaxation.
To keep skin *tight;* lightly exercise facial muscles. (See exercise chapter.)
To keep skin *clean;* cleanse, hydrate, tone and moisturize morning and evening, and anytime after you have been outdoors. Cool or tepid water nourishes the skin with moisture, so hydrate your face frequently during the day.

CLEANSING

Ideal skin: Cleanse with pure soaps such as Ivory, Dove, Aveeno Bar, Regular Palmolive and lukewarm water. Rinse, rinse, rinse with tepid water (at least 30 splashes). If you prefer cream, use the water soluable creams. If using an oil based cream, remove with moist washcloth and finish with a gentle toner or freshener.

Dry skin: Avoid soaps and use water soluable creams or cleaners such as the imitation, super-fatted soaps: Lowila Cake, Basis and Oilatum, or Dove which is milder, less fatty and will not cause drying. *Use no skin toners or fresheners.* Beware too hot or too cold water. Dry skin requires gentle pampering. Do not irritate it with extremes in temperature or with rough treatment. Dry face gently. Pat rather than rub.

Oily skin: Young skins do not handle excessive oil well. They tend to break out with acne. Aging skins develop a natural tolerance for oil and youthful conditions generally improve with maturity. The more you wash an oily skin the better! Facial saunas which steam clean are excellent. Wash at least three times a day with Ivory, Neutrogena for Oily Skin or with specially formulated soaps for oily problems. Degrease as much as possible. If excessively oily, soak a cotton ball with water and add astringent. Some astringents or toners, as they are called, have an alcohol base which helps to degrease. Use sparingly to avoid over-drying.

Combination skin: Steam the oily "T-zone" (chin, nose and forehead) with warm terry cloth. Wash with gentle soap and lukewarm water. Rinse well with cool water. Close nose and chin pores with ice-cube wrapped in cloth. Use a toner or freshener on oily "T-zone." Use a water soluable cream or gentle cleanser on cheeks. Do not use toners or fresheners where skin is dry.

If you are too tired after a long day or evening to cleanse your face, fight it! It is worth the battle. Skins stay youthful and beautiful with consistent care. Always cleanse and moisturize before you go to sleep. The more often you cleanse, the better your skin will look.

Many actresses and those whose careers make them particularly visible maintain youthful skins for a long time, simply because they cleanse and moisturize more often than the average woman. In the cleaning and moisturizing, the skin is gently massaged which helps keep it toned and tightened.

Cleanse, moisturize and apply makeup with upward and outward strokes. This helps prevent "down" lines. Think happy thoughts while you do this, and notice how your face lifts. Be gentle while cleaning around the eyes. The skin there is thinner than elsewhere and should never be rubbed.

CLEANSING MASKS

Masks are deep cleansing, pulling surface impurities from the skin, conditioning it, and making you feel fresh and dewy. Make masks part of a weekly, deep cleansing routine. Put them on in the tub where you can relax in tepid, perfumed water, regenerating your face, and relaxing your mind and body. Take a portable radio into the bathroom. Turn on the softest, sweetest music you can find. Sink into water silkened with bath oil, while your face sheds its dead cells. Many good commercial masks are sold and you can experiment with an enormous variety. But if you wish to save money, make your own.

Dry skin mask: Use mayonnaise, Fuller's earth (a powdered clay cleaner sold in drug stores), 1 egg yolk. Mix 4 teaspoons oil rich mayonnaise and 1 teaspoon Fuller's earth. Make a paste. Cleanse your face first as you normally do. If you have super dry skin, or your skin is mature, brush a thin layer of pure egg yolk on *before* you apply the mask. Apply mask and leave on face for 10 minutes. Rinse gently with lukewarm water. Rinse finally with cool water (at least 30 splashes).

Oily skin mask: Use honey, plain yogurt, Fuller's earth, mint extract, bicarbonate of soda. Mix 1 teaspoon honey, ½ cup yogurt, 1 tablespoon Fuller's earth, 2 drops mint extract and a pinch of bicarbonate of soda. Blend well into smooth paste. Apply mask to clean face. The yogurt softens the skin, the Fuller's earth and honey pull top layer impurities from it. Close your eyes, relax for 10 minutes. Rinse off mask with lukewarm water, then cool (at least 30 splashes).

Almond Meal scrub: If you do not take time to make "masking" a weekly routine, substitute Almond Meal scrubs. Do not use on dry skins. You can either make a mask of almond meal and leave it on for 10 minutes, or you can gently massage the almond meal into your skin and remove it with a warm terry cloth and cool water rinse. There are a number of different types of Almond Meal scrubs, some made with honey. You will find them in health food stores and at cosmetic counters.

MOISTURIZING

Moisturizing keeps skin soft, supple and young by creating a barrier which prevents natural cellular water levels from diminshing. In essence moisturizers act as sealers. A sealer need not be heavy to be effective. There is increasing evidence that heavy creams clog pores and actually damage delicate tissues under the eyes, therefore moisturizing is often the most misunderstood part of the cleansing, toning, moisturizing routine.

Moisturizers work best on damp skin and the perfect time to apply them is after a bath or shower, because they seal the added moisture created by the shower. Using moisturizing cream in this fashion has the added advantage of stretching a little dab a long way, which not only assures you of not putting too much on, but in the long run saves you money.

Moisturizing by misting the face with mineral waters is another technique popular with the "spa-set." A status affectation, spritzing the face with mineral water is no more effective than splashing it with water from the tap or using a dampened terry. What you seek is the wetness that feeds the skin, so water it frequently.

Fresh water swimming is fantastic for the face! All exercise stimulates circulation which feeds the skin, but swimming multiple laps with your face immersed in water offers the bonus of moisturizing which keeps skin youthful.

Climate, geography and the type of skin you have determines how much you need to moisturize and what type of cream or liquid is best. It takes experimentation to find those that are most effective.

I change moisturizers according to where I am and what I am doing. In winter, skiing in the East where it is cold and damp, I use a rich, lanolin based cream, layering it heavily around my mouth and on my cheeks where I am driest. Since my lips are the driest part of my face due to years of winter exposure, I wear a natural ingredient, colorless lip cream, under lipstick all year round. When I ski out West in high altitudes, I use a special high altitude cream which contains sunblock. During the summer or while on speaking engagements in Florida I use a sheer, light, aloe-vera liquid with sunscreen. In cities such as Phoenix, Tucson, Salt Lake, Boise, or wherever it is dry, my moisturizer changes again. I find the best moisturizer to be water and my skin feels superb after swimming 50 laps. Immediately after my rinse-off shower I coat my entire body and face with the aloe-vera liquid.

If you live in salt laden air, rinse your face in lukewarm and then cool water often during the day and moisturize lightly morning and evening. When traveling, keep small packets or a vial of cream or liquid in your handbag so that you can rinse and moisturize enroute. Pressurized airplane cabins are excessively drying to the skin. When on a cruise or vacationing at the seashore, rinse frequently and moisturize.

Sunshine is splendid. It lights the day, lifts our spirits and is the source of life. *But it is deadly to the skin!* If you enjoy sports and participate actively, if you are a sun-worshipper, make sure you wear a good sunblock cream at *all times.* Nothing ages the skin more than sunshine. The ultra-violet rays are dangerous and can cause skin cancer. Do not sunbathe between 11 A.M. and 3 P.M. when the rays are harshest. Save sunning for early morning and late afternoons if you want to maintain a youthful skin.

Now that cosmetics are labeled you can identify what you are paying for. Many expensive brands contain the same ingredients as less costly items. Most have a mineral oil base. The ingredient listed first makes up the majority of the formula, with all others in descending proportion. Therefore if you are paying a great deal of money for a very special cream and you find that particular ingredient listed last or close to last, you know that there is very little of it in the product.

I buy many of my cosmetics from a mail order house which specializes in vitamins and naturally based products. But these too contain almost the same ingredients you find in those sold in department stores. That is why I find reading labels fascinating. Those touted as being "natural" contain the very same substances, because almost all cosmetic ingredients are naturally derived from plants and animal oils.

"Natural" oils are in your kitchen cabinet. One of my ski friends uses only safflower oil on his face. Another swears by olive oil. A woman I play tennis with uses mayonnaise. Whatever works best for you and is least expensive is what you want. Examine, explore and experiment. It is fun, especially visiting cosmetic counters for consultation and trying on new faces. If you do not live near these facilities there are numerous individualized makeup services such as: Mary Kay Cosmetics, Avon, Merle Norman, Beauty Control, whose representatives will call on you at home.

Who is the fairest one of all? One who knows what to do and does it! When you see a lovely, well-groomed woman you are looking at someone with a *finished touch*. When she awakes in the morning, she does not look any better than you. But she has learned the art of coordination, grooming and makeup.

MAKING UP YOUR FACE

Makeup begins with foundation because foundations even color and improve skin texture. Some women prefer powder after using a moisturizer. Others prefer a balanced liquid foundation and no powder. I have not used powder in many years. I prefer the natural, more youthful sheen of a liquid foundation. Liquid foundations are water-based, or oil-based and can be used on all skin types. The amount of coverage is easily controlled. Liquid makeup is making cream and cake makeups as obsolete as rice powder and cake mascara.

Foundation looks most natural when it is kept as close to skin color as possible. You want to match the color of your face, not your neck or wrist. However, there are times when foundation color can create special effects and camouflage as well as enhance.
For example:

Colorless foundation smooths fair, porcelain type skins.
Pink-toned foundation brightens sallow skins.
Peach-toned foundation looks best on mature skins.
Beige-toned foundation compliments healthy, outdoor faces.

The difference between whether you look "madeup" or "marvelous" is often the choice of foundation color and your own dexterity in applying it. No one should be aware that you are wearing makeup. If you choose it carefully and work at applying it subtly, no one will! The following is a quick-easy-minutes-only routine for a fantastic face. (sketches 57 and 58)

1. *Foundation*

Dot on foundation working with fingers. Blend over face using up-ward strokes. Do not scrub or pull skin. If foundation does not have enough "slip" mix it with mineral water, or plain water and moistur-izer in the palm of your hand before you apply it. Blend a second coat to cover trouble spots.

2. *Concealer*

To cover darkness under eyes and to camouflage lines, dot conceal-ing cream under eye area. Warm your fingers first in hot water. The warmth will melt the cream slightly, making it easier to apply. Be gentle. Avoid a too-white look.

3. *Rouge*

Smile. Dot cream rouge on highest part of cheekbone. Blend towards hairline. Do not blend close to eyes or middle of face. If you use a dry blush-on, follow the same technique, using brush. If you are "setting" your face with dusting of powder, a touch of blush-on atop the powder will brighten up your cream rouge. (do this after step 4)

4. *Set*

To set makeup, use either powder, water or an ice-cube. If you choose powder, use a light, translucent shade and texture. Brush away excess with a thick makeup brush. I prefer the sheen, the glowing look which is achieved by a spritz of mineral water, a dash of plain water, or by running an ice-cube lightly over my face.

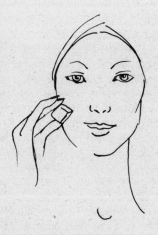

WITHOUT A DOUBT, THE EYES HAVE IT!

Unless a woman is endowed by nature with vivid eyes, thick, dark lashes and well-shaped brows, a woman without eye makeup is like a hot fudge sundae without fudge. Something's missing! No amount of makeup however, will do for the eyes what good health habits will.

Rest, a nutritious diet; and protecting the eyes at work, at play, outdoors, all add up to eyes sparkling with vitality. Our moods; happiness, unhappiness, a positive attitude, or lack of confidence, are all reflected in our eyes. Eyes need daily doses of tender, loving care to keep them healthy.

If you are tired, or have a busy evening ahead, lie down with your feet propped up. Place cotton balls soaked with witch hazel on your closed lids. Unwind. When your eyes tire, "palm" them. Cup the palms of your hands over your eyes. Shut out all light with the cupping. Think . . . black velvet. Sink deeper and deeper into the black velvet. If you have been working steadily or driving, your eyes need this momentary rest. You will be amazed at how refreshed they feel after five minutes of "palming."

Wash your eyes each day, just as you brush your teeth. Use mild boric acid solution, commercial eye wash or eye drops. It is especially important if you use your eyes a great deal in your work; if you live in air-polluted cities; if you have been confined in a smoke filled room; if you have been at the beach. And wash your eyes before you put on eye makeup.

Eye exercises keep eyes bright looking and youthful. They stimulate circulation to the eye and help maintain healthy eye muscles. Do the following anytime, anyplace:

1. Move a pencil slowly left, then right, then up, then down. Follow the pencil with your eyes. Do not move head.

2. Close eyes tightly. Open wide, wide, wider. Blink, blink, blink. Most nearsighted people do not blink often enough.

3. Put arms straight out in front of you. Make two fists. Slowly spread fists apart as you watch each fist move with each eye. Do not move head. Move fists only as far as eye can follow. Return to center, eyes following.

4. Sitting straight, slowly begin to circle eyes, without moving head. Look up, to the right; down to the left. Circle slowly five times, then reverse.

5. The elephant swing relaxes the eyes and the mind. Drop head. Let arms hang and shoulders droop. Feel like an elephant with a huge head hanging. Relax. Swing body wide and easy. Shift weight from foot to foot as you swing. Pick up momentum and give into the swing.

Eye areas wrinkle first because the skin around the eye does not manufacture its own oil. Use a light eye cream at all times. Sleep with it on, and wear it outdoors. Apply it lightly under makeup. If you intend to spend the day sailing, skiing, sunning, swimming or riding on a motorcycle, put a generous layer on. Do not ever rub eyes or rub cream into the skin around the eyes. Pat gently. Exercise stimulates circulation under eye areas and a light tapping with your fingers as you apply eye cream is beneficial.

EYE MAKEUP

The basic eye look should be flattering, chameleon-like, good in all light and relatively quick to do. As with clothing, neutral palettes provide more versatility. They avoid questioning whether to match eye shadow to eyes or to clothes. Browns, greys, taupes and surprisingly neutral mauves enhance all eye colors, are softer in daylight and kind to mature eyes. They provide a muted setting which allows natural eye color to shine forth. Save color and brighter eye shadows for dim lights and festive occasions. They are to play with, not for harsh sunlight or office lights. Avoid frosted shades. They give a harsh look, can cause allergic reactions and make older eyes look older. The idea is to highlight the eyes by softly defining them, rather than riveting one's attention to "Aegean Blue." If you love eye color and what it does for you, tone it with a soft beige over the color.

Eye coloring is so varied you have a host of options: creams, sticks, pencils, liquids, tubes, pressed powder. Some find pressed powder shadow the easiest to apply. It blends well and is long lasting. I cannot use pressed powder shadow or mascara when I wear my contact lenses. Even the most minute particle flaking off causes irritation. I stick with cream eyeshadow in pencil type tubes and wear false eyelashes when I wear contacts.

To apply eye makeup:
Required tools: eyelash curler,
brow brush, eyebrow pencil or
powder, mascara, grey crayon and
Q-tips.

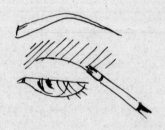

1. Apply light tone neutral shadow
to clean, dry eyelid.

2. Apply darker tone neutral shadow in crease and slightly above.
Blend upward so that there is no
demarcation line. Add shadow to
outer corner of bottom lid.

3. Curl lashes. Gently grasp lashes
in curler. Squeeze for several
seconds.

4. Powder lashes. Use a brush to remove excess. Apply mascara sweeping lashes upward to separate them. Repeat if needed. Using the tip of mascara wand, coat bottom lashes lightly. The most efficient way of applying mascara is to look down into a mirror and brush up. Several thin coats, followed by separating and brushing the lashes is more effective than one heavy coat.

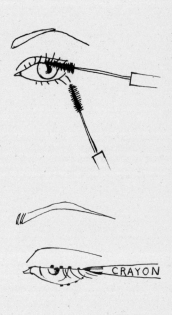

5. Eye liners are meant to make lashes look thicker. Make dots close to lash with eye crayon. Smudge with Q-tip to achieve a soft, smoky effect. Avoid hard lines. Line the inside rim of the bottom lid with navy blue liner. It relieves redness in the eye, makes whites whiter and the eyes look brighter. Widen close-set eyes by applying liner emphasis to outer corners only.

6. Brush eyebrows upward. Fill in space with brow color. Arch should match natural curve of the eye. Tweeze wild hairs. Brows should never be exaggerated either in shape or darkness. Too strong an eyebrow accent detracts from the eye. If you have heavy, straggly brows tame them with a touch of moustache wax.

Skillfully applied, eye makeup makes the face more expressive, and helps to camouflage less than perfect features as effectively as clothes camouflage the figure. Eye contouring creates the following effects:

Deep set eyes: Use light (white or beige) shadow under brow. Apply shadow sparingly on outer corner of lid. Line upper and lower lids lightly with eyeliner. Mascara upper lashes only.

Close set eyes: Run a line of light shadow from tear duct to middle of brow. Do not use shadow close to nose. Apply liner, mascara or false eyelashes towards outer edge, away from inside corner of eye. Apply mascara more heavily to outer corner of upper lash, lightly to outer corner of lower lash. Eyes look further apart when makeup begins away from nose.

Baggy eyes: Lighten deep crevices under bags with light toned shadow or foundation. Brush a darker eye powder or use a darker foundation on puffy bag. Line and mascara upper lids only; avoid all harsh lines.

Bulging eyes: Use darker shadow on entire upper lid to deepen the look. Line and mascara upper lids only. Keep the look soft and smoky.

Wide set eyes: Apply shadow to entire upper lid. Line upper lid fully. Mascara upper lashes and outer half of lower lashes. To create the look of wide set eyes, apply shadow from center of upper lid outward, line and mascara from center outward.

FALSE EYELASHES

By all means, try false eyelashes. I became a devoted user years ago. My natural lashes are blond and baby-fine. Without false lashes my eyes look bald. With them I *feel* more attractive. They are worth the time I spent learning how to put them on.

It was doubly difficult for me since I wear contact lenses and I could not figure out whether the lashes should go on first, and then the lenses; or pop the lenses in and then try to glue the lashes. At times the lashes wound up on my nose, more often I lost the lenses!

Putting false eyelashes on takes practice. I find it easiest when I close my eye, look into the mirror with the other eye and place the lashes just under the fold that lies between my natural lashes and the lid. Curve the lash to the shape of your eye before you begin. Make sure it fits. If too long, cut from *outer* end. To make eyes look wider, place lashes slightly away from inside corner. Demi-lashes that are not quite as long are good for people with close set eyes. To curl false eyelashes, wet them and let dry wrapped around a pencil.

Squeeze a small amount of surgical adhesive on a pin. Draw a fine line of adhesive along edge of lashes. Place on eyelid. Press lash gently in towards lid. When adhesive sets, press your own lashes and false eyelashes together. Mascara.

A more natural looking alternative to strip lashes is the individual lash sold in clusters of long and short hairs. They are more time consuming to apply than strip lashes and take more practice, but they look exactly like your own. Use them as fill in or for emphasis wherever you wish. They create the illusion of thickly lashed eyes. Do not place them close to inner corner of eye, no matter what your eye shape.

To apply:
Begin at middle. Pick up lash with tweezer. Dip base into adhesive. Affix artificial lash to base of lid or to base of natural lash if you are lengthening it. (Some makeup experts place artificial lash one third of way down on natural lash. While it looks fine from a front view, it looks false from all other angles.)

If you are satisfied with the placement of the first lash, continue until all lashes are affixed achieving the look you wish. *Check each lash after placement.* Look straight into the mirror. Look down. Look at lashes from a profile view. Make sure lash is securely in place. Apply individual lashes after curling your natural lashes and before using mascara. The results are more natural than strip lashes with the added bonus of meeting your personal needs.

EYEBROWS

Eyebrows lend animation, expression and balance to the face. Unless you want to raise eyebrows keep them as natural as possible. Pluck brows only if they are wild, shaggy, sit too closely over the eyes and cannot be tamed. Do not be a promiscuous plucker! Make sure each hair really should come out.

To pluck: Brush brow and continue to brush as you go along. Cream the area generously, and sterilize the plucked area afterwards with alcohol. Make sure alcohol does not get near your eyes. Run an ice-cube over brows to prevent swelling.

LIPS

No matter what the trend, the only people who look attractive without lip color are women under twenty and men! For a youthful, dewy look, use soft-toned lipsticks in muted or frosted shades.

Lipsticks come in four basic colors: Reds, Browns, Pinks, Oranges. *Reds* highlight the colors you wear and are the most important of the four basic shades. Reds are best with strong colors, and to create special effects. Reds look warm and vivid under night lighting and liven colors that need bright complement. Bright reds also enhance stylistic type clothes, such as a 30's look.

Browns neutralize and tone down the colors you wear. They look best with textures, tweeds, wools. Brown tones are more natural looking and more appropriate during the day or for the office.

Pinks can be paradoxical. Some softly minimize the look. Others like fuschia center attention on your lips and pull the eye away from what you are wearing.

Oranges are difficult to wear because they look as unnatural as Tang tastes. Coral is kinder to the face and easier to accessorize, since it is a deft blend of orange and pink.

The main consideration of lip color is that it harmonize with the rest of your makeup, (no burgundies or bright magenta with brick blushon!) and that you achieve color compatibility with the clothing nearest your face. Almost any color lipstick can be worn with black, navy and white, but other colors and shades need an educated, talented blending.

Do not throw old lipsticks away just because you have tired of them, or the color that looked so great at the cosmetic counter now seems all wrong. Save used lip gloss pots to create your own colors! Crush old lipstick into pot, add a bit of your new favorite color (slice it from the top with a razor blade). Mix thoroughly with a lip brush. You have created a new custom color and saved money on a new lipstick! Dig favored, used up colors out of tube bases. Put into lip gloss pots and mix up a new batch.

To make up your mouth:
Begin by outlining lips. Many makeup artists like to use a pencil darker than the lip color and an all over application of lip liner. I find this approach creates a hard, artificial look. A more believable mouth is created by using two pencils: one slightly *lighter* than your lipstick and one slightly *darker.* The lighter shade is used to define the lips and keep lipstick from bleeding into the tiny crevices surrounding the mouth. Do this first. The darker pencil is for emphasis after main lip color is in place. Highlight top center "M" and center bottom of lips with darker pencil. This creates a sculpting effect with color.

After lining lips, apply lipstick directly from tube or with lipstick brush. To complete lip makeup, apply gloss to the *center* of bottom lip. Any other placement of gloss will wear away too quickly and gives a greasy rather than moist appearance. Use the ever faithful Q-tip to clean any smudges.

Whatever makeup you choose it must be compatible with your body chemistry. Many are allergic to various cosmetics and the new labeling law is helpful in determining what the actual ingredients are.

Take time to experiment with makeup. Try many brands until you find that which suits you best. You will be amply rewarded for the time spent with a glowing, finished look that makes you self-confident, beautiful and secure!

11

The Crowning Touch

Is it not ironic that I, the victim of confused and cranky chromosomes, which must have been kissing cousins to Telly Savalas, should be writing a chapter on hairstyles and hair care?

The ultimate irony is that my hair is so poor it has supported me handsomely for 22 years. It is the keystone of my show. Without my miserable hair, the show would be less funny. What I thought was soft and silky as a child, I now know is horrid. How it came about is a mystery. Experts tell us the quality of our hair is genetic. My parents, grandparents, uncles, aunts, cousins, all have thick, beautiful hair. My sons' hair is incredibly handsome. My daughter had lovely hair until she went out West to ski for two years. After months of steady skiing in high altitudes and bright sunshine without protecting her hair or scalp, her hair is now like mine: limp, thin and baby-fine.

My research indicates my hair is the result of a hormonal imbalance with which I was born. During my pregnancies my hair grew thick, lustrous and long. Three months after my children were born, it would begin to fall out in handfuls. Since it was inconvenient to stay pregnant all the time, I have learned to cope, although I have never accepted having ugly hair. I read all I can about hair and hair care. I take vitamins. I watch what I eat. I balance the stress in my life. I seek professional advice. I do all the right things. Does it help?

Not a whit! All I can hope for is that in my next incarnation I come back as Farrah Fawcett's grandchild.

I remember years back making an appointment with a leading hair stylist who I hoped might devise a cut I could handle. I was so ashamed to have him see my hair as it actually was, I went to a local shop *first* to have it washed and set! When the "great one" looked at my hair, he shook his head, lifted his scissors limply and sighed, "I'll give it a try!"

Another time on the Dinah Shore show, when one of the world's most famous hairdressers was challenged to do a hairdo on me, he laughed and put a wig on my head instead!

Because of my hair I am ultra-sensitive to the importance of hair in creating the crowning touch to the finished look. A handsome head of hair, beautifully styled makes one look sensational. And how great it makes one *feel!* Without lovely hair, one looks unfinished and unattractive.

Pick parents with heavy, lustrous manes if you want to have a fantastic head of hair. (Mine didn't help me at all). It is the only way you are going to get it, for the hair you are born with is the hair you will have! You can never have more, no matter what some may promise. Your body allows only the number of hairs your genetic printout calls for, and no amount of brushing, oiling, shampooing, conditioning and dressing is going to change that.

Without proper care, you could lose what you have even with a good genetic heritage. Chemicals, air pollution, poor nutrition, smoking, excessive stress, over-bleaching, over-permanenting, over-anything that is harsh hurts hair.

The hair, like the rest of our body is fed by the bloodstream. If important nutrients are missing, vitamins, trace minerals, oil, protein, the hair will not flourish. The hair bulb passes these nutrients on to the nucleus of the hair. If the nourishment is inadequate the hair stops developing. When the bulb becomes diseased or toxic, the hair stops growing and falls out.

Did you know that our scalp has muscles? The Arrector Pili muscle keeps hair erect and anchored to the scalp. Like all muscles it contracts, which allows hair to move as it grows. When this muscle tightens due to spasms caused by stress or poor nutrition, it locks hair in place and the hair stops moving. This can often be painful. If these muscles weaken, hair becomes limp and falls out.

Hair shafts contain a medulla and cortex. The medulla is an inner, center chamber. It is the nucleus of the hair. Surrounding and protecting it is the cortex, which maintains moisture and oil. When we change hair color chemically we bleach the cortex of its pigment. In addition, each hair strand consists of a number of layers stacked one on top of each other which protect the cortex. The outer layer is called the cuticle. It is the number of these layers which determine hair thickness, density and quality. The loss of layers leads to thin, brittle, damaged hair.

Thick hair has as many as 20 layers. My hair probably has three. The layers consist of a hardened type of protein which is almost plastic-like. It can melt, soften, crack, be colored, reshaped and can dry out becoming brittle.

When hair is colored, the dye collects in the third layer. Since the layers are translucent, color shows through the layers above. The follicles which emerge from the scalp have various degrees of curving as they follow exit pathways. The curving causes slits in the outer layer of the hair as it is bent. These slits give the hair flexibility, and the sharper the curve of the follicle, the curlier the hair. Slits are formed as the hair is bent in different directions when styled and combed. Permanent waves slit the outer layers to form new, flexible shapes. Once the hair shaft is slitted, it becomes vulnerable. Straight hair is much stronger than curly hair because it has few slits. Evidence of this is the incredibly strong straight hair of the American Indian and the Eskimo.

The sebaceous gland, which manufactures oil, connects to the follicle and is located close to where the hair exits from the scalp. It lubricates the shaft reducing the friction caused by the emerging process. The oil also protects the scalp from the elements. Unfortunately the sebaceous gland manufactures mostly saturated oil and the body seeks to rid itself of it by dispensing it to various glands in excessive amounts. When the sebaceous gland overproduces, one has greasy, oily scalp, hair and skin. Diet, rather than shampoo controls this gland best.

The scalp must be kept clean, pliable and moist if one is to have healthy hair. If the scalp becomes tight, hardened, waxy, it loses its mobility and the muscles lose their tone. The follicle openings close, the hair suffocates and falls out. Therefore a consistent program of scalp massage is necessary to keep scalps pliable and pink. A pink scalp is a healthy scalp. A white, tight scalp is a danger signal. Whenever you think of it, run your fingers through your scalp and massage it with a gentle, rotary movement. Begin at the back of the neck and work up and forward. It takes only a few moments and you will feel your scalp tingle. Make scalp massage a daily habit.

Keeping hair healthy is simple if you know the facts. If the nucleus of the hair is harmed by poor nutrition, excessive stress, disease, chemicals and physical abuse the hair will atrophy and fall out. New hairs actually grow side by side with the hairs they are replacing, but they too can be deficient and loss will occur. Many times due to illness, hormonal changes, stress, we lose large amounts of hair. Once the problem is corrected new hairs will grow, but remember, *new hair exits from already existing follicles,* and we have only the specific number *we were born with.* If the follicle opening is closed or has been destroyed, that is the end of that particular hair.

TO KEEP HAIR HEALTHY

Eat a well balanced diet of nutritious, natural foods. Balance the stress and pressures in your life through exercise, meditation and relaxation. Keep hair clean and conditioned. Since many shampoo advertisements refer to ph scale, it is wise that you know to what they are referring. The ph scale between 0 and 6.9 is acid. Seven is neutral. Alkaline ph ranges from 7.1 to 14. Experts approximate that the healthiest ph for hair would be 5.5. If you eat a lot of acid forming foods such as meat and dairy products, hair and scalp will have an acid ph. If you eat mainly vegetables, grains and fruits, hair and skin are closer to neutral.

Massage scalp daily.
Protect hair from the elements by keeping it covered in hot sun and wind.

Avoid the following physical abuses:

Combing or brushing wet hair.

Excessive shampooing and rinsing. Hot water forces its way into the slits and cracks of outer hair layers, loosening them and draining the layers of natural lubrication. Some of the water can even find its way to the nucleus and cause permanent damage, which leads to thinning hair.

Washing and rinsing hair under high pressure showers. Never use a shower massager on the hair. It shatters hair layers with its force. Water force also stimulates sebaceous glands to produce more oil, making hair greasier. If you wash and rinse hair in the shower, keep water pressure gentle and temperature tepid.

Rough toweling also damages hair layers. You strip the slitted outer layers with rough towel drying. This causes remaining layers to lift, attracting positive electric charges from the atmosphere which create static electricity and flyaway hair. Use a towel in one direction only.

Chemical processing — bleaching, frosting, straightening, permanent waves — anything that alters hair structure and color affects the protective layers, softening and loosening them. If you, like I, use these chemicals, then you must also use preventative measures to condition the hair.

Hot air drying and styling.

Keeping tight rollers in hair for long periods.

Tying hair back tightly or in pony tails.

Sleeping on one side of the head.

Most harmful of all to hair is that which ages the skin: sun, wind, and a dry atmosphere. When moisture is removed from the scalp it triggers the sebaceous gland to produce even more oil. At first this normalizes the hair, but then it becomes excessive and the hair becomes dry, causing a flaking, itchy scalp and lifeless looking hair. The answer is to use a humidifier in winter and to cut back on air conditioning in summer. Adding raw vegetable oil to your daily diet is also helpful.

BEAUTY PRODUCTS FOR THE HAIR

As with the skin, you have to know the kind of hair you have and its condition before you haphazardly use shampoos, rinses, conditioners, hair colors, tints, permanents, etc. The effects of many hair products can be surprising and harmful. For example: cream rinses act as softeners. If your hair is already overly soft, using a cream rinse can damage it. Some hair conditioners contain thickeners.

These thickening agents saturate the slits in the hair layers and cause the layers to become loosened. The layers will eventually fall off, which is the opposite of what you want.

Harsh shampoos to control oil could overdry your scalp and hair, aggravating the problem. If you have problem hair: soft hair, split ends, the frizzies, or you "can't do a thing with it," have it tested by a professional who can determine its density, thickness, and the condition of the hair layers. Then you will have a prescription for hair care that is individually tailored to your needs.

Read also, Philip Kingsley's excellent book on hair and hair care: *The Complete Hair Book* (Grosset & Dunlap, 1979).

If you have the kind of hair my sons have, thick, curly, indestructible, browse hair cosmetic counters with abandon. Enjoy experimenting with whatever strikes your fancy!

HAIRSTYLES

Contour is just as important in hairstyles as it is in clothes. Hairstyles balance the total look, doing for the face what clothes do for the figure. Bangs, for example, help conceal a long, narrow or too-wide forehead. Short bangs lengthen the face.

Hair that looks non-structured, natural, loose, carefree makes you appear younger than a tightly coiffed head. Little tricks with hair camouflage, reproportion and fool the eye:

Avoid too long, or too full styles if you are short and plump. Keep hair short, high and soft.

For those who are slender and young, loose, shoulder length styles look sensational.

If you are keel heavy, keep hair high and somewhat wide at the crown.

Those with swan-like necks look good in longer styles and fuller cuts; those whose necks are short do better with short hair, brushed up off neck.

If you have crow's feet, fluff hair at temples, waving it near the eye corners to conceal lines.

Center parts are for those with almost perfect, oval faces. If one's nose is Nefertiti-like, or one's face moon-shaped, steer left or right of center parts.

Low side parts and hair brushed high soften square faces and help reproportion those with avocado and round-shaped faces.

Extreme hair styles such as the small head look demand finely chiseled, even features. If you have easily managed hair that responds well to styling, try whatever new look comes along. It keeps you on top of the fashion scene and those you know can never take you for granted!

HAIR PIECES

For those of us who cannot change hairstyles as we would wish, wigs and other hair pieces are the answer. Wigs, falls, chignons and curls are fun, convenient and add variety. Some like myself are dependent on them for a dressed-up look. Others who have lost hair due to illness and cancer therapy depend on them for full time wear.

The secret to a natural looking wig, is to choose one that is loose, with hair falling slightly over forehead and about the face. Make sure no hard, "wiggy" line can be seen. Blend wig color with your skin color. Note, I did not say, "hair color." Why wear a wig the same color as your hair? You can of course, but it is much more fun and intriguing to wear a different shade, as long as it harmonizes with your skin tones. Try a daring shade, one that will change your outlook and personality.

Synthetic fiber wigs are terrific. They require little care, look best when shaken and brushed rather than combed and are oftentimes less costly than a cut, wash and set in a salon.

And you can try on a new color and style without having to change your own hair! If you contemplate changing your hair color or style, try on some wigs first before making this important decision. You might even buy the wig closest to what you want and live with it for a while to see if it really suits your mood and needs.

Wigs are wonderful for traveling, especially if you will be gone for a period of time and your hair begins to change color at the roots. If you are reluctant to have your hair treated enroute, a wig solves the problem.

Wearing wigs constantly is not good for your own hair, but wearing them occasionally is pure pleasure!

People have become so accustomed to me in my wigs, even my closest friends forget it is not really my own hair. While skiing a wooded trail one Sunday with my friend Sandy and my sons, a low-hanging tree branch snagged my wig from my head. I threw myself into the snow as a shrill scream sliced through the cold. Sandy, rounding the bend behind me, seeing me in the snow, my hair in the tree, *fainted!* The boys, embarrassed, skied on down the mountain pretending we were total strangers!

I hope all I have written so far will make you feel and look special, and will save you money. It is time now to get to the nitty-gritty, to determine what lurks in your closet so that you can easily coordinate what you have with the ideas presented.

12

Closets . . .
Putting It All Together

One time after a show, a man came forward tugging a woman along. "I'd like you to meet my wife, Meg," he grinned, "she has two closets filled with nothing to wear!"

Meg smiled sheepishly. "I can never throw *anything* out, yet whenever something important comes up, like tonight, I never have anything I *want* to wear!"

Meg is one of those millions of women with closets of collectibles they are reluctant to cull. I understand fully. Whenever I give something away or sell it, I then need it. Since I enjoy recycling and redoing clothes, it makes it doubly difficult to heed the wise inner voice which nags, "Clean it out, Judy, clean it out!"

It takes determination to discard that which clutters our closets and stamina to redo them, but before you shop for new clothes you should know what lies in their depths . . . so let's clean them out *now!*

Look at it as an adventure. You will find treasures you've long forgotten and you can make money on discards and duds by selling them or giving them away and taking a tax writeoff. For a clean, new feeling about your closet, why not repaint or repaper the interior, so that your collection, both old and new, has a bright, cheerful, organized place in which to shine?

The lift you get when your closet is freshened is fantastic. It reflects itself even in the way you look around the house, for you will wear clothes you have forgotten about and to which you will add new life and a new dimension. You know how good it feels when you've cleaned up that mess in the garage? Cleaning out a closet is even *better*. It is the ultimate high of housework.

The only way to reorganize a closet is *all the way*. Halfway measures won't work. Choose a time when nothing will interfere, when you can be alone for a number of hours. Turn your favorite music on and begin by taking *everything* out.

Prepare the room first for the clutter. If you have a portable clothes rack, set it up. If not, arrange chairs, clear the bed and have cartons handy in which to place clothes in their category together.

As you remove a garment, try it on. If it still fits your figure, your personality and your lifestyle and is in tune with contemporary fashion, it is a collectible. Keep it. If you find, however, that you have not worn it for years, chances are you won't and unless it is a special treasure you wish to keep as a memento (which should be stored and wrapped in tissue paper) sell it, or give it away and get a receipt for its value so you can write it off.

The compunction to keep fine quality clothes is strong and if you are a good recycler that's fine, you will appreciate the recycling suggestions offered later in this chapter. But if you cannot thread a needle and the thought of altering anything makes you dash to Dunkin' Donuts, keeping clothes with the intention of redoing them is unrealistic.

Major changes to duplicate new styles are expensive if done professionally and chancey unless you are skilled. Therefore be realistic about what you wish to keep when you restructure your closet, recycle your clothes and reorganize.

How can anyone function with an unlit closet? A lighted closet is essential and battery lights are fine if you do not wish to invest in professional wiring.

Unbelievable clutter surrounds you. Was this all in your closet? you ask. What do I do now? Organize!

Coats first. Hang them by color, weight and texture. Use good quality, padded hangers. Hang the coats you use most often the easiest to get to. If you have an entry closet, put all your coats there, with the exception of lightweight wraps that are an integral part of an ensemble.

Separate skirts from suit jackets. Categorize all separates: skirts, jackets, pants, blouses, vests, jerkins, tunics. Hang pants by the cuff,

Sketch 61

Sketch 62

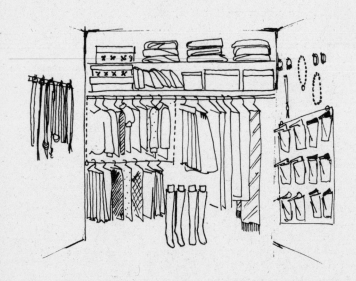

skirts by the waistband. Folding skirts and pants over hanger bars creates wrinkles. Arrange the separates according to color and weight. Hang them so that you can easily see what goes with what. One jacket can coordinate with many skirts; blouses and shirts can be worn with a number of skirt, pant, jacket combinations. If you hang jackets, vests and blouses on half bars above skirts and pants it will make selecting separates a cinch.

If you are renting or are subject to frequent transfer you may choose not to permanently or professionally refit your closet. Hanging rods are available in notions departments which double your hanging space by creating two halfway levels. Other closet extenders include hangers which have several clips for skirts and pants and several shoulder bars for shirts and blouses.

Hang dresses so they face separates section. Placing dresses and separates in close proximity enables you to experiment with interesting coordination. Why not add a jacket or blazer to a dress; wear a blouse which has a straight, finished hem open as a third layer, or tie the tails of a shirt at the waist? Vests, jerkins, sweaters, tunics, scarves, belts all add interest to dresses extending your wardrobe into the unexpected. Try not to crowd clothes. Let them hang freely to prevent wrinkling.

Place folded sweaters on the shelf above separates. Make one stack of pullovers, one stack of cardigans. If you have two-piece knitted suits make sure you either hang them on a well padded hanger, or fold them as you do sweaters. Keep two piece knits in separates section, because they can be combined with other articles in your wardrobe. Do not think of a two piece knit merely as a single outfit. It is a separate! Wear the knitted skirt with a blouse and belt it; the top with a tweed skirt and jacket, and both with a blazer.

Categorize clothes by color and weight rather than season since many clothes today are transitional and can be worn year round. Good visibility in your closet is important because seeing all your clothes makes it easier for you to coordinate creatively. Arrange articles so that you can see and identify them. I use clear plastic boxes for shoes, scarves and jewelry, placing a label in the front of each box which helps me identify the contents more easily. I have a vast collection of scarves and I categorize them by color, keeping like tones in one box. My non-valuable jewelry is categorized as to season and kind: e.g. all summer bracelets in one box; necklaces another; pins another. Shoes are stacked according to season and color.

I do not keep garment bags in my ready-to-wear closet but in a storage closet where I store out-of-season and out-of-use-at-the-moment clothes. I label these bags as well. Small, clutch type handbags are in a clear plastic, hanging bag with shelves which I purchased in the notions department. My larger handbags are arranged by color and texture on the shelf above the plastic shoe boxes.

When my friend Sandy lived in Greenwich Village she had only one meager closet, but it had high ceilings. She had a carpenter install an extra rung above the standard rod where she hung her out-of-season clothes, reaching them with an old-fashioned hooked stick. At one time I lived in an apartment which had a small, but deep closet. I installed an extra rod, behind the original.

Belts are best on belt rings or hung on hooks where you can see them. The idea is to keep everything up front, for seeing what we have makes us use it more. So many of us tend to store things away and then forget about them. Many closets are of the sliding door type which prevents you from using the insides of the doors for hanging accessories. Make use of a sliding door by having it mirrored on the outside. It not only makes the room larger and more attractive, it give you a good sized reflection in which to check your creativity.

RECYCLE—RENOVATE—RE-USE

Almost anything can be altered, updated, resurrected.

Long dresses and skirts can be shortened and the extra fabric turned into a sash, scarf, or when trimmed with fringe, worn as a shawl.

Short, outdated dresses can be cut into overblouses or worn under skirts. Ruth, an early morning walking enthusiast and a retiree on a fixed income, cleverly wears her daughter's cast-off short dresses as blouses under sports skirts. Ruth also updated a pair of out-dated culottes by ripping the seams, refashioning them into a skirt, top-stitching a new seam down the center.

Tuck too-short pants into boots. Wear them as knickers, or cut them shorter and wear as gauchos. Add top-stitching or trimming to let-down hems so that original hemlines do not show. Turn a daytime dress into evening by hemming it with boa. Update old blouses by stitching new buttons on with embroidery floss in a color to match or contrast with the fabric. Replace buttons for a newer, more contemporary appearance. Wear old shirts and blouses under sweaters with only the collars and cuffs showing. Try an old lacetrimmed slip under a silk blouse which is worn open for a provocative evening look. Insert or remove shoulder pads according to current styles. Turn coats into box jackets. Refashion old furs into vests, jerkins, or as linings for outerwear.

If you are a skilled seamstress, update suit jackets and coats. Narrow or widen lapels, shorten or lengthen jackets and hems depending on current styles. If the suit is of excellent quality and you are unskilled, have an expert do it. Add a pin, a flower, a scarf or a belt and suddenly what you intended to discard has taken on new life!

I've adopted a number of my son's cast off shirts, especially old velours which I love to lounge in. Longer than my own shirts, the old velours are dandy pajama tops on a cold night. The dress shirts are great for casual wear. Since the sleeves are too long, I cut and hem them and wear them rolled. If the collars are frayed I remove them and top stitch the neckline for a collarless look. I either cut shirtails off and hem them straight or I wear them folded up with tails tied around my waist. The shirts are good quality cotton, and comfortable casual wear under sweaters, and with sports clothes.

The gold color chain I use as a necklace or belt in my show was once the handle to a handbag. When the handbag wore out, I detached the chain. When the ruffled look was the rage years back, I had kitchen curtains I yearned to get rid of, but my frugality prevented me tossing them out for no reason. Priscilla style organdy, they were trimmed with yards and yards of lush ruffles. I made collars and cuffs to create a ruffled look and use them to this day.

Hundreds of recycling possibilities lurk in your closets. With the soaring cost of clothes, renovating is not only fun, it is money smart! If you enjoy recycling old clothes and buying antique items Diana Funaro's excellent book *"The Yestermorrow Clothes Book"* (Chilton 1976) offers detailed drawings and instructions.

CARING FOR CLOTHES

Some people care for clothes like my daughter. Wherever they drop, they lie, to be picked up days (or weeks) later and cleaned hurriedly, all in a bunch.

Years of performing and the need to have clothes on-the-ready have instilled discipline. I hang my clothes immediately and check them for soil and needed repairs *before* I put them away.

I think my system is easier. My daughter thinks I am compulsive. When I watch her anguish as she tries to press a wrinkled skirt moments before an appointment, or wash ten loads an hour before departure, I am grateful for the discipline I have developed.

It is much easier to care for clothes with a consistent program than to toss them all into the closet for "Sunday." Save little repair jobs such as ripped hems, loose buttons, split seams for your favorite talk shows. Iron to music, its cadence lending rhythm to your strokes. Wash, iron, repair and send to the cleaners as the need arises. Do not wait for "Sunday or someday," which comes all too soon. Then the mountain of clothes which need care becomes so depressing you either spend the whole day cursing or you raid the refrigerator.

Check clothes for soil and spots and check handbags and shoes as well, polishing and cleaning them *before* you put them away. Putting good leathers into the closet soiled lessens their life.

Oil or polish shoes and handbags frequently to keep them looking lovely. Stuffing shoes with tissue or using shoe trees helps maintain their shape. If you are caught in a downpour as I was with a favorite pair of Ferragamo leather pumps, stuff them with tissue or newspaper until they are dry and then use mink oil to restore suppleness. I find that Jubilee Kitchen Wax cleans white or light colored leathers beautifully.

A lesson I have learned in 22 years of travelling and lecturing is to lay out clothes the night before. Wrinkles generally disappear when clothes are laid out. When on the road, I hang them in the bathroom before I retire, steaming them out by turning the hot water on. This is especially effective for velvets and other napped fabrics. If you do not travel with an iron and you have no time to steam your clothes in the bathroom, every hotel room has an object which works as an iron . . . the light bulb in any lamp! Turn the light off, remove shade, dust off the bulb. Turn light back on and as the bulb warms, quickly run the area to be smoothed over the warming bulb. The hotter the bulb gets the faster you must work. It is an excellent emergency measure.

Pressing clothes is an art, and while I am not the best of ironers, I have learned a few hints which work.

A good steam iron that does not spit and a sturdy, well padded board is essential. Treat yourself also to a sleeve board and a shoulder mitt. They make it easier for you to do a professional job. Turn garment inside out, or if you iron on the right side, use a cotton pressing cloth.

To prevent press marks showing on the right side when ironing seams flat, place an envelope or a double sheet of paper, *under the seam allowance,* as you iron. If the garment is lined, iron inside first, turn to right side and use a pressing cloth. If there are stubborn wrinkles in the seat or in the sleeves, use a damp cotton press cloth. Purchase pressing cloths, sleeve boards and shoulder mitts in the notions department.

I travel with an iron and steamer (for my hats) and I use large bath towels doubled, placing them either on the floor or on a table for ironing needs.

Those on tight budgets should consider the cost of dry cleaning when purchasing garments which have DRY CLEANING ONLY tags sewn inside. While I do wash my silk scarves and on occasion have washed my silk shirts in cold water and Woolite—hand washing silk shirts is a chore and requires *careful pressing.* IT IS MUCH SAFER TO DRY CLEAN SILKS. Woolite diluted slightly and applied deftly also does a good job on fabric handbags and shoes.

Light colored clothes, unless they are easy-to-care-for synthetics can put a crimp in budgets. Whites and pale colors look lovely only when they are *bright* and *clean,* and natural fibers will require frequent dry cleaning. Therefore if you love the natural fabrics, plan to spend more money on maintenance.

Linings too must be considered. The status of a handsome suit or coat is diminished by a soiled or ripped lining. Replace linings that have aged in good quality clothes.

Since moving to the cabin I use bulk dry cleaning machines for sweaters, slacks and other garments which do not require professional pressing. It is less expensive than paying for dry cleaning by the piece. After a while however, dry cleaning woolen sweaters robs them of their texture. Washing is best for woolens, for wool is a natural fiber which responds well to water. Wash good woolens in cold water with Woolite, adding a teaspoon of baby oil to the rinse so that the wool retains its softness. Block away from heat and allow to dry naturally.

If you have synthetic clothes which have "pilled," I pass on a hint given to me by Penny, a young executive who is successful in a male-dominated industry while maintaining an attractive and soothing femininity. Penny uses cheap, about-to-be-discarded razors whisking them lightly over clothes which have pilled. I tried it on an Orlon sweater and the pills disappeared!

Your closets are now freshened and organized. All the chaff has been discarded and you have a good idea of what you own and what goes with what. You have also promised yourself to be consistent about clothes care and maintenance. All this industrious effort deserves to be rewarded and what better treat than shopping for something new to add luster to that lovely uncluttered closet!

Let's explore the lively art of getting the most for your money!

13

Getting The Most
For Your Money

Getting the most for your money, and buying the best for your needs is a game of skill rather than luck! Shopping is a national pastime for some and a dreaded chore for others. To shop successfully requires training. It means developing an educated eye and the discipline and endurance of a long distance runner.

Shopping for clothes is a costly, time-consuming undertaking and should begin with a structured plan. It is amazing to me how women who appear completely practical, efficient and moneywise will become impulsively emotional when they shop for clothes for themselves. I know women who never make a mistake when choosing things for their family, who shop for food loaded with lists and cents-off coupons, spending hours in supermarkets to save pennies, only to blow it all at Bloomingdale's on fashions they will wear once or twice and then tire of.

Buying does stimulate our emotions and to strike a happy balance between mind and desire takes discipline, determination, *and a plan*. Shopping impulsively is risky. One incident comes to mind.

Years ago I fell mindlessly in love with an orange sherbert, nubby wool suit. It was perfect in every possible way, except one . . . *it was all wrong for me*. But, blinded by the beauty of the fabric and mesmerized by the markdown (it had been so drastically reduced the tag hypnotized my eyeballs and levitated my charge plate to the clerk), I bought it anyway. I rationalized all the way home, refusing to acknowledge the persistent drone in my head which nagged, "Orange sherbert nubby wool? You'll look like a melted cone!"

My son Jeff, home from school, took one long look at me in the suit and boomed, "Boy, Mom, you're getting fat!"

I went to the phone immediately and dialed my next door neighbor, a pompous woman with an irritating, pretentious attitude. I judged giving her the suit in recompense for her frequent jibes. She loved it (as I knew she would) and I enjoyed the way she looked in it as she waddled to the elevator.

Stores play on our emotions with clever merchandising, enticing displays and "packaging". And how persuasive "packaging" can be! There is little you have ever bought in any category that has not been carefully researched and "packaged" to stimulate your senses, to play on your emotions so that you could not help but buy it!

Even the tossed about tables and stacks of racks in non-glamorous discount stores are part of "packaging." Their chaotic clutter leads you to believe that you are getting a bargain and so you barrel through them, impulsively buying much you do not really need.

How vulnerable we are and how well merchandising executives know our weaknesses. Their profit depends on your impulse purchases. All the oh-so-clever stimuli are intended to make you buy without *thinking* because an impulse purchase is pure plus for a store. Not that all on-the-spur-of-the-moment buys are bad. Seeing something on sale that you really need and buying it is being sales smart. But becoming diverted by budget breakers when you've planned to buy something else is nothing more than giving into your emotions and adding double digits to your deficit budget.

The pressures on a woman when she shops are enormous for not only must she deal with the seduction of her emotions by merchants, she has to cope with her self-image, her status, her means, her reflection in the mirror, and too often, sales clerks who enjoy putting her down!

Is it any wonder that many women detest shopping claiming: "It gives me a headache," or "They never have anything I can wear," or "The clerks call their friends and by the time I get there, nothing good is left," or, "I get confused, I just can't decide what I want!"

Frustration, insecurity, fear and fury often overtake a woman when she shops for clothes, because the decision she makes affects her appearance and the money she spends is so important to her.

Twenty-two years of being on the road has given me the privilege of browsing and shopping in stores all over the country, as well as the extraordinary opportunity of observing thousands of women of all ages, backgrounds, interests and incomes. This, plus millions of miles of boring plane trips which have offered contemplation and countless copies of the latest magazines, have helped sharpen my fashion focus and my shopping skills.

Successful, money-saving shopping requires a game plan.

PLAN AHEAD

Now that you have reorganized your closets, know what contours and colors suit you best and have determined what you need to coordinate with what you have, hone your fashion skills with continuing exposure. Before you buy, scan the ads in fashion magazines and in the newspapers. Magazine ads more accurately *forecast trends,* as do the articles which also offer valuable "how-to" information. Newspaper ads give you the *specifics* of where to find what you want.

Attending fashion shows also enhances expertise because clothes on a runway look totally different than when hanging on a rack. Movement adds a dimension to clothes you cannot see on a hanger, and outfits in fashion shows are professionally put together, coordinated to make the most of their color, shape, texture and purpose. Even if you feel the fashions in the show do not relate to your needs, it is a show of ideas as well as design and you can adopt many of the accessorizing concepts and color combinations.

Alert your senses to incoming and outgoing lines and how they can be modified so that what you buy will not become easily outdated. Balance what you have with what you want and need, *and plan a budget.* A realistic, flexible budget is important as is a *written list* of what you intend to buy. Before you set out with checkbook and credit cards, spend a day or two just *browsing*.

BROWSE BEFORE YOU BUY

Stores carry similar items at varying prices and browsing helps you establish what is in style and what you will be spending. Unless you have a super keen memory, take a small notebook along and jot down where the best buys are.

Browsing sharpens sensitivity and helps evaluate merchandise. There is nothing wrong with saying, "I'm just looking." Most sales-clerks leave you alone when you tell them this. Browse even the super select shops and design departments where clothes are generally not displayed. When you tell clerks that you are considering a purchase and wish to think about it, they are generally helpful, especially if you ask for their card. If you should come across an arrogant person who tries to do a number on you, establish unswerving eye contact and firmly express what you wish to see. When you have finished, simply say, "Thank you, I will be back when I have made a decision."

You may be pressured to buy, especially in smaller shops. Remember . . . *make no decision on major, expensive purchases without sleeping on it first.*

In 1969 I wanted a white fur coat. I needed a new coat and I decided that a casual white lambskin would work best with my clothes. I set a price over which I would not go. It was October and I was engaged to appear in San Francisco for the National Association of Realtors. I was staying at the St. Francis and since my show was the following day and I had the afternoon free, I headed for Ghiardelli Square to meander through the shops. On a mannequin in a small fur salon was just the type of coat I wanted. I tried it on and it was perfect, but it was $200.00 more than I had planned to spend. When the clerk put the pressure on saying it was "one-of-a-kind, hard-to-get, could-not-be-reordered, looked-so-beautiful, I-would-never-find-another," I countered with what has saved me all these years. "I never make a decision about anything that costs this much unless I sleep on it. Thank you, I'll be back."

He was annoyed but I left, fully intending to be back because I loved the coat and wanted it. I just had to think about spending the extra $200.00, which in 1969 was a good deal of money.

The next afternoon, following my show I headed for the American Express office on Union Square to cash a check so that I might buy the coat. I had decided it was worth the extra two hundred. Adjacent to American Express was an interesting boutique which had vivid sales signs all over its windows. It was going out of business. In the window was a white fur coat . . . MY WHITE FUR COAT . . . the very same design, the very same type of fur I had seen the day before.

I just stood and stared. So much for "one-of-a-kind!" I went in and tried it on. It fit as perfectly as the other had. Cautiously I asked the price and when the clerk told me, I gasped. It was $200.00 *less* than

212

the coat in Ghiardelli Square. It was *exactly* the price I had set as my limit. I bought it immediately and I still enjoy wearing it.

Browsing enables you to try on a new image, clothes you would not ordinarily think of buying, but which may be exactly what you need for a change of pace. One needs to step into new lines, new designs, new looks, occasionally, and browsing is the easiest way to experiment. Psychologically you know you are not planning to buy, so you feel much freer, more confident and you give yourself more of a chance than when you actually put cash on the line.

KNOW YOUR STORE

Familiarity makes you confident and knowing the store you shop in frees you from uncertainty and timidity. Many stores cater to a particular kind of customer and have established identities relating to quality, price and the variety of merchandise they offer. Walking into a large, unfamiliar store is upsetting and confusing because not only are you unaware of the kind of clothes they sell, but you have no idea of where the various departments are. Many department stores have become a series of small boutiques and specialty shops, each featuring specific styles at varying prices. Thus, browsing becomes more important so that you familiarize yourself with these new departments and the choices available to you.

At one time, only major cities had a variety of interesting shops to explore. Today, outlying complexes offer suburban and rural women unlimited options. Not only are there many specialty shops in malls along with one or two anchor stores, but super stylish complexes which feature unique, ingenious selections have opened. Water Tower Place in Chicago; The Mayfair in Coconut Grove; New Market in Philadelphia; the Omni and Bal Harbour Shops in Miami; Market Place Square in Boston; Place Ville Marie in Montreal; Rodeo Drive in Beverly Hills; Peachtree Plaza in Atlanta; Ghiardelli Square in San Francisco and similar shopping areas all over the country offer the browsing shopper a vivid showcase in which to experiment.

Rate the stores you shop in by what they offer you. Do not waste time in stores that are unsuitable. Some woman adore burrowing through bargain basements. Others detest it and require splendid surroundings and pampering. Still others are not happy unless they know they have gotten it "wholesale" or drastically reduced. Some women become so dedicated to one store they neglect to explore new arenas in which to shop, missing many opportunities for adventurous clothes hunting. Specialty shops and boutiques tend to limit their wares to specific tastes and sizes, but that does not mean there won't be something special for you.

I once thought the avant garde boutiques in Greenwich Village too exotic for me. One day while visiting Sandy, I went by a shop I had passed many times on other visits. I enjoyed their windows, amused by the unusual designs which made me wish I were years younger. In the window this time was a simple wool pant suit in muted tones of lavender. I went inside and began to browse, and to my surprise found a number of items I could wear. I bought the lavender shirt and pants and have the shirt in my wardrobe to this day.

Factory outlets offer savings on clothing and accessories, but one must be observant and knowing, because outlets deal in "seconds," merchandise which has a flaw and cannot be sold through regular channels at the established price. But you can find marvelous buys in them. I bought three velour shirts at 65% discount simply because there was a mistake in the weaving on the cuff. I cut off the cuffs, restitched the sleeves and wear them bracelet length or rolled.

Antique and second hand shops; Army-Navy stores; garage and yard sales; flea markets, are treasure troves . . . challenging market-places filled with collectibles at attractive prices. These haunts have been known by money-wise women for years and are now being actively shopped by the young because of the collector's type items which can be found. Crystal prisms from old chandeliers make sparkling earrings and pendants. Look for antique mesh or beaded handbags for evening. If the handbag is badly worn, buy it anyway. The frames, made usually of silver, bone or tortoise, are of great value. Make new pouches for antique frames out of velvet, brocade, silk or any scrap of exotic fabric.

Old tuxedo jackets which may be bought for as little as two dollars make sensational boleros when the tails are cut off and the bottom resewn. Even if you cannot do this type of tailoring, a tailor can, and the cost is far less than what a new, silk bolero would be. Feather boa, antique fans, hair combs, stick pins, all make interesting accessories. Old draperies with beautiful silk fringes, or any silk velvet you find, can be made into long or short evening capes. There is no velvet around today which compares to the lushness of the old silk velvets. Don't worry if it looks old. There is a beautiful patina on older velvets, silks, and leathers that make a true fashion statement when worn. Some things really look better as they get older and develop fading and wrinkles . . . just look at Paul Newman, Charles Bronson, James Coburn and Sean Connery!

Old petticoats and ruffled slips in fine, combed cottons trimmed with lace, coordinated with batiste camisoles, ballet slippers and slender satin ribbons in a young woman's hair create a fragile, Degas-look for a summer evening. If the slips have turned yellow, dye them and wear them with an undershirt. Add a stretch belt or a colorful cummerbund and you have an outfit!

While the two previous ideas are for the young, no matter what age you are, you can modify any look for the stage of life you now enjoy. Those who have saved items from the 20's; 30's; 40's and 50's now find that young people seek them out, avidly collecting these classics. Now is the time to bring collectibles out of the closet! Use them, wear them or sell them!

No matter what your age, if you are looking for quality, but cannot afford it, shop the resale stores. Some wealthy people change wardrobes four times a year and regularly sell their clothes to second-hand shops.

Just after the war, I married a handsome, elegant man who was descended from Russian royalty. His mother, Anna, the youngest daughter was the only survivor of a distinguished noble line. Anatasia-like, and against her will, she was spirited from Southern Russia to safety in Turkey by a young man who worked as a gardener on the family estate and who adored her from afar for years. He saved her life, married her and though they had four children she refused to acknowledge his presence, seldom speaking to him directly. She never truly accepted her life as a commoner and raised her two sons to be the noblemen they would have been in Russia. Both men reflected their mother's aristocratic teachings with superb, gallant manners and demeanor, as well as a penchant for only the best in life which neither could afford.

My husband, Michael, was the elder son. He was the assistant manager of an exclusive hotel in New York City and had to maintain an extensive and handsome wardrobe. It was he who introduced me to second-hand shopping. His silk and wool hand-tailored suits; herringbone overcoats; fur trimmed stormcoats; pima cotton shirts;

215

silk ties, beaver felt Homburgs and Derby's were from Sulka's, Finchley's, Countess Mara's, Sak's and other fine stores . . . but he bought them all in tucked-away shops scattered through the city, spending only a fraction of their true value.

Once our children came, Michael could not face up to the responsibility of a family and in 1949 when our sons were less than two and three years old, he walked out and I have never heard from him since. I had to return to work *instantly.* Maintaining a fulltime job and two pre-school children in that era was not easy. To save money, I shopped second-hand for my clothes and the children's for years . . . for one person's discard is another's treasure!

MAIL ORDER SHOPPING

Mail order shopping is a tradition in the United States from the early days of Sears Roebuck when its hefty catalogs were as much a part of rural America as the family Bible, to today's elegant, beautifully produced pieces which feature sable coats, million dollar condominiums and helicopters. With a gallon of gasoline soaring to where it too may soon be featured in the Neiman-Marcus catalog, buying through the mails will become increasingly popular.

People busy with burgeoning careers and family demands who do not have time to shop enjoy sinking into an easy chair to peruse handsome, enticing catalogs, but mail order shopping can be risky. Often the articles advertised are overpriced and disappointing. I have found that merchandise ordered from well known store catalogs is of better quality than that ordered from those firms which are merely mail order houses. Most major department stores today issue sales catalogs in addition to the annual Christmas book, and these offer well known labels at substantial savings. Generally mail order items cost more than what you pay in stores and you also pay delivery charges. But, if you compute your time as money, plus the cost of transportation for in-store shopping, you save shopping at home. Beware of mail order firms which advertise outlandish bargains. Make sure the company you are dealing with is reputable, and if you do not like what you receive return it for a refund.

SHOP IN COMFORT

Do not plan a buying trip if you are in a harassed state. Plan enough time out to shop unhurriedly. If it is the kind of day in which the baby-sitter has run off with the paperboy, or the boss really means, "Just an hour for lunch, please," put it off.

Plan enough time not only to shop, but to coordinate color and accessories. You might also have to arrange for alterations. With time to shop, explore other sections in the store to seek out unusual, cost-saving finds. You might chance upon a fantastic, slinky evening dress in the lingerie department! Why not lacetrimmed satin camisoles and slitted slips worn with boa or open silk shirts doubling as jackets?

Or take a plunge in the swimwear department and surface with swim suit and skirt coordinates which double as evening wear under a tropic moon. Leotards and satiny halter-shorts sets are great sea-dressing and cost so much less than bathing suits.

Good savings are found in children's and teen's sections. If you are tiny why not shop there for classic separates such as shirts, sweaters, skirts and blazers.

Many prefer to buy pants, especially jeans, in boys' and men's departments. Men's pants have more pockets and alterations are *free*. Shirts, sweaters, vests and hats in boys' and men's departments are excellent buys. Explore for odd items in departments other than where you would ordinarily find them. You may save money and find interesting ways to wear new ideas.

Wear comfortable shoes while shopping, even if they do not flatter you. Carry an extra pair for trying on clothes which require a higher heel, or for a later social engagement. If you intend to match a color or pattern, take the item you wish to match with you. And . . . make sure you carry a roomy, zippered pocketbook. No tiny clutches or super elegant purses which can easily be stolen while shopping. You need a secure, work-a-day, zippered handbag that you keep with you, tucked to your side or on your shoulder, *in sight at all times.* It is incredible how skillful pickpockets are! I had my purse pilfered at a major store and discovered it only when a woman exclaimed, "Your handbag is open." It surely was, and my wallet was gone! I could not believe it had happened. There was no bumping, no sensation, nothing! Since then I always shop with a zippered bag and keep it tucked close.

Dress for shopping as if your psyche depended on it! Unkind mirrors and glaring lights do little to help your self-esteem. How can anyone have a confident, positive attitude about themselves when they stand, sans makeup, hair disheveled, undone, before a three-way mirror? Especially when a gorgeous vendeuse dressed in the latest styles give you a pitying smile.

Look as attractive as you can when shopping for it not only bolsters your self-image, it results in salesclerks being more courteous and helpful. Why salespeople play the "put-the-customer-down-game" puzzles me. They should enjoy helping customers. While some customers can be selfishly demanding and arrogant, and clerks are put upon and harassed, there is no excuse for the supercilious power plays some of them pull.

Living and working in the country tends to keep me in jeans and sweaters. Sometimes I have "just-run-into-town-for-something" and noted an unexpected sale in the local store. How differently I am treated when I am dressed *deshabillée* and when I look my best, and how differently I feel! I avoid mirrors. If I spot anyone I know, I head the other way!

CONCENTRATE ON YOUR PURPOSE AND SHOP WITH CONFIDENCE

Try not to be diverted by having lunch with a friend, or stopping for an unexpected Cuisinart demonstration. Keep your mind on your agenda. Head *directly* for those departments you have browsed which you *know* contain what you want. Finish shopping for what is on your *written list first,* before you allow for delightful diversions such as Trigere fashion shows or tea in the Trellis Room.

Unless you have a longstanding relationship with the person waiting on you, *do not ask for their opinion* concerning what you want to buy. It makes you vulnerable and you have no idea of what their day has been. They could be very helpful and honest and then again, they may want to get rid of you as fast as possible. Realistically, recognize that a salesperson's job is to get a sale over with as quickly as possible and go on to the next person. You have by now established your own expertise on what's best for you. Depend on your gut feelings. Have confidence in your decisions and buy what you *know* is best for your figure, your face, your needs and your budget!

LEARNING SALES LINGO HELPS

Knowing the difference between *"Reduced for Clearance,"* *"Special Purchase,"* *"Job Lots"* and *"Draw Lines"* helps you determine whether you are really saving money.

"Reduced for Clearance" is the best way to buy good quality merchandise at the lowest possible price. When browsing or shopping it always pays to investigate a *"reduced for clearance"* section. This is merchandise the buyer wishes to clear away, to make room for new lines. You will find odd sizes and colors, whatever is left over from regular stock. Unless it is marked *"as is,"* it will be perfectly good merchandise provided you can find your size and the style you like. If you wait, *"reduced for clearance"* items keep nosediving.

At the beginning of a sale, merchandise may be marked down 20–25%. As the sale progresses and the goods do not move, the markdowns escalate and discounts can soar to 75% and more! Waiting for larger discounts is risky. You might not get the item at all. The way to play this waiting game is to scan the sales items. If there seems to be a good supply in a number of sizes, styles and colors, wait, they will be reduced even more. If, however, there is very little stock left and what you want is truly special, grab it while you can.

Be leery of items that bear the signs . . . *"drastically reduced."* Reduced from what? Check to make sure that it is indeed a sales item, and not a *"special purchase,"* which are goods bought at close-outs specifically to draw you into a store.

"Draw lines" are what the name signifies; special items put on sale to bring you into the store. To cash in on *"draw lines"* you have to be there early and be part of a milling mob. While *"special purchases"* and *"draw lines"* can be good value, they are not generally first class merchandise which has been reduced to make way for new goods. Many *"draw lines"* and *"special purchases"* are not the regular line of merchandise, but neither are they *"seconds"* or *"as is."* Sometimes a manufacturer has cut more than he intended. Other times a major account has cancelled an order leaving the manufacturer with extra goods on hand. These are the items which become *"special purchases"* and *"draw lines."* If they are seconds or irregulars it must be stated as such.

"Job lots" are most often found in bargain basements and discount stores. *"Job lots"* and those goods bought for *"draw lines"* and *"special purchases"* are similar.

"Job lots" represent a substantial amount of stock which has been bought at a close-out. Always check items you buy when it is a *"job lot"* sale, because the merchandise can be either perfect or irregular.

"Regularly Priced" may mean merchandise marked so high originally that the sales figure represents the actual value and not the discount. Be wary also of *"Selling at Cost."* No retailer can stay in business if he constantly sells at cost. *"Going out of Business"* and *"Fire Sales"* may be genuine sales, or sales of shoddy merchandise to draw you in. For these types of sales knowing the store and its reputation is important. *"Made to Sell For"* is another sales gimmick. The way to stay ahead of this ploy is to know your labels, fabrics and quality.

"I Can Get It For You Wholesale." Unless you have a personal contact with a well known manufacturer, wholesale buying is actually retail buying of generally average merchandise at the normal retail price. When you buy wholesale there are no return privileges, often you cannot try the merchandise on, and the selection is limited to what the manufacturer wants to sell.

IRREGULARS: Save substantially and regularly by buying irregulars in clothes which do not make a fashion statement. If you need trousers for cycling or gardening what does it matter if they have a misweave? Hoisery, underwear, lingerie, pajamas, nightgowns, shirts and other such items wear just as well in irregulars. Irregulars sales are frequently advertised. Shop them to save. Wear irregular panty hose under slacks and save good quality hosiery for dresses and suits. Sometimes the irregularity is so barely visible that only you know it is there.

Some years ago I came across an Oleg Cassini dress in the specialty shop at the Greenbrier Hotel in White Sulphur Springs. I do many shows at Greenbrier and I like shopping resort stores because they feature styles not available locally. The low price tag intrigued me. The sales clerk then pointed out an irregularity in the geometric print, whose vividness had caught my eye. There was a misprint on the *underside* of the sleeve. It was barely visible. I bought the Cassini. Are not misprints valuable to collectors?

BUY OUT OF SEASON: Inexpensive, cheap clothes destroy your image and make you feel insecure, unimportant. Yet one need be realistic. You may be young parents paying off a high interest mortgage, or a single parent. Perhaps you are just starting out on a career. You might be a military wife, the wife of a policeman, fireman, steelworker, automotive man, or teacher. You could be a retiree. You might be able to afford only one or two good choices a year, if that! The way to solve this dilemma is to *BUY OUT OF SEASON!*

Buy shoes in January and June at clearance sales. Today's merchandising is so competitive that shoe sales are held more frequently. Wait for them and save on good leathers in shoes and handbags. Buy swimsuits in August, winter coats in January, and all other clothing at closeout sales.

Try not to buy clothes for yourself before Christmas, and give Christmas gift certificates to those you love. After the holidays they can almost double their value by shopping during after-Christmas sales. I know people who regularly return Christmas gifts and take credit slips which they use after the holidays. Shopping in-sale and out-of-season enables you to buy better clothes and get the most for your money.

14

On The Move . . .
Light Hearted
And Lightweight

Seems I've been on the move all my life, although I did not begin to travel until my thirties. Growing up in the depression, children of poor families had little opportunity to test their wings. The yen to travel was strong, but it was a dream I spun as I leafed through endless copies of the National Geographic in our neighborhood library.

Reality for me was not glamorous Bon Voyage parties on the *Normandie* with caviar, champagne and chocolates. A nickle bought me a ride on the Staten Island Ferry and New York's harbor became my North Atlantic and penny candy my stateroom treat. The Ninth Avenue elevated was my 20th Century Limited as I went "downtown" each Saturday to meet my mother, who was off work at noon. I was only six years old, but a seasoned veteran of New York City's trains and ferries.

The long, low whistles of northbound freighters as they snaked along the Hudson, the sharp no-nonsense hoots of oceangoing liners stacked along West Street's piers called to me. At fourteen I polished planes at Floyd Bennett Field for flying lessons and fantasized being Amelia Earhart. At fifteen I signed on as cook's helper on a freighter bound for the Orient, but my ever watchful mother found out my plans just before we cast off (thank goodness) and prevented fantasy becoming tragedy because war was declared just two weeks later. At sixteen I tried to join the WAAF's, those courageous women who

ferried planes to Europe, but one had to be twenty-one, and by that
time I was so immersed in New York's incomparable theatre and the
Stage Door Canteen, I thought anyplace ten miles west of Broadway,
wasteland.

It was not until I began to perform in "I HAVEN'T A THING
TO WEAR!" in 1958 that the world of travel opened to me. Since
then I have flown in all kinds of weather to every major city in the
United States and to towns so rural, the only way in is by two-seater
Cessna and then an auto. And the six Hershey Bar flights I have
known! Mountain waves and the plane dropping 2,000 feet, fogged
in Oil City, Pennsylvania and turning back to Pittsburgh after three
tree top approaches could not find a runway hidden by ceiling zero,
Dodge City, Kansas and the pilot taking evasive action as a tornado
suddenly swirled off the port engine; despite all this, I am ready to
take off at anytime!

My first trip West was in 1960. I had completed 150 shows since
the previous September and had given birth to my daughter in October, 1959. That was the year of the chemise and audiences were never
sure if I was or I wasn't. I had always dreamed of camping my way
west with the boys, but I had never been able to take a summer off.
With a new baby it seemed that if we did not do it then, we never
would. I set off June 19th with my dear friend Wanda Getter, Jeff
and Jonathan who were 11 and 13 years old, and a bright, seven
month old cherub who by the time the trip was over recognized every
ice cream and gasoline sign from Pennsylvania to California.

Wanda's husband and mine, both of whom hated camping and
disliked auto travel even more, made bets we would be back in a
week. We were on the road thirteen weeks and covered more than
13,000 miles, at first camping in a tent, and then in a trailer which
we bought enroute. It was such an incredible experience, we set forth
again in 1962, this time through the northern tier of the United
States headed to the Seattle World's Fair. We would have gone on to
Alaska except that I had to return early for a fall lecture season.

Being on the move is when one must muster all the organizational
talents one has, recognizing that comfort and convenience are essential, and most importantly, learning to travel as light as possible. Our
1960 trip almost ended five days out, because I took too much,
including a typewriter I intended to use each evening after the tent
was pitched to record the day's adventures. I faced up to reality one
bleak, rainy morning in Kentucky, packed the typewriter and many

other non-essentials and shipped them home. After that we began to enjoy the journey. I still work to pare my travel needs. I am always unhappy if I take too much and I keep trying to lighten the load.

No matter where you travel, even if it is only a day trip into town, or home for a short holiday stay, the cardinal rule is to be comfortable and to look attractive. I'll never understand why some people disembark in cities noted for their culture, their sophisticated ambience, looking as though they've just fallen out of bed, in outfits more suited to spring cleaning than to strolling Fisherman's Wharf or the Via Veneto.

And the people picking up people at airports! I will not dwell on the sights I've seen, but it would seem to me that when one greets a loved one or a guest, she would want to look her best; attractive in a pleasant, casual way, complimenting the warm, friendly smile on her face. I doubt that Jonathan and I shall ever forget the way Jeff greeted us when we arrived at the Honolulu Airport for my appearances in Hawaii for the American Bankers Association meeting. Jeff had left for Hawaii in September to work on a book, and had been there six weeks when our plane landed in mid-October. He wore white bathing shorts, thongs, a deeply bronzed tan, and six lush, fragrant lei around his neck. His hair, golden from the sun, gleamed against the magenta, purple, white, yellow, and red of the orchids, plumeria, and carnations which made up the heavy, beautifully strung garlands. Not a costume for New York or San Francisco, but absolutely perfect for Hawaii and as he loped to us and draped the leis about our shoulders every head turned. His was a Hawaiian greeting true to tradition and one which had disappeared along with the Matson liners.

You can be casual, chic and comfortable at the same time! Comfort need not be equated with looking rumpled and shabby, patched jeans splitting, and plaid shirts flopping over waistbands. Knits, crease-resistant cotton or silk blends, soft, sheer wools, eased, softly-flowing dresses, skirts, and suits in wash and wear, make for handsome travel ensembles assuring you of elegance no matter how long the journey. A turban, silky head wrap, beret or cloche keeps hair in place (or hidden) and affords an extra touch which adds distinction and prestige.

A good travel wardrobe should include both natural and synthetic materials. Natural fibers breathe and drape better, especially when weather gets hotter. But to be practical about the care and appearance of clothes while traveling, look for garments with a small percentage of synthetic fibers which will discourage wrinkles and make maintenance easier. Trousers are terrific, but not as good as skirts for traveling, because if pants are cut properly, they hug your figure and begin to bind when you sit in them for a long period of time. Bias cuts, eased A-lines in skirts and dresses are more comfortable. Separates, shirtwaist dresses, two-piece knit suits are super when on the move. Add a belt, scarf or jewelry for a variety of looks.

How I would love to leave on a trip as my friend Joan once did. Dashing into my office late one Friday afternoon, with a wicked glint in her eye, she said, "Do you mind if I leave early, I'm flying to Puerto Rico at six!"

"Wow!" I exclaimed, "when did you decide this?"

"Five minutes ago," she laughed, "when Norman phoned and asked me."

"You won't have time to get home and pack in Friday traffic," I cried.

"Don't be silly," she sang out gaily, waving the toothbrush she took from her desk drawer, "I'm leaving from here, I'll buy what I need when I get there!"

That's going in style! For those who can afford it, it is the ideal way to travel, but for the rest of us who agonize over what to wear and how to pack it, the following is intended.

Consider climate first when planning what to take. The mean temperature of where you plan to visit is your best guide. Ask your travel agent for this information. Other factors create variable weather conditions in places of identical latitudes so be aware of: altitude, humidity, and the closeness to oceans, and large bodies of water whose breezes and currents affect local conditions.

The second consideration are the customs and ambience of the city or country you are visiting. Its mood is set by traditions and history which mold its character and those of its people. Cities such as New York, San Francisco, Dallas, Chicago, Washington, D.C., Boston, Atlanta, London, Tokyo, Copenhagen, Paris, Rome, Brussels, Stockholm, Amsterdam, Vienna, Mexico City, Rio, Buenos Aires, Montreal, Toronto, Vancouver have a formality and air of sophistication which call for on-the-town clothes rather than casual sports clothes. Los Angeles, Miami, Kansas City, Phoenix, Portland, Seattle, Houston, Winnipeg, New Orleans are more casual. Colors in cities and countries vary. While brightly colored silks may be sensational in the Far East, India and Los Angeles, a more subdued color is better in London and Madrid. Latin countries have a long tradition of conservatism and strict social decorum, and black is an important fashion color, but black in San Diego is out of sync. Do not make the mistake that because you are on vacation, you can wear vacation type sports clothes such as shorts and slacks in a metropolis. I've often wondered how the men and women tourists I've seen in major cities wearing shorts would feel if tourists dressed as they visited their home town. Few people would go downtown in their own cities in shorts or shirts hanging out over sloppy pants, why then do they stroll streets in major cities in such poor taste?

Good manners are important everywhere and at all times, and it is rude to dress with disrespect for a country, its customs and its people. Dress in every city as if it were your own, in clothes which make you feel attractive, comfortable and confident.

The third and major consideration are the clothes you plan to take. Are they comfortable? Are they convenient? Will they travel easily? It is best not to go out and buy special clothes for a trip, unless you are planning to go on safari or attempt an assault on Mt. Everest. It is more fun to save all you can for shopping on your journey, buying little treasures in the places you visit. At one time, clothes bought abroad were less expensive than what one would find in comparable fabrics and quality in the States, but no longer. Your best buys are in the United States, but there are special items indigenous to various countries which are good fashion investments if you can afford it. We mentioned some of these items in the section dealing with ethnic clothes.

In connection with ethnic clothes, a semblance of an ethnic look as accent on the clothes you wear is fine, but do not dress totally in the obviously ethnic dress of the country you visit, because you may seem pretentious. The local people know you are American and may resent your attempt to simulate what to them are not costumes, but every-day garb.

Your closet probably contains all you really need for any journey. If you live in or near a major city, this is undoubtedly so. If your lifestyle is rural and completely casual you might have to add a few items, but begin first with what is in your closet and dresser drawers.

Do not change your basic style for a trip. You are what you are, you know what you feel most comfortable in, and a journey which can be arduous is not a time to create a totally different you. Select

On the Move—Light Hearted and Lightweight _____

your favorites, those clothes which have always done the best for
your figure, face and varying moods. Employ the concepts . . .
COMFORT . . . CONTOUR . . . COLOR . . . CLASSICS . . . coordination to expand and make better use of a travel wardrobe.
Remember to include and use the scarf and coordination ideas
suggested, and most of all, work with color!

Choose one or two neutral shades as your basic wardrobe and
splash other colors and shapes with accessories. My favorite travel
colors are black and white. I find this combination suitable in any
city, any country, any time. Working with one or two neutral shades
enables you to limit accessories in shoes and handbags which weigh
the most.

If black and white is not your style, try taupe, beige, camel and
other earth tones. Whatever basic color you choose, it is far easier
to coordinate with one or two shades than to take a number of
unrelated colors which might require their own accessories.

Consider climate when choosing colors and fabrics. Lighter colors,
bright sunny shades and lightweight fabrics are for warm, sunny
places. Deeper rich tones and wools, both lightweight and sturdy, are
for northern climates. No matter where you travel, even if it is to
Miami in August or India in September, take a sweater or shawl for
evening. Air conditioning, ocean breezes and desert winds make
sweaters and shawls advisable.

To dress for daytime in cities all over the world follow the same
rules you would adhere to in any American metropolis. Wear
smartly tailored, crease-resistant suits in lightweight wools, cotton or
silk blends, two piece silk or wool knits, layered separates of blouses,
skirts, jackets or vests, simply cut, classic dresses. Coordinate with
the appropriate accessories and accents. Do not choose clothes cut
too straight and tight. You need fashions that walk with comfort and
enable you to climb stairs. Select skirts with eased bias cuts, A-lines,
inverted kick pleats and other type pleats. Clothes that move freely
with your body and give you a sense of freedom are more attractive
than tight fits which tend to ride up and crease through the waist and
hip.

If you are traveling in early spring, late fall or winter to cities in the
north temperate zone include two dresses of sheer wool. One might
be cut low at the neck and be sleeveless or with short sleeves, and
have a cover-up jacket. The other could be long-sleeved. If these
dresses are uncluttered, understated, and are of a darkish color, they

can be worn for sightseeing or business by day and with just a slight change of accessories become ideal changelings for after five.

Always pack a simply beautiful, simply cut silk dress that flows liquidly, sheathing your body in luxury and softness. Choose a rich, medium shade that flatters your skin and you have a perfect dress for late afternoon engagements or dinner at someone's home, as well as a short evening dress for theatre and night clubbing. If your plans include a number of evenings on the town, take a long evening skirt with which you can wear daytime silk shirts, scarves, sequined tube tops and other separates.

If you are planning a 21-day "if this is Tuesday, it must be Belgium trip" you may have to pack for a range of climates. Lightweight wool worsted is a nomad's best friend, and desert dwellers have worn lightweight wool burnooses for centuries to shield them from hot sun and to keep them warm when desert temperatures plunge at night. Wool does not wrinkle, it holds its shape, affords warmth in chilling damp and is cooler than synthetics when the sun blazes. Lightweight wool, and sleeveless cotton or cotton blend dresses with little jackets or a sweater work well in warm, sunny places. Unless you are going to Russia, Eastern Europe, or Scandinavia in winter or skiing in the Alps, leave furs at home. Cloth coats are more versatile, as are lined trenchcoats in cold climate. If it is summer, unlined all-weather coats are handy and the classic trench coat in black, cut with great flair and style, can be used after-dark.

Pack lightly and travel light-heartedly. How carefree it is to travel with one compact case! Slide it under the seat and forget about waiting in baggage claim. Better yet, when you arrive your luggage is with you . . . not off to Nome as you disembark in New Orleans. And . . . you save money on tips when you carry one small case.

Should you be traveling standby to save additional money, and you do not make the flight, you need not haul heavy suitcases back and forth. Traveling lightly gives you mobility, you can change your mind about where you want to go and how, instantly!

The "duffle" wardrobe for a two week trip anywhere can be packed into a case 9″ × 14″ × 22″ which fits under airline seats (sketch 63):

two pair pants
two skirts: one dressy, one tailored

one dressy blouse
two shirts
one cardigan sweater
two T-shirts
one dress
three silk scarves in varying sizes
one lightweight Qiana type robe to sleep in or lounge poolside
one bathing suit (Danskin type can double for dancin') and rubber
thongs (double as slippers)
two or three sets of underwear and hosiery
one pair sandal style dressy shoes
one small clutch bag, preferably one that folds flat
travel umbrella, cosmetics

Let loose with all your coordinating skills to assemble a one case wardrobe. Your educated eye, and your talent for combinations will create compatible outfits. Blend and contrast colors. Choose fabrics that are a cinch to care for. Wear an outfit of separates on board which coordinate with what is in the case such as a wool blazer, skirt, shirt, belt and perhaps a vest or another light, pull-over sweater. Fling a lightweight raincoat over your arm in a glossy, colorful fabric or a traditional neutral. Take a couple of good books and a small camera which you can stow in the raincoat pocket. Shoulder a sturdy, roomy, zippered bag. Wear comfortable walking shoes, and you are off, lightweight, lighthearted, ready to have the greatest time of your life.

If you are one who cannot feel secure on a journey unless you travel with a lot of clothes, the following wardrobe offers a number of options and is suitable anywhere. The weights are approximate, and the articles proposed, along with your suitcases (you will need two), still weigh less than 44 pounds.

1 lightweight wool suit	3 lbs.
1 silk or silk blend suit	1½ lbs.
2 dresses	3 lbs.
1 cashmere slipover type sweater	½ lb.
1 lightweight wool cardigan sweater	1 lb.
3 blouses	2 lbs.
2 shirts (one of which doubles as bathing suit topper)	2 lbs.
1 extra skirt (long or short, but dressy)	¾ lb.

3 pair shoes: one pair walking shoes with medium, heel,

Duffle Wardrobe

	one pair dressy shoes, one pair sports shoes	3½ lbs.
1	bathing suit (two if you swim a lot)	1 lb.
4	pair underpanties and bras	1 lb.
2	slips, 2 camisoles	1½ lbs.
2	lightweight foundation briefs if you wear them, or you might prefer control top panty hose	¾ lb.
1	nightgown	½ lb.
1	lightweight robe (which can double for beach)	1 lb.
6	pair hosiery: 3 pair daytime shades and weights, 3 evening sheers (if legs tire easily take support hose)	¼ lb.
1	all weather or lightweight wool coat	2 lbs.
2	hats: one rain or storm hat; one all purpose beret, cloche or turban. If you will be in sunny, warm climates, include a beach hat	1 lb.
4	scarves of varying sizes	½ lb.
1	wool or challis shawl	1 lb.
2	belts	½ lb.
1	pair casual pants	1 lb.
1	pair well tailored trousers that coordinate with suits	1 lb.
3	handbags: a sturdy, zippered tote, large enough to contain all that you carry aboard. A medium size, zippered shoulderbag for sightseeing which blends with your walking shoes and brightens the neutral shades of your wardrobe. In summer, this bag could be of straw or bright fabric; in fall and winter it could be russet or burgundy leather. A dressy clutch that packs flat and is of leather, silk or other fabric, for evening.	2 lbs.
1	umbrella	½ lb.
	cosmetics and toiletries	2 lbs.

The above weighs approximately 34 pounds. Since you would be wearing one of the outfits, possibly your suit, and one of the pair of shoes, carrying your coat and tote bag with cosmetic and toiletries, you would be packing less than 25 pounds.

Vacationing at a resort or taking a cruise enables you to enjoy all the dressy and resort wear you may own or wish to buy. Since you will not be hefting suitcases in and out of hotels, pack as much as you want. Extended cruises offer the opportunity to wear all the glamorous collectibles you've stashed and have little chance to use. While there is no baggage allowance on ships, there is a space problem (with the exception of first class on the QE2). Depending on who you share your cabin with, you may have to travel light or sleep with some of your clothes!

To climatize clothes for variable and fickle weather, use separates and layering. Layering not only gives you the warmth or coolness you want, it adds and subtracts for dressy or casual needs. Coordinate travel wardrobes to make the fullest use of separates.

The bag you carry on board should contain all you need for a comfortable flight: a pair of soft slippers, or slipper socks, cosmetics and toiletries to freshen up (especially moisturizers to counteract the drying effect of pressurized cabins), any medications or vitamins you take, a light sweater, jewelry (never pack it), camera, binoculars, a good book plus a small, insulated case containing fresh fruit, almonds or pecans and small plastic packets of raisins or sunflower seeds.

Airline food even at best has always been "toy food" and with inflation, airlines have cut back on the quality and quantity of the food they serve. Some "no frills" flights do not have free meal service. You can obtain better quality food if you request a special meal at the time you book your reservation. I find no-salt meals the best. They are fresher, less plastic and always contain fresh fruit. If you are a die-hard for salt, the trays contain salt and pepper packets anyway. Kosher, dietetic, vegetarian and other special meals are generally better quality as well. On short duration, connecting flights all you get is an abysmal "snack," therefore carry fruit, nuts and cheese for nourishment. Protect your health and energies while you travel because becoming ill on a journey is nothing but a hassle.

The regulations concerning luggage weights on most overseas flights departing from the United States are as follows: Up to 70 pounds in one bag is allowed with each passenger permitted to ship two bags for a total of 140 pounds to their destination and return. In addition, one carry-on bag which is not included in the 140 pound allowance is permitted. *This allowance is to the first overseas stopover only.* For example: you may fly from New York to London, connect there for a flight to Paris, connect in Paris for a flight to Greece and arrive in Athens with 140 pounds of luggage at no extra charge. If you were to stop overnight in London, your luggage allowance on the balance of the trip reverts to 44 pounds economy class, 66 pounds first class for *all pieces including your carry-on bag.*

If you will be visiting various cities, take no more than 44 pounds economy, 66 pounds first class. Airline personnel in foreign countries weigh luggage assiduously. If you plan to spend two weeks skiing in St. Anton or sunning in Rhodes, you could, if you are hardy, cart 140 pounds to your destination. It is better to take as little as possible and use the generous 140 pound allowance to bring back all sorts of lovely, hand made articles, clothing and art objects.

Skis, golf clubs and other sporting equipment take up the allowance of one 70 pound bag. Regulations allow for only one pair of skis, one pair of poles and one pair of boots. Avid skiers know one pair does not suffice and they cannily purchase double ski bags (Rossignol makes one of the roomiest) to enclose additional equipment. I take one pair alpine skis and one pair cross-country skis plus two sets of poles, and cross-country boots stuffed with knee length socks in a double ski bag. I wrap either a ski jacket, ski underwear or windshirts around the bindings to protect them and to save additional room in my suitcase. My alpine boots, stuffed with socks and mittens, are packed into a special boot bag. Ski bags are not checked to determine if there are more than one pair in them, and you can cram the bag with many necessities without having to pay for overweight. It is not the weight airlines are concerned about, because today's larger planes can carry enormous amounts; it is the space. Since a ski bag takes just so much space, stuffed or unstuffed, it will pass. When I take golf clubs I fill the pockets of the bag with shoes, socks, golf gloves, balls, hand towel, etc.

Place identification tags inside your suitcase as well as on luggage tags. If your suitcase is not easily identifiable, tie a colorful ribbon or put a decal on it, so that you can easily pick it out from others coming down the carousel. Remove old routing tags. Some people love to save these to show how many places they've been, but it confuses confused baggage handlers even more, so take them off.

Few people read the notice of baggage liability limitations which is printed on the back of every airline ticket. Nor do they read the limitations on the loss of life or injury. If they did, they would carry yearly travel insurance. The type you buy at airports is too costly when bought per trip. Yearly insurance is more comprehensive and less expensive. It is also wise to purchase additional baggage insurance. Baggage on overseas flights is weighed for insurance purposes, because baggage is insured by the *pound,* not by the *piece.* For most international flights, which includes any domestic portions of the international journey, the allowance is approximately $9.07 per pound, which means that if your 44 pound of checked luggage is lost, you will receive approximately, $399.08. Unchecked baggage (your on-board possessions) is insured up to $400.00 per passenger. If you carry aboard a Nikon camera and lenses and something happens to them you've blown the insurance allowance. On domestic flights (travel wholly between U.S. points) the limitation is $750.00 per passenger on most carriers, but some have lower limits, so it is important to check.

Baggage insurance costs little in comparison to the trauma one has when luggage and possessions are lost. Making a claim for lost luggage is annoying and time consuming, therefore keep all receipts on what you buy so that you will have them in case it is necessary to make any insurance claims.

Losing my luggage would be disastrous for me, because my entire show is packed in one 26 inch suitcase, and while I could carry it off, not having the clothes and accessories to highlight the program would be disappointing to an audience. I believe the reason I have not ever arrived for a show without my suitcase in all my years on the road is because I check it through to the final destination, *only if it is a non-stop flight,* or if making a change, *I do not change airlines.* Since most of my flights require a number of changes, I check my bags point-to-point and pick them up at each stop and personally transfer them to the next carrier. It is a hassle, but worth it. Every person taking a trip should invest in a folding, wheeled, luggage-carrier. It takes very little room, is light, easy-to-handle and superb when racing through airports to make close connections. If you plan a trip abroad do not go without one. The money you save on tips covers what you spend on a carrier.

CONVENTIONS, MEETINGS, SEMINARS

The fashion needs of women attending conventions, meetings and seminars vary as much as the places in which they are held and the season. Ninety percent of my appearances are at such events and I meet women from 18 to 80 who fall into three categories:

a) The woman attending with her husband whose participation, while primarily social, has a business purpose in the personal contact and exchange of experiences which strengthen business relationships.

b) The woman who goes to conventions and meetings as a participant attending business sessions, and whose social contacts are purposefully business oriented.

c) The woman, generally a young executive, on duty in the booth and exhibit area for her company.

The woman attending a convention as pure pleasure should pack clothes that suit the many social functions programmed into meetings; cocktail parties, visits to hospitality suites, and the annual banquet. Also there may be a luncheon with a speaker such as myself, and possibly a tour which will take her away from the hotel for most of the day. Often these tours are combined with time for shopping. If the convention is in a resort area she will want sports clothes, bathing suits and pants outfits. Many times meetings in major cities are followed by three or four day side trips to resorts and resort cities. A flexible wardrobe which affords variability will enable her to create outfits for both. The classic standbys of cleverly coordinated separates offer the best choice. Since her function at the meeting is social, she can wear more relaxed lines and brighter colors. Even if she attends business meetings to hear particular speakers, she can put together a handsome, understated outfit from her classic coordinates.

The woman who attends a meeting as pure business would wear more businesslike clothes for daytime events, and softly feminine, dressy clothes for the social functions. To maintain her prestige, she should avoid evening clothes that are too bold, too brash or too décolleté. The chapter which follows offers ideas on how to create a positive fashion image for business. Since conventions are a time for important business contacts the fashion statement you make at a meeting should be pleasing, and instill confidence.

The young woman on duty in her company's booth or exhibit, should deftly balance subtlety with a dash of color and verve. She is a salesperson, greeting people visiting the exhibit, describing her company's products and services. She needs to reflect enthusiasm, brightness, cheerfulness, as well as an aura of reliability and dignity.

Trade exhibits are very competitive with hundreds of companies offering wares and services. You want prospective clients to remember your company and you. Wear a unique touch, an accent that is unforgettable and in good taste. Perhaps a flower in your lapel, or a single, smashing colorful accent such as a silk kerchief in the pocket of your blazer; or a warm, rich color that highlights your eyes in a handsome, well tailored dress. Unless your company has a convention uniform or a particular dress code, plan to wear something different each day so that you keep your enthusiasm revved up. Manning a booth for many hours over a period of three or four days can be boring and tiring. Clothes which make you feel alive, attractive and happy will help. Comfortable, good quality shoes in low to medium heels are essential. Keep an extra pair in the booth to change off. After exhibit hours, if you participate in the social activities or are required to be in the hospitality suite, you will want dressy, feminine clothes which are not too daring. Do not antagonize the wives of the men your company deals with by wearing a dress cut to the bottom line.

PACKING

If I could but accept all the offers I receive to help people pack, I would earn enough money to circumnavigate the globe via Concorde. Unpacking my case before an audience was a happy accident. I never planned it. As a performer, I knew that one should be prepared for an audience, but on one of my very first engagements, my car broke down and I arrived late. I had to unpack on stage before a very large audience of top management executives and their wives, and the reaction was so great, I have kept it part of the show ever since. When audiences see all that I take out of one 26 inch case, they keep asking if it has a secret bottom. Many stay behind to see if I actually repack all that I have removed.

Knowing how to pack might be a genetic trait. My Dad packed a Model A Ford and took off on a three month cross-country camping trip in 1928. My son Jeff packs a car so that it holds as much as a truck. Our little ski cabin, which was intended for weekend use, has become an accordian as more and more books, paintings and manuscripts inundate it.

The secret to packing is not to leave any space for clothes to move around. All the little valleys must be filled in. Softsided suitcases should be packed so tightly the sides bulge. The other secret is to compartmentalize. Put different items into plastic bags and containers so you have what you want *instantly*. Also carry a steamer or travel iron (with adapters for overseas) to freshen clothes.

Begin by assembling the following aids: tissue paper, or dry cleaner's plastic bags; plastic envelopes in a variety of sizes with and without zippers; plastic containers for cosmetics. I prefer a separate cosmetic bag which has its own containers and which I compartmentalize further with small plastic envelopes in which I place individual items so that I can easily take out whatever I need without having to burrow through a jumble of emery boards, lipsticks, eyebrow pencils, etc. Include three or four flat plastic hangers (depending on how many suit jackets and dresses you take) and collect Crown Royal liquor bags. They are super for shoes and jewelry!

Categorize the clothes you are taking. Separate hard, bulky items such as shoes, handbags, belts, umbrella, etc. from the softer articles. Put each category in its own plastic case. Add a bit of fragrant sachet or a little piece of cardboard on which you've put a drop or two of your favorite perfume (like the cards advertising perfume enclosed with department store monthly bills). Stuff shoes with the pantyhose or stockings you wear with them. Put each shoe in its own sock or Crown Royal bag. Place all heavy items in back of the suitcase so that when the bag is picked up the heavy articles are at the bottom. If taking belts, wind the open belt around diameter of case. Make a flat, even layer by filling in valleys with odd items. Decide which clothes you intend to wear most often and which are for special occasions. Pack the special occasion clothes first, with the heaviest articles on the bottom (e.g. suit jackets, sweaters, trousers).

Place suit jackets and dresses on flat, plastic hangers. When you unpack, simply hang your clothes. Many small foreign and American hotels never have enough hangers.

On the flat surface you have created, place buttoned jacket, collar towards back of case, front facing you. Place layer of tissue paper or plastic dry cleaner's bag across jacket. Cross sleeves, turn up part which extends over case, *over* the tissue or plastic.

If skirts must be folded to fit in case, fold at waist rather than hem. If skirt creases, the fold marks will be covered by the jacket or blouse you wear with it. Put tissue or plastic on the skirt and make fold *over* it. If the skirt is very full or has a center seam, fold in half *lengthwise;* fold marks will blend with center seams or will be camouflaged by the fullness of the fabric.

Place dresses on flat, plastic hanger in case, *front facing you.* Smooth out collar and shoulders. Cross sleeves, put tissue or plastic over dress and fold at *waist* to fit in case. Close all zippers and buttons on clothes. Vary the way in which you place jackets and dresses: jacket #1, collar to back of case; jacket #2, collar to front. Dress #1, hem on top; dress #2, hem on bottom, etc. This makes for flat, even layers. Make as few folds as possible, covering the widest area you can. Stuff all empty spaces with small items such as film, rolled up bathing suits, rolled up plastic envelopes containing lingerie, tissues, costume jewelry. If you have a very special suit or dress, stuff sleeves and bodice with tissue. Keep lightest items on top. If your dresses are heavier than the plastic envelopes containing blouses, lingerie and scarves, pack the envelopes on top. If the dresses are sheer and lightweight, pack so that only your nightgown and robe top them. Your nightclothes and robe should be the first items available when you open your suitcase.

If you use a hanging case, fill bottom with handbags and shoes. When you hang clothes, fold sleeves and any extra widths to center. Double up dresses, skirts and jackets on hangers. If you have more than the hangers can hold, place clothes flat without putting them on hangers. I have a handy accessory with its own hanger for my case. It is a series of plastic pockets in which I place lingerie, scarves, and other soft items. When I arrive at my destination, I hang it and have everything I need at the ready, without unpacking!

Some people like to roll their clothes and if using a duffle this works well with sweaters, knits, jeans and soft sheer dresses. I have a filmy chiffon which I always roll. Another traveler I know packs in layers. She stands her suitcase on its platform, unzips the top and places everything in layers, while the suitcase is *standing*. When the case is flat, she can see all the items by color and texture. Clothes have to be folded narrowly to pack this way.

Pack cosmetics and toiletries into individual containers and then into separate plastic bags so that if anything spills it does not ruin your clothes. Seal bottles such as nailpolish, polish remover, mouthwash, etc. with tape. When you remove the tape to use the contents stick it around the bottom, so that it is always handy. Do not fill any bottle more than two-thirds because liquids expand in altitude and will trickle out.

If you take medications or vitamins, take enough to last your entire journey, with a week's extra supply should there be unforeseen delays. Carry a supply on board in your tote in case your luggage is lost or delayed.

There are so many different types of luggage available, I could not possibly cover it all in one chapter. I have been using French luggage made in Covina, California since I first went on the road. It is expensive, but it has given me remarkable wear. I recently sent the case I purchased in 1960 back to the factory and they reconditioned it for about $100.00. It has strong, sturdy sides and frame with zippered top. Top and bottom are flexible allowing for expansion. It is heavier than most soft-sided lightweights, but for extensive travel and overseas journeys, you need a sturdy bag. Soft-sided nylons are immensely attractive and easy to carry, but they afford little protection.

Always travel with a *locked* suitcase, and the combination locks are convenient, provided you do not forget your private code. I fantasize paring the show to such degree that I could travel around the world with naught but a knapsack, but until then I pack a light, nylon day-pack with my luggage for unexpected jaunts and spur-of-the-moment shopping.

Knapsacks have so many uses. Check your luggage at the hotel and take off for a weekend jaunt into the country. For shopping they can't be beat. Cram them with all your collectibles for the trip home. Even the day packs are spacious. The adventurous traveler is wise to pack a lightweight, nylon knapsack with his or her luggage; it folds flat into the suitcase and takes no room.

The less you take, the less you worry about what to wear! When you have very little, necessity charges your coordinating talents and you make up your mind quickly. Thus, you can concentrate on the joys of the journey, the sights, the new experiences, rather than on what to wear. So, set forth with as little as possible. You will then have the space and the reason to buy whatever strikes your fancy enroute!

15

The Power
Of A Positive
Fashion Image

I was in the VIP cottage at Fort Polk that had once been used by General Patton when Mary Ellen picked me up for a radio interview on KLLA in Leesville, Louisiana. I was to speak later that day for the Fort Polk Officers' Wives Club and had agreed to do the radio interview before the luncheon. When Mary Ellen stepped from her Mercedes her positive appearance immediately told me that here was a smart lady, a woman of varied interests. She maintained a career, as well as being a military wife. Her step quick and confident, her eyes alight with enthusiasm, Mary Ellen on that nippy January morning was a perfect example of the power of a positive image. She was handsomely put together in a navy wool jacket, muted plaid skirt of burgundy and navy wool, burgundy blouse, burgundy leather handbag and shoes. Her personality was as brightly engaging as her outfit and I knew I would enjoy our time together.

I have been privileged to meet women like Mary Ellen all over the United States, in Canada, England and Ireland. I wish I could name them all. Women you've never heard of, whose names do not appear in Liz Smith's column or Rona Barret's newscasts, but women with such style, such verve, they make celebrities pale by comparison. I am in awe how women (and you are one of them) with humor, love and incredible fortitude take all the curve balls life throws and smash them into the stands for home runs. The military wife in particular deserves mention. She has been stereotyped, maligned and misunderstood and it was not until I began an extensive tour of military bases that I came to know these able, dedicated women as they really are: accomplished, creative, flexible, good humored, concerned not only about their family but the world around them, and fascinatingly, the most attractive audiences for whom I have appeared. I find more beautiful women amongst military wives than any other group, and I have spoken to well over 3,000 audiences in 22 years. Their beauty is not the hard-edged rivalry and shafting sleekness of Beverly Hills, Palm Beach, Southampton, Park Avenue and Grosse Pointe, but softer, kinder, more truly womanly, despite the insular, competitive society in which they live.

And their resilience! Can you imagine uprooting your family, your home, and moving gracefully, 15 times in 20 years? And their self-control! During the Vietnam war, when I was an anti-war activist, the military wife not only had to deal with the anguish of her husband killed, maimed, missing-in-action, or a prisoner of war, she had to cope with the villification and the insensitivity to her position by all those opposed to the war.

Military wives essentially are like women everywhere: human beings besieged by the pressures of living in an uncertain world. They live constantly with the knowledge they are affected first in a national emergency. Every screaming headline that you and I ignore is to them a danger signal. And this tension makes them extraordinarily appreciative of the times they spend with their families. They bring a sense of gaiety to their daily lives, and they work hard to look attractive. I have never seen a frumpy military wife! I've seem them overweight, underweight, older, irregularly featured and irregularly shaped, but they are well groomed and wear clothes with flair and élan.

There are three types of career women, one of whom is not generally recognized as being a true career woman although her job demands more effort, expertise and dedication than most careers. The woman who devotes full time to a home, husband and family is a career woman whose replacement would cost over $40,000 a year. Unfortunately career homemakers seldom recognize their value. There are an infinite number of women who prefer being full time homemakers and have no desire for an outside job. For them the fashion image is more relaxed. They can wear more casual clothes and spend less money on daytime wear. When on the town shopping or lunching, they wear freer, more eclectic fashions, bolder colors and more varied designs. Yet the homemaker should recognize the power of her fashion image just as much as the woman in the commercial marketplace.

The second type of career woman falls into two categories: the single person who loves her job and does not plan to marry and raise a family, and the single woman working only to mark time before marriage. For both, their wardrobes need a dual personality; a sleek efficient look for day, and a soft, feminine image for an active social life after five.

The third type of career woman has the most complex situation. She juggles a career, marriage and family, and must function in all three areas with vitality and attractiveness. She needs a fashion image that bolsters her throughout a busy life.

For all three, the power of a positive fashion image makes the job easier and more enjoyable. People, even the closest members of your own family, have a totally different attitude when you look attractive, well groomed and in charge! We are all painfully aware of how people react to us when we look less than our best. I deplore this emphasis on facade, but it is a fact we must recognize and with which we must cope. People react to power! They respect, and are considerate of those who look important, act confident and are in charge!

How do you establish a positive fashion image? What we have discussed in the book so far concerning: the importance of comfort and classics; knowing your body; how to choose color, fabrics, clothes for special occasions and travel; ideas for coordination and using accessories; how to shop; how to cull your closet and establish a system of maintenance . . . all these are tools which strengthen the power of your image.

The statement you make through the language of clothing not only reveals what you look like on the *outside,* but indicates the way you think *inside.* Some women dress from the outside in, using clothes to create a person who does not really exist. Insecure women tend to do this, and you can recognize them by the uncomfortable way they behave in their clothes, by the furtive glances they cast whenever they pass a mirror; by the way they avoid your eyes when you speak to them.

Others, content and knowing, dress from the inside out, in clothes which express their inner feelings. Because these feelings change and grow, these women change with ease. They are comfortable adapting or not adapting to new trends, ready to listen, to learn, to experiment. They create their own style ignoring designs they know do not work for them. These women meet your eyes warmly, they grasp your hand with vigor, they smile with true sincerity, they cannot be intimidated.

A positive fashion image bolsters confidence, and confidence creates a liberated outlook. Liberation lies not in magazines, fashion or feminist, or in self-help books, or in the strides one makes on the job. Liberation is in your head, and the way it works for you from the inside to the outside shows in the way you dress, talk, walk, and function.

I disagree with much of what John Molloy says in his *"Dress for Success"* book. The needs of women in business are too variable for his rigid philosophy of putting people in equal clothing so that they are on an equal footing and one does not overshadow the other. Who is he kidding? Business is competitive and filled with competitive, innovative, creative people who cannot be confined to man-tailored, three-piece corporate straightjackets. Any woman with moxie knows what is appropriate in an office. If she has to be told *exactly* what to wear, how can she be a leader, a creative innovator? When a woman seeking a job enters a corporate personnel office in clothes more suited to a Laverne and Shirley episode, she won't get much further than filling out forms anyway.

Women in business dress as differently as women at home. The fashion atmosphere in advertising, publishing, television, movie and theatrical offices, art galleries, interior design showrooms, and other offices which deal with the arts is freer, less structured, more eclectic and light years apart from the "dress for success" concept. People in these offices express themselves in a clothing language which makes full use of individualism combined with good taste.

Those in the fashion industry have an image apart from most others. Models, fashion magazine editors and writers, department, specialty store and boutique personnel, manufacturer's and designer's showroom people would no sooner be caught in a "dress for success" stereotype than they would in last year's hemline. What they wear publicizes today's look and forecasts tomorrow's trends.

Women in professional careers, corporations, banking, finance, real estate and other male dominated businesses are most vulnerable to Mr. Molloy's philosophy. Their clothes should reflect the dignity and responsibility of their positions, but that does not mean they have to be drab and lack individuality. There is no reason why a woman cannot look feminine, pretty and businesslike. *Any man worth his title* should not be intimidated or distracted by an attractive woman who performs in a dignified manner. *If he is, that's his problem, not hers.*

Being dressed for business means looking well put together, chic, confident and comfortable. No matter what your position, secretary, file clerk or executive, dress with a touch of class. Subtlety and quality are the key words for business clothes. Boldness, blatancy and bad taste are as out of place in the business world as elsewhere.

The better the quality of the business clothes and accessories you choose, the better they will look throughout the day. And a good business wardrobe should not bankrupt you. Earlier we wrote of how to skillfully blend less expensive clothes with better quality garments; how to create illusions with colors and fabrics. That's the way to build and stretch an attractive business collection. Choose natural fibers blended with a touch of synthetics for easy care. Accessorized with good quality handbags and leather shoes, business dressing can be livened with the touch of a silken scarf, a dash of color, the unique way you wear a simple gold pin. Pay close attention to being well shod. Some people notice shoes and handbags before they notice anything else. One major personnel director told me he observes men's socks and the watches they wear. A woman president confided she makes a decision about a new employee based on their shoes and heels, as well as the watch.

The watch business was fascinating to me, because I had heard it from too many people to mark it down as mere coincidence. The jewelry you wear to a job interview is carefully scrutinized. Business jewelry should be the best you can afford and held to a minimum. Wear none at all, rather than something cheap. Junk jewelry destroys an otherwise elegant, sophisticated look.

People react to you in so many different ways when you are being interviewed for a job. Grooming and body language are as important as the clothes you wear. The way you sit, use your hands, place your feet, make eye contact, communicate verbally and listen, all reveal your confidence or lack of it. Sometimes just a simple little touch makes all the difference in the world.

I'll never forget my first interview for an advertising position. I had not been trained for anything other than theatre and when in the fall of 1949 my husband walked out and left me with two sons less than two and three years old, I had to find work immediately and acting jobs were scarce. I literally had only twenty-five cents the morning I left for that interview. Since I had few office skills, I decided I would seek something creative and found a promising ad under "advertising assistant." I planned to be there early.

I carefully computed how I would stretch my twenty-five cents: ten cents for carfare to and from my apartment on the lower East Side of Manhattan; ten cents for a Nedicks lunch and five cents in reserve, in case I had to make a phone call.

I dropped my sons at the Virginia Day nursery and crossed the street to catch the uptown bus. An old woman stood at the corner, a shawl around her shoulders, despite the warm September sunshine.

"A rose," she cried, extending a beautifully coiled tearose. "Only a nickel for a rose!" People hurrying for the bus passed by.

I stopped and smiled. "Good morning, I'll take one," I said handing her one of my precious nickels. (I'd just have to eliminate the necessity for a phone call.)

Her wizened face broadened into a grin as she pinned the delicate bud to the lapel of my black suit. I turned towards the bus, just as it pulled away.

There was a long wait for the next bus and I arrived late. The entrance to the New York Merchandise Company was dreary. The back room in which a number of young women were seated was even bleaker. A shirt-sleeved man with slick dark hair handed me a slip of paper with number "eleven" on it. I sat down and waited. Finally a voice crackled over an ancient intercom, "Number Eleven!"

I was ushered through a vast room with wall-to wall display tables, much like a department store, then up a spiral staircase to a narrow balcony overlooking the cluttered downstairs. The balcony was dark and dingy. A lightbulb in a hanging green glass fixture shadowed the face behind a rolltop desk in the corner. A long, fluorescent tube lit a rough, wooden worktable.

The man behind the desk was handsome, in a steely, grey haired, grim way. His desk was so crowded with papers and objects the top was no longer visible.

I handed him my filled out application form. He barely glanced at it, his eyes were on the rose. He forced a tight-lipped smile and motioned me to sit down.

"Where'd you get the flower?" he asked abruptly.

"From a street vendor," I replied.

"Do you know anything about advertising?"

"No," I said, looking him directly in the eye.

"What makes you think you can do this job then?" he probed.

"I can do anything I set my mind on," I answered straightforwardly, "and I need a job, now!"

He looked at me for a long moment, glanced at the application and flicked the switch on the intercom, graveling into it, "Stanley, let the others go, I've just filled the position."

"But," I began, "don't you want to test me?"

"Know everything I need to know," he said. "This job requires someone with an eye for details. Any woman who would take the time to buy a flower and wear it to a job interview would take the time to do a job well. Let's get started."

Years later, long after I had left his employ, I met Sam Bloom at a convention in Chicago. He told me he had never forgotten the yellow rose.

I had bought that rose innocently, to make myself feel better during a difficult time. I did not realize then how much of an edge it gave me over the competition. The first impression we make is the strongest. We can do much to alter first impressions later on, but we can never *erase* them. Therefore choose what you wear with great deliberation and be meticulous with your grooming. Know your market and dress for it.

Do not wear tight fitting or body hugging clothes to a job interview or in the office. Not only are they out of place and in poor taste, they ride up, crease and look weary after you have been sitting in them all day long.

Wear clothes which move with easy grace, flowing about your figure in a flattering line. Separates offer variety and enable you to look individual. Shirts, blouses, sweaters, skirts, jackets, vests and other third layers exercise your coordination talents. If you prefer dresses, choose shirtwaists, two-piece knit suits, sweater dresses and the changelings: classic, uncluttered lines which can be easily accessorized and accented. If in doubt about an accent, don't use it. The very doubt in your mind is signal enough. Better less than more.

Whatever clothes you choose, grooming is the ultimate accent. It must be meticulous. Hairdo, makeup, nails, perfume, the fit and appearance of your clothes and accessories reflect the power of your positive approach to the way you see yourself, and your job.

As I was finishing this page, I received a letter from Tricia, a young executive who attended my show in New Orleans last week. Her letter was heartwarming and I quote a passage which seems timely at this moment:

"It was not idle talk when I told you I wished I had seen your presentation before the convention, because for the most part, clothing myself has always been a bit of a trial. Somewhere in the inner recesses of my mind, there has always been a rebellion against trying to squeeze my body into someone else's concepts of how it should be shaped and adorned! Not to mention the money I would much rather spend on any number of other things. I know that my attitudes have changed radically since watching your presentation. This gal's suitcase will forever be different as a result of the two hours spent listening to you!"

Thank you, Tricia.

All that you have been working with in this book now comes full circle. Create a fashion image you are proud of, and most comfortable with! When you are on top of it all, you will look it!

And when you feel healthy, strong and vigorous you will do a better job! Taking care of the inner body is essential if you want to look attractive and have the energy to enjoy life to the fullest. To build and maintain good health requires work, just as creating a positive fashion image requires attention to details.

The section which follows outlines a practical program of nutrition and exercise that will show remarkable results, even if you adhere to only a part of it. I've entitled it WINNING . . . and that is your reward, WINNING a healthier body, a happier outlook, and a more beautiful, positive, enthusiastic, energetic and youthful YOU. I fully expect you will be a WINNER!

Part 3

Winning!

16

Life Is An Olympics

The greatest high of all is WINNING! Nothing beats the surge, the joy of *SUCCESS,* and what better game than LIFE!

LIFE is the ultimate OLYMPICS, and to participate, and in the long run . . . WIN, requires as much dedication and discipline as preparing for any championship!

How can anyone expect to engage in such an important event without training? Athletes train for years for competition. Is not LIVING the greatest competition of all?

Years ago when people lived a more simple, resourceful life, when they worked physically, ate unprocessed foods, spent their evenings quietly, retiring early to sleep peacefully until daybreak, there was little need for physical training programs.

Today life is more complex, more stressful, with days and nights filled with activities, with demands upon one's energies which can quickly drain physical and mental reservoirs.

To stay healthy and vital in today's strobelighted, punkrockblasting, wheelspinning, tirepeeling, interestsoaring, spaceshuttle world takes work! Yet, what an exciting time to be alive with the 21st Century just *five Olympic games away!*

If you want to make it, as I do, then you are wise to begin training now, for the physically fit person lives longer! The physically fit cope with stress more healthfully, their bodies can better handle life threatening traumas. They are much keener, their reactions quicker and better coordinated. Active, physically healthy people are more youthful, maintaining a spirit of adventure and an appreciation of self-worth well into advanced years.

YOU CAN BECOME PHYSICALLY FIT! No matter what your age, no matter what condition you are in now, you can _improve._ YOU CAN BE A WINNER, and even if you do not make it to the year 2000 Olympics, you will feel better every day of your life!

All it takes is a simple, daily routine which becomes easier each day you do it, just like jumping hurdles: only the first one is tough. Your daily training program will balance exercise, nutrition, rest and mental attitude. It becomes more enjoyable the longer you stay with it, because it makes you _feel so good!_

As you become fit, your muscles become stronger. Your heart pumps more blood with each beat and begins to work more slowly, more efficiently. Your circulation improves and increases. Your lungs take in more air with each breath, nourishing your bloodstream, bringing a natural shine to your skin, a spark to your brain and a glorious feeling of well being! You become more supple, more graceful and your every step exudes vitality. You have the energy to love, to finish the unfinished, to backpack up Mt. Whitney. You have the confidence to create!

Your sensualities awaken! The more healthful you feel, the stronger your sexual appetite, and good, strong, loving sex makes you sparkle, makes you happy, attracts others to you because you are FUN to be with . . . YOU ARE A WINNER!

THAT'S WHAT GOOD HEALTH IS ALL ABOUT. It is not an unobtainable goal. _IT IS POSSIBLE._ . . . provided you _work_ at it. Begin now, all you have to lose is lassitude!

You begin this four-pronged WINNERS TRAINING PROGRAM of exercise, nutrition, rest and the strengthening of one's emotional and mental attitudes by making it a part of your everyday routine. It becomes a way of life after a while, almost involuntary, like breathing.

Exercise forms part one of this training program because unless your body responds to your needs, all else becomes difficult. Understand, however, that this is an all-encompassing program; one part is no more or less important than the other. Exercise, nutrition, rest, relaxation and the development of a positive outlook are all a circle, strengthening each other because of their _indivisibility._

Exercising consistently forms the foundation from which good health and physical fitness grow and daily exercise need not disturb your busy days. It becomes PART of that day, as natural, as easy and as relaxed as awakening. The exercises suggested and illustrated are divided into segments designed to coordinate with your daily routine. Do not think, "I DO NOT HAVE THE TIME." The time *IS THERE,* you are being trained to recognize it and *USE IT.*

It is not necessary for you to do all of the exercises outlined in this chapter. Choose those which most easily fit in with your schedule, and stick with them. If occasionally you find more time, add another segment or vary the segments. The more you do, the better shape you will be in.

Exercises fall into four categories:
Isometrics—Exercises which move muscles without moving joints. For example: pressing hands together to enlarge breasts.

Isotonics—Exercises which move muscles and joints. For example: calisthenics.

Anaerobics—Exercises which make quick demands for oxygen but are cut short. For example: running, cycling, swimming a short distance, swimming one or two laps quickly, running for a bus. These exercises demand a large amount of oxygen quickly without building a steady training effect. They are used by competitive atheletes to build up speed, and *should not be part of anyone's average physical fitness regime.* The word "anaerobics" means without oxygen.

Aerobics—The exercises which work the inside muscles, the ones we cannot see. Aerobics strengthen heart and lungs building a healthy cardiovascular system and endurance. *They are exercises we should practice every day,* if we want to stay healthy and youthful. "Aerobics" means with oxygen, and are: rapid walking, jogging, running, cycling, swimming laps, all at a brisk pace for a specified length of time. The best books on aerobic type exercises are: *Aerobics* by Dr. Kenneth H. Cooper and *Aerobics for Women* by his wife, Mildred Cooper.

Aerobics are the most important of all the exercises and should be part of a daily program or practiced at least five times a week. It is not difficult to fit aerobics into your daily life. All it takes is a brisk walk of at least two miles at 15 minutes per mile to begin a steady training program that will strengthen your cardiovascular system and build endurance. This means just one half hour out of your day, and you can walk in the early morning, at lunchtime, or after dinner.

Walking briskly is the healthiest form of exercise. It places little strain on joints and muscles and can be safely indulged in at any age. Some prefer running and jogging, but before you begin a program of this type, *make sure to check with your physician first.*

Bicycling, cross-country skiing, handball, racketball, tennis, golf (no cart), dancing, are all aerobic type exercises which keep heart and lungs healthy and add youth to your step. Even if you choose not to do any of the isometrics and isotonics outlined in this chapter, for your life's sake, begin a consistent program of aerobic type exercises now!

To prove how easy it is for you to get in shape, our exercise program begins at the very beginning, *in bed,* where you were born!

When Mark Twain said, "Everytime I think of exercising, I lie down until the thought goes away," he did not realize there is no better place to begin a new day than with simple, stretching movements in bed, *before you get up.* It is the most comfortable place of all, and the results are immediately recognizable. For people with arthritis, back and joint problems or athletic injuries, it is imperative to begin here. The following exercises should be done on a firm mattress; the firmer the sleeping surface the healthier it is for your spine.

Waking up quickly and *jumping* out of bed is a shock to a newly aroused body. Chinese philosophy tells us the long journey from sleep to awakening should be broken only in the most loving and gentle manner. Chinese women for centuries were taught to caress their husbands awake. If you share your bed, caress each other awake and do the following exercises together. If you sleep alone, be content to awaken by yourself. Stretch, stretch sensuously and massage your own body.

1—Breathe deeply. Run hands over your body toward your heart. Massage gently. Work around the back of your neck with a kneading motion, up into the scalp using your fingers in a circular movement. Work around the entire head and feel your scalp tingle and your brain come alive! (Marvelous for the hair.) Massage your hands, rubbing them over each other. Work up your arms, deep into the shoulder areas. Lift one leg with knee bent. Beginning with ankle, massage up to the thigh, working completely around leg. Repeat with other leg. Do this slowly, allow body to awaken gently.

2—Place fingertips together on diaphragm. Breathe deeply, pushing diaphragm out as you inhale; in as you exhale. Feel fingertips move apart as you inhale. When you exhale, they will come together. Count as you exhale and see how many counts you can work up to before fingertips come together. Think only of the breathing, filling lungs deeply each time. Do five, slow deep breathing movements. Listen to the rhythm of your life's breath soaring into a new morning.

3—Raise arms overhead. Stretch, stretch, stretch, first one arm, then the other. Stretch feet to foot of bed. Try to touch end. Stretch toes, curl them, alternate. Clench fists, release. Stretch, release a number of times. Think of something lovely, like winning a lottery or waking up 20 pounds thinner! (sketch 64)
Note: If your legs should ever cramp while sleeping or while stretching, *curl toes*. Then stretch gently and curl. Stretching and curling, eliminating sugar from your diet and drinking two glasses of skimmed milk a day should do away with leg cramps.

4—Pull stomach in, hard. Hold to count of five. Relax. Repeat five times.

5—Clasp arms overhead. Bring one knee to chest bringing arms up, over and clasping hands over knee. Repeat with other leg. Breathe in when arms are overhead, breathe out as you bring knee to chest. Repeat five times alternating legs. When you become stronger, bring both knees to chest at same time and lower slowly. (sketch 64)

6—Stretch arms out, shoulder level. Raise head, look at toes, turn head (still raised) slowly to left, then right. Lower head to bed. Repeat five times.

7—Close eyes, open wide. Roll eyes in complete circle, right to left, left to right, up and down. Close eyes again, look at a distant object in the room. Look at something close. Repeat a number of times. Close your eyes, take two deep breaths. Think blue, think green, think serene. Open your eyes slowly. Think of what a GREAT DAY THIS WILL BE . . . SMILE . . . and then, GET UP!

While these exercises may not be as satisfying as Chinese caresses, they stimulate circulation and tone stomach, back, neck, facial and

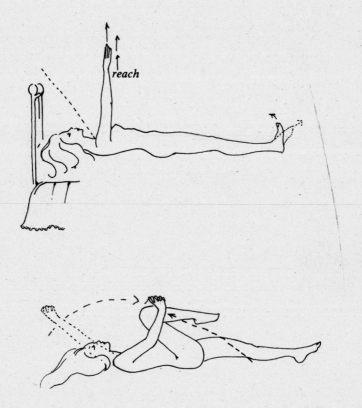

reach

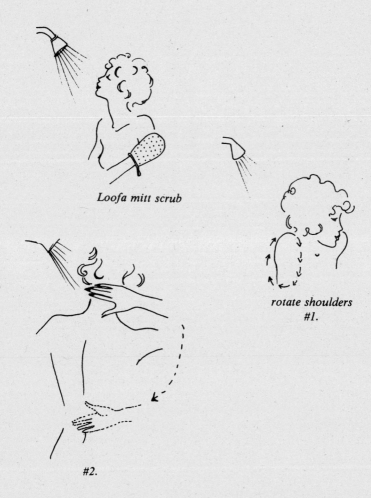

Loofa mitt scrub

rotate shoulders
#1.

#2.

eye muscles. If you are a diehard who insists, "I have no time to exercise in bed," or "I *must* get up *before* my husband and the children," then let a morning shower awaken and stimulate you!

Showers are terrific for massage and other exercises! Use a loofah mitt or a rough terry cloth briskly. Begin with arms; run mitt or cloth from fingertips to shoulder, massaging in a circular motion. Work under, over and up the arms, around neck, across top of chest (never massage the breasts roughly), down the sides, under bosom, around waist, stomach, hips, buttocks and down legs. Come up, massaging vigorously, yet gently.

1—Rotate shoulders forward, around back, and up. Do ten rotations. Reverse direction, rotating shoulders, backwards, down and forwards. Do ten. (Keeps shoulders young and prevents fat from building up at back of neck.) (sketch 65)

2—Place palm of right hand on back of head (elbow bent). Reach down and back, placing hand, palm out in center of back. Do five times. Repeat with other hand. Fantastic if you have ever had a shoulder injury. (Helps to keep upper arms youthful.) (sketch 65)

3—Bend over from waist. Place hands on knees. Allow the relaxing warm water to caress your lower back. Pull stomach in hard, rounding back and dropping chin to chest. Your knees will straighten. Hold for a moment. Relax stomach, raising head, arching it backwards. As back arches, knees will bend. Repeat this tightening and relaxing of stomach and back at least five times, making sure to drop chin to chest and arching head as back arches. (This is the all important pelvic tilt which keeps backs strong and vaginas youthful.) (sketch 66)

4—With the shower aimed at the back of your neck (gently), turn head to right and rest chin on right shoulder. Feel the stretch of neck muscles. Hold for a moment, turn slowly and repeat to left. (sketch 67)

5—Place right hand on right side of face. Drop head to left shoulder. Try to raise head, while at the same time right hand resists. Be gentle, do not force, just resist. Repeat with left hand, dropping head to right shoulder. (sketch 67)

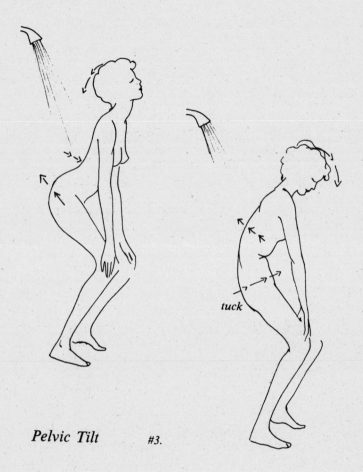

Pelvic Tilt   *#3.*

tuck

6—With water still cascading gently on back of your neck, rotate head allowing it to drop fully onto chest and fall backwards as you come around. Feel like a ragdoll. Relax. Feel the water fall on your face and the back of neck. Reverse the rotation. (sketch 67)

Gradually cool the water, accustoming yourself to the cooler temperature by allowing it to spray the *base* of your spine *first*. This seems to set a body thermostat that makes taking a cool shower easier. You might then wish to try what Frenchwomen have been doing for years to help keep their bosoms youthful. Run cool, cool water on your breasts to tone and tighten. (This should never be done by anyone with a heart condition.)

If you are taking a shower with one you love, the possibilities for hand massage are infinite. Enjoy it even more knowing that not only is it a terrifically sensual experience, it is also healthy!

Pulsating shower heads are excellent for stimulation and circulation, but heavy, pulsating jets can be harmful if used indiscriminately, or by those who have disc or joint problems. Be careful and do not overdo.

What you have done with these shower exercises is to awaken your spinal column to a new day. The central nervous system is encased in the spinal cord, and the peripheral nerves emanate from there. Maintaining a healthy lumbar and cervical spine is essential to good health and physical fitness, and helps soothe injuries, arthritis, and other problems which beset the spine.

I was 19 when I first injured my back, foolishly attempting an advanced exercise before I had warmed up sufficiently. At that time I was physical director of Dr. Robert Anderson's health camp near Peekskill, New York. Even though I had a daily routine in which I conducted four lengthy hikes, taught three calisthenics and two swimming classes, I sustained a sacroiliac injury when I attempted a difficult movement before my body was ready. Because I was young and physically fit, I healed quickly, though painfully.

In 1967 I suffered another back injury and this time I was past forty. I was told I would not be able to continue to ski, run, play tennis or golf. The orthopedic specialist recommended a back operation. I refused and he put me into traction for ten days. When I was released from the hospital, I began a daily program of back exercises and since my apartment was only a block from the YWCA I swam each day during lunch hour. When I was on tour, I would find a local

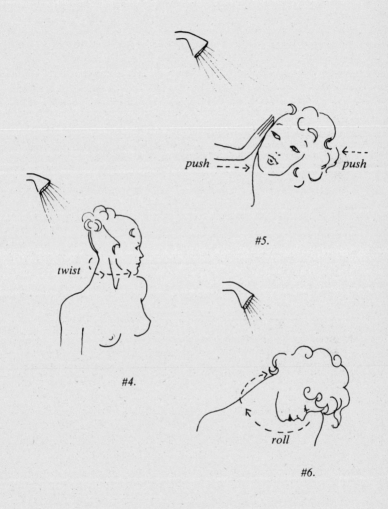

push - - - → push

#5.

twist

#4.

roll

#6.

Y and swim before or after my shows.

I worked up to swimming one half mile five days a week and continued this for three years, until I moved to the Pocono Mountains where swimming is not that convenient.

Today, I can bend over from the waist with no difficulty and touch my hands flat to the floor. In 1973, I joined the teaching staff at Camelback Ski Area, just ½ mile from my home and taught skiing on the weekends I was not on tour. In 1978 I won my first Silver NASTAR medal in a ski race at Steamboat Springs. Two years ago I took up cross-country skiing. I walk at least four to six miles a day and do a full hour of advanced calisthenics three times a week. I also play golf, tennis and cycle whenever I get the chance.

I had four grandparents who died of heart disease and high blood pressure while in their early fifties. Genetically I am not a good risk, but I continually work to better my odds.

I begin each morning that I am home in a warm tub, using a whirlpool machine for twenty minutes while I exercise. I have had no hint of back trouble since my '67 injury and I feel stronger than when I was a young woman. My tub routine has worked so well for me, I hope that you will make time for it. Get up a half hour earlier, it is worth it!

Buy an eyeshade. Pour bath oil or perfume into a warm, warm tub. (I use camomile blossoms tied in cheesecloth.) Cleanse and moisturize your face. Leave the cream on. Soak two cotton balls with witch hazel, or use two cucumber slices. Place over eyes, cover with eyeshade. Invest in a portable whirlpool machine which sits on the rim of the tub. It is well worth the money. I bought such a model from Sears for less than $100.00 nine years ago and I have used it constantly. Turn the whirlpool on, aiming jet at your lower back.

1—Sink into swirling water, so that back is flat, knees bent. Contract stomach muscles tightly, forcing small of back to tub. Hold, release, repeat. Do 100 contractions the first day, eventually working up to 500. While you do these contractions, move the whirlpool arm so that the jet reaches various parts of your body. Keep your mind free of thought, concentrate only on the contractions. If you have no whirlpool, just do the exercise, it's great! *Note:* A delightful bonus to this particular exercise is that you are also strengthening sphincter and vaginal muscles. Your love partner will find you tighter. Doing these same contractions during the love act brings stimulating and sensual excitement to both partners.

2—Aim jet at ankles, or if you do not have a whirlpool machine, turn faucets on and let a stream of swift running water massage ankles as you exercise them. Bend feet forward and back. Stretch toes, curl them. Rotate ankles right and left. Do these ankle exercises anywhere. If you have been shopping or touring and your feet hurt, sit down somewhere and do them. Ankles not only turn men's heads, they hold you up, and when your feet hurt, it shows in your face. (sketch 68)

3—Sink hands into tumbling water. Try to grasp and hold the whirling liquid. Extend fingers, make a fist, extend, stretch. Rotate wrists, right, left. Exercises make the hands lovelier, stronger, and younger looking. *Note:* If fingers are arthritic, gently massage joints under water. Doing this daily will help to alleviate pain and keep fingers from stiffening further. (sketch 68)

4—Sit up (eyeshade still on eyes). Aim whirlpool jet at your knees. Make sure pressure is not too strong. Contract thigh muscles. Hold, release. Put hands on thighs and feel the muscles working. Strong thigh muscles are important for knee strength. Do ten contractions working up to twenty.

5—Bend elbows. Clasp fingers tightly. Try to pull hands apart. Resist. Hold for five counts, relax, repeat ten times. (Tightens arms and bust.)

6—Extend arms forward. Turn palms to outside. Tense. Hold five counts, relax, repeat ten times. (Keeps upper arms firm.) (sketch 68)

All of these exercises can be done without a whirlpool, but the whirlpool is a definite plus and should be considered. Once a week, apply a facial mask while you do this tub routine. *Note:* If unfortunately you are bedridden due to illness or injury, all of the foregoing exercises can be done while confined to bed. They will help maintain muscle strength. Check with your doctor before you begin.

If exercising in bed, in the shower, in the tub is not for you, then try the kitchen. THE BROOMSTICK will keep you fit. No specific number of repetitions appears in this segment because these exercises should be done rhythmically without bothering to count. Do what feels good!

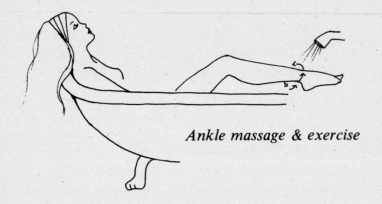

Ankle massage & exercise

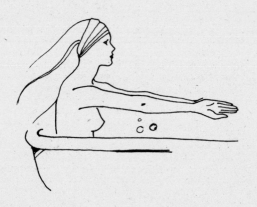

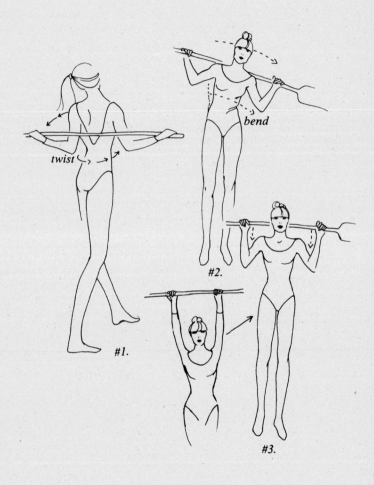

twist

bend

#1.

#2.

#3.

1—Place broomstick across upper back. Twist slowly from side to side. Pick up a nice, easy rhythm. (sketch 69)

2—Same position. Bend sideways, alternating sides. Slowly stretch from the waist. Keep hips loose to prevent pulling waist or back muscles. (sketch 69)

3—Reach broomstick high over head. Lower it behind neck and shoulders (as far as you can go). This helps straighten posture and prevents ugly fat deposits known as "dowager's hump." It also tightens and tones back of upper arms. (sketch 69)

4—Hold broomstick out at shoulder level. Turn right foot to side. Keep left foot straight ahead. Bend knee and slowly lunge over right knee in fencing position. *Do not bounce.* The idea is to stretch inner thigh. Get as low as you can comfortably. This is not to be done quickly. What you want is a long, long stretch for inner thigh. Repeat with other leg. (sketch 71)

5—Hold broom vertically, sweeper end up. Pretend it is a sturdy cane. Swing leg back and forth attaining rhythm and height. Stay loose. Do not strain. Begin kicks slowly and do not go too high. Your leg should be a dead weight which swings freely in a pendulum motion. Alternate legs. (sketch 70)

6—Same position. Raise right leg to side. Slowly, stretch. Then begin slow side kicks, gradually raising height of kick. Do not strain or you could pull a muscle. Alternate legs. (sketch 70)

7—Hold broomstick out at shoulder level. Raise knee, try to kick stick. Alternate legs. Begin slowly and work up to a lively tune to tone hips, legs, abdomen. (sketch 70)

8—Hold broomstick out at shoulder level. Bend knees slightly. Keeping back straight, push pelvis forward, lower and raise body gently. Do not go too low. Feel the stretch and pull in your thighs. This partial, stretching knee bend is far better for you than deep knee bends. Women with varicose veins should never do any deep knee bends, nor should other women. (sketch 71)

9—Raise broomstick overhead. Slowly bend forward from waist, *knees bent.* Reach broomstick towards floor. *Do not bounce.* Do not

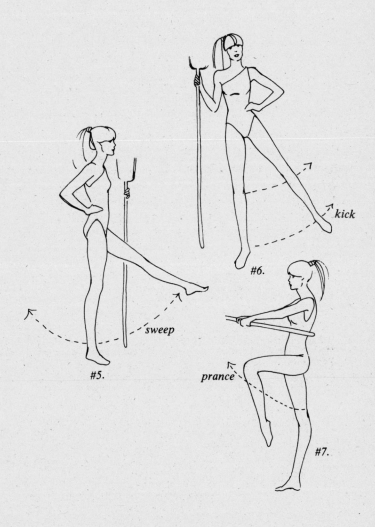

kick

sweep

#6.

#5.

prance

#7.

arms
chest level

head & back
straight

pelvis
forward

#8.

#4.
fencing lunge

attempt to touch floor if you have not exercised in years. Be patient. Slowly raise from knees until legs are straight. You are stretching the back muscles and the legs. Breathe out as you bend towards the floor. Inhale as you come up, raising broomstick high over head. Stretch up, lift your ribcage. As your suppleness increases, straighten your knees *slightly* as you bend towards floor. Eventually you will be able to touch floor with straight knees. Always do this exercise *slowly* stretching from the waist. (sketch 72)

10—Hold broomstick horizontally, chest high. Extend arms straight out. Bring them back. Extend again; bring back a number of times. This tones and firms upper arms. (sketch 72)

11—Same position. Turn broomstick so that alternate ends face ceiling. Twist and turn broomstick rapidly, holding arms straight out. DO NOT BEND ELBOWS. This exercise keeps arms and breasts youthful. (sketch 72)

12—Put broomstick down. You are finished with it. Finish off with jumping jacks. With hands at sides, feet together, jump feet apart, raising arms and clapping hands over head at the same time. Work up to twenty jumping jacks. You will feel vital for the rest of the day! (sketch 73)

If you have no broom, get a *board! A slant board!* If we lived in a weightless world, perhaps nothing would sag, and at sixty our body would look as lovely as it did at twenty. Since we are earthlings and subject to its gravity, slant boards help to combat downward drag. If you have no slant board, an ironing board placed on the edge of a chair, its forward end on the floor, will work. You can also lie down in the slant position for a few moments each day by elevating your feet on a chair with pillows propped under your back. The slant position sends blood to the head, stimulating facial tissues, nerves and muscles.

1—Arms overhead. Raise arms and clasp knee to chest. Alternate legs. When you feel strong enough, do this exercise raising both knees to chest. Breathe in when arms are overhead, breathe out as you bring knees to chest. (sketch 74)

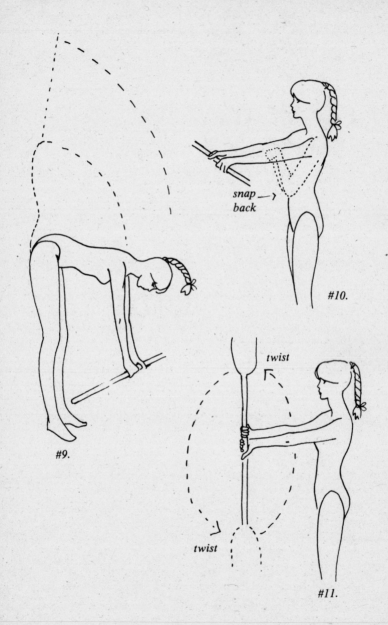

snap
back

#10.

twist

twist

#9.

#11.

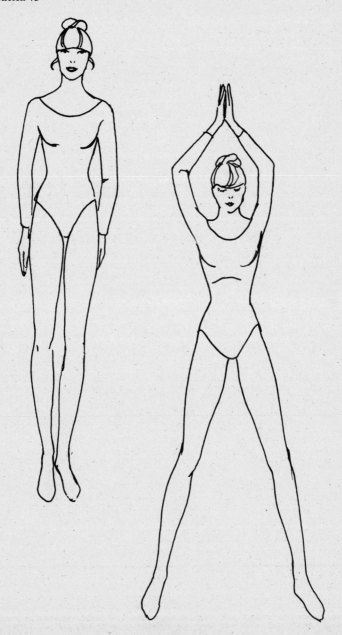

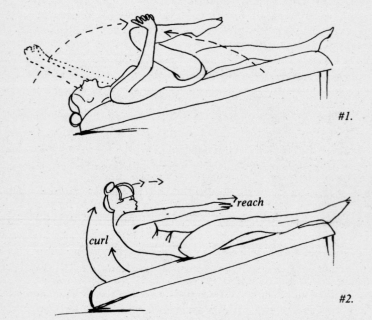

#1.

#2.

2—Arms overhead. Slowly raise body and try to touch toes with fingertips. Exhale as you sit up. Inhale as you slowly return to starting position. *As your strength increases, fold arms across chest and raise body, touching head to knees.* When you are truly strong, place arms behind head and sit up. Work up eventually to twenty-five situps. Breathe in when body is lowered. Breathe out as you come up. (sketch 74)

3—Hold onto slant board grips. Raise both legs slightly. Cross right leg over left in side scissor kick, spreading legs as far as possible with each crossover. Keep knees straight. Alternate; begin with ten working up to twenty-five crossovers. This strengthens abdominal muscles and trims inner thigh. (sketch 75)

4—Hold grips. Raise each leg slowly as high as you can. Work up to twenty with each leg, breathing in when prone, breathing out as leg is raised. Alternate. (sketch 75)

5—Hold grips. Raise both legs high (slowly). Lower legs to board (more slowly still). Feel stomach muscles tighten! The slower you do this, the stronger the pull on the stomach muscles. Breathe deeply and evenly, inhaling and exhaling as above. (sketch 76)

6—Raise head. Hold. Turn slowly from side to side. Lower head to board and repeat. (sketch 76)

If you feel you cannot take time to do either the broomstick or slant board exercises, know that beneficial exercises can be done any time of day and in almost any situation. For example, if you are waiting for a bus, in line at a supermarket, or in your car waiting for the light to change take a few moments for a terrific stomach tightener: pull stomach muscles in hard. Hold, hold, hold. Relax.

Cleaning house? Stretch, bend, reach while doing chores.

Hanging clothes? Set the clothes line higher than normal, so that you have to stand almost on tiptoe to reach it. This stretches arms and helps to keep them toned and youthful.

Ironing? Smooth out your rear too! Place feet twelve inches apart. Bring one leg out to side, then back a bit. Keep hips straight, do not

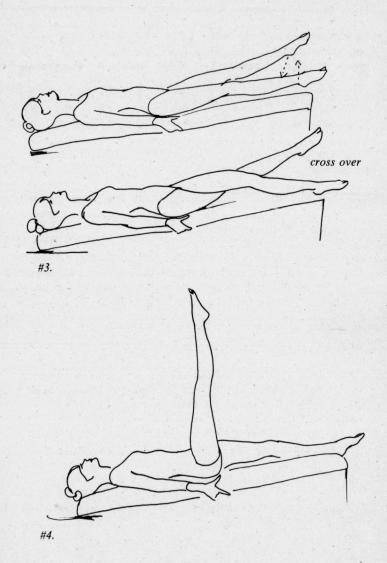

cross over

#3.

#4.

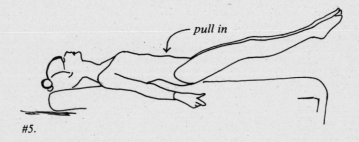

pull in

#5.

#6.

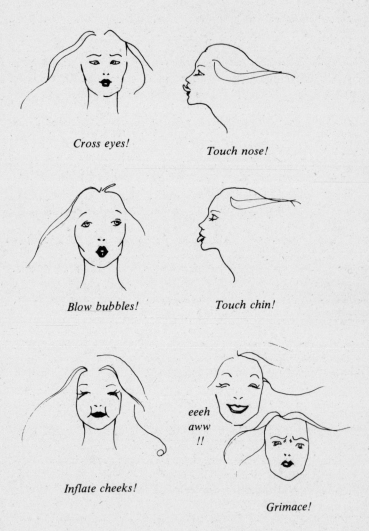

Cross eyes!

Touch nose!

Blow bubbles!

Touch chin!

Inflate cheeks!

eeeh
aww
!!

Grimace!

turn them. Tense buttock muscles. Hold for a count of six. Repeat with other leg. Keep this up while ironing and you will not feel so tired.

Dressing? Reach, reach, for that zipper. Raise arms overhead when pulling on a sweater or blouse. Twist and turn in front of the mirror to make sure of the fit of clothes. When putting on hosiery, sit on a stool or chair, lift your leg, reach out with straight arms, suck in your stomach, round your back and pull your hose on. Do not bend, reach out.

Brushing your hair? Bend forward keeping back flat with feet flat on floor. Brush hair overhead with long, sweeping strokes. Stretch lower back. Then, bend to the side and brush.

Sitting at a desk? Clasp palms, interlace fingers. Turn hands outward, palms facing away. Keep elbows straight. Raise arms overhead, stretch, stretch. Keeping arms overhead with elbows straight, bend and stretch to each side. Lift ribcage.
Unlock hands, bend to side, touching fingers to floor. Repeat, alternating sides. Stretch fingers as you reach to floor.
Stretch legs out horizontally under your desk. Wiggle toes, rotate ankles. Do this frequently whenever you have been sitting for a length of time. Particularly helpful when you have been confined to a narrow, cramped seat on a long plane flight.

Tired after typing for hours, driving long distances, or pouring over books while studying? Lift shoulders, rotate them forward. Rotate backwards. Turn head from side to side. Roll head around clockwise, then counterclockwise. Place hands behind head, bend forward, then side to side. Do all of these slowly and feel tensions ebb away.

Watching television? Don't just sit there spreading, do leg lifts. Raise each leg a number of times. Raise both legs together. With legs raised, swing them wide apart, then cross over in a scissor kick. These are excellent for circulation, stomach and thigh muscles, and are movements that elderly people can do easily.

Brushing your teeth? Keep your face youthful with exercises which keep facial muscles taut and springy. Become a clown! Inflate cheeks. Blow out. Blow bubbles. Grimace. Whistle. Go eee-awww, eeeh-

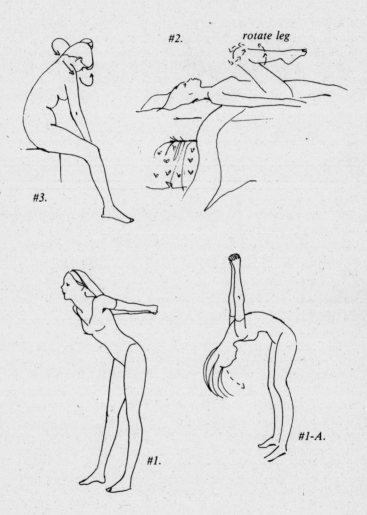

#2.

rotate leg

#3.

#1.

#1-A.

awww. Open your mouth wide, wider. Close it! Try to touch tip of nose with tongue. Try to touch chin. Close your eyes, open them wide, wider! Look at your nose, roll your eyes! (sketch 77)

Achy and tired after a busy day? If you do no others, make these three exercises part of your daily routine. They are particularly effective if you plan to go out for the evening. They relax you so that you can take a short nap and awaken refreshed, ready to be a vibrant companion.

1—Clasp hands behind back. Stand straight, stomach in. Slowly, *without bending forward,* raise hands as high as you can. Keep head back, while raising hands. Drop head, bend forward slowly from waist, keeping clasped hands high behind back. Drop head as close to knees as possible. Hold, then slowly come up, inhaling deeply as you raise head and lower arms. Release hands and feel the sensation of the blood flowing back down to your wrists.

This exercise has multitudinous benefits. It relaxes the muscles of the neck which tighten when you are tired or upset. It tones and tightens upper arms and breasts. It stimulates circulation to the face, and, most importantly of all, it helps correct poor posture. (sketch 78)

2—Lie down. Bend knees. Raise one leg at a time with knee bent. Rotate leg from knee. Circle left, then right. Alternate legs. Do at least twenty circles in each direction with leg. Do this in bed before retiring. It relieves leg strain and helps prevent varicose veins. This is an important exercise for anyone who does a lot of standing or sitting. It is especially important for pregnant women. (sketch 78)

3—Slump in a chair or on edge of bed. Don't sit, *slump,* like a ragdoll. Relax completely. Let your mouth drop open. If you are relaxed, it will. Allow eyes to close. Roll head around, easily, slowly. The weight of your head will carry it around. Roll, roll. If you become dizzy, reverse direction. Reverse anyway after ten rolls in one direction. Soon you will yawn. This proves it is working. Lie back and take a short nap or go to sleep for the night. (sketch 78)

YOU CAN BE A WINNER IN THE OLYMPICS OF LIFE! Take time to stay fit. Dying is easy, anyone can do it. It takes *work* to stay ALIVE! Exercise is fun and you do not have to limit yourself to set patterns. Join an aerobic dance class. Exercise in the swimming pool; taking a walk in waist high water does wonders. Flexibility keeps one youthful and to maintain suppleness, stretch, bend, *move* every day of your life!

17

Foods To Keep
You Young

"Oh to be young," sang out the lady with a lovely cloud of white hair as I loped by. What an up! To be called *"young."* But that is Florida. In Aspen I would be old.

Feeling young is feeling like a sunburst! Every streak vibrates with the pulse of life. New ideas, new thoughts tumble over each other. No day is long enough!

The body is incredible! Even if you meet it only half-way with good nutrition, exercise, rest, and a positive mental attitude, it responds with vitality. When you are without pain, at ease with yourself, content that you are doing your best, your mind becomes serene and responds alertly to your needs. You become confident, positive, *powerful.* All the annoyances, setbacks, disappointments and stress that everyone experiences become manageable.

Why would anyone permit themself to feel draggy, depressed, sick, when feeling *good* is so *great?* The *zoom* you get with good health is worth all the effort it takes!

And, despite your genes, despite your habits, you can build good health *right now, at this very moment,* with this easy-to-follow guide for nourishing foods which will help you create a healthy lifestyle.

Live foods keep you young! Fruits, vegetables, grains, legumes and seeds in as natural a state as possible, when combined with proteins: nuts, soy and other beans, fish, fowl, meat, eggs, milk, and cheese, nourish your body and mind with vital nutrients that make you feel terrific! You are eager to get on with the joy, the excitement, the adventure that is life!

This chapter reflects thirty-eight years of a spirited commitment to the health movement. It is a condensation of reading and studying countless books, articles and medical papers, of questioning and *doing*. It mirrors my enthusiasm, bred from experience, of how terrific I feel when I follow the laws of nature. I have observed at close hand how the health of others has improved when they adopt a healthier lifestyle. The key to good health, at any age, is *prevention*. Practicing a consistent program of preventative health care will enliven your life, for when you feel fantastic, all seems possible!

Simply put, we are a complex biochemical factory. Our vital organs, glands, brain and nervous system are encased and protected by bones, muscles, sinew and skin. All are fed by the bloodstream which nourishes the cells with oxygen, proteins, carbohydrates, vitamins and minerals. The bloodstream in turn is nourished by the food we eat, the water we drink and the air we breathe. We absorb and utilize these nutrients. We excrete wastes through the kidneys, colon and skin. The healthy body functions resiliently with a beautiful, ongoing rhythm. When all is in balance, the cadence correct, body and mind work in harmony. We feel alive, super-charged, sensational!

However, when you flood the system with the cumulative effects of poisons: junk foods, alcohol, caffeine, nicotine, drugs, chemical preservatives and additives, excess sugar and salt, environmental chemicals, mental and emotional stress, fatigue . . . the cells begin to change. They no longer receive the harmonic balance of nutrients they require. Their signals go askew. The biochemical chain that is our very life becomes off-balance, and we begin to experience breakdowns in the way we feel, the way we function. Disease takes root. The changes which are subtle and mostly unrecognized while we are young, become more pervasive and evident as we mature. Sadly, disease due to the factors described are occurring more and more frequently in the young. An inordinate number of babies are being born with genetic damage, and an inordinate number of children are victims of crippling, chronic diseases.

While at this time, we cannot radically change cell death and the aging process, we can slow it down. Sound nutrition keeps cells alive and vital. Exercise stimulates circulation, nourishes the bloodstream, and keeps the body supple, flexible and youthful. Rest regenerates and recharges life. And, a positive mental attitude brings serenity, and the confidence to make it all possible!

When I first became interested in natural foods in 1942, I was considered, "strange," . . . "on-the-fringe." Now I am in the mainstream of a vast, growing movement. More physicians today recognize that you are indeed what you eat, and that many annoying symptoms and illnesses are nutritionally based.

How lucky I was to experience healthful eating and living at the age of nineteen! I had been a sickly child and no wonder. I never ate a raw vegetable or tasted a tomato or strawberry until I went to live with my Aunt Helen at the age of ten. When I rejoined my mother a year after my grandmother's death, I was eleven years old. Since Mother was at work, I was unsupervised and unknowing. I ate cake, candy, ice-cream and loads of chocolate. My lunch was most often Pepsi-Cola and canned peas. My dinner, overcooked meat and soggy potatoes. I had measles five times and a constant cold, no matter what the season. Many times during the year I was plagued with "pink eyes," awakening each morning, my eyes glued shut with mucus. My hair was thin, brittle; my nails spotted with white marks and cracks.

I credit my off-the-wall interest in sports with building a fairly strong body, despite my diet. No one in my mother's family enjoyed or participated in any type of physical activity and she tried to discourage me because I had been born with a heart murmur. My father and his brothers were athletically active, but I saw them only twice during the years I grew up. The genes were strong, however. I was on the school track team; I joined a swim team at eleven and progressed to pre-Olympic training. I bought my first bicycle with the money I earned in a dress factory at fourteen

My bicycling companion, fellow plane polisher and budding pilot, Mordy Rhodes, had had eczema as a child, and his wise mother who had given up on doctors and drugs after years of no results, sent him to a health camp, where through diet, sunshine and exercise, his skin cleared completely. Mordy returned incredibly handsome, hearty and filled with determination to change his coke and pizza pals into celery chomping converts.

I, like the rest of the gang, resisted, enjoying every gooey taste of mozzarella as it dripped, laden with tomato sauce, hot pepper and oil from a crispy, curling crust. Mordy kept after me and finally, after one particularly miserable bout of "pink eyes," I promised to contact his health doctor. Even though I am not Jennifer O'Neal, the summer of '42 changed my life. I went off to work as physical director for Dr. Robert Anderson just as Mordy went off to war. Dr. Anderson was one of the early nutritionists and a naturopath who operated Camp Hygiology, a vegetarian resort which used to nestle on the banks of the Hudson at Verplanck, New York, just south of where the Indian Point nuclear power plant is today.

Dr. Anderson had been stricken with tuberculosis in his early thirties and had cured himself through natural means. In his seventies, he could still clear a field of underbrush better than his young helpers. I worked for the Andersons for three glorious summers and returned with my two young sons years later for another season.

Although my family made fun of me when I became a vegetarian, they were amazed and delighted with the results. I lost more than twenty pounds. My constant cold disappeared and I no longer sounded like Lily Tomlin at the switchboard. My hair grew shiny and reached its ultimate length, an inch below my ear. My nails stopped splitting and the white spots (a sign of zinc deficiency) disappeared. I felt sensational! Every day was a song, and over much too quickly. After Hygiology closed that first summer, I entered the American Academy of Dramatic Arts and began a whole new life!

The lessons I learned there have stayed with me and have helped keep me healthy despite a poor genetic heritage, despite a difficult childhood, despite the stress of raising three children without the emotional and financial support of a husband, despite a demanding work schedule and despite my impulsive, emotional nature which often finds an outlet in sweets and overeating.

While I did not remain a vegetarian, I eat little meat, preferring fish and fowl. The bulk of my diet is just that . . . bulk . . . mostly raw or slightly cooked vegetables, fresh fruits, fresh fruit and vegetable juices, whole grains, seeds, sprouts and nuts. I also take vitamin and mineral supplements and liver protein pills.

A DIET TO KEEP YOU YOUNG AND VITAL

The ideal diet, one which will keep you young, vital, energetic and enthusiastic is a natural diet containing: complex carbohydrates, proteins, vitamins and minerals. It is comparatively low-fat, free of sugar, salt and additives. To be realistic, it is not easy to give up that which we have traditionally eaten, those foods we have come to love, and those luscious dishes which add such zest to our lives. Most people change their diet only when they are overweight or illness becomes so pervasive that there is no alternative.

There is an alternative now! By easing into eating natural, healthful foods, you will find it less difficult to give up those favorites that form such a special part of your life. You can learn to select foods carefully, achieving a compromise you can live with that incorporates healthful, natural foods. Then, occasional forays into foods that are less than perfect, but perfectly delicious will do little harm.

Most important of all is to recognize and admit how harmful refined sugar is and how it pervades almost all the foods we eat. Refined sugar is *not a food!* It is a chemical compound extracted from sugar beets and sugar cane. It resembles cocaine and heroin and can be just as harmful. Refined sugar, like drugs, produces psychological dependence and addiction. It has no vitamins, minerals, fiber, protein, fat, enzymes, trace elements or any semblance of what constitutes food. Refined sugar upsets the vitamin-mineral balance of the body, robbing it of calcium, Vitamin C, and the essential B vitamins. Refined sugar is absorbed into the bloodstream quickly causing the pancreas to release insulin at an inordinately high rate resulting in surges of blood sugar levels which then fall rapidly, setting off a chain of uncomfortable symptoms which if unchecked and uncontrolled are frightening and can become life-threatening. Refined sugar causes obesity and lays a fertile foundation for diabetes, hypoglycemia, heart and kidney disease, arthritis, tooth decay, blindness and a host of other illnesses.

Nutritionists, some physicians and researchers now recognize blood sugar disturbances as the cause of emotional, mental and behavior problems in children and adults. These facts are well documented in books such as: *"Body, Mind and Sugar,"* E.M. Abrahamson; *"Psycho-Dietetics,"* Dr. Emanuel Cheraskin; *"Nutrition and Your Mind,"* and *"The Psycho-Chemical Response,"* both by George Watson; *"Sugar Blues,"* by William Dufty; *"The Ortho-Molecular Approach to Learning Disabilities,"* by Dr. Alan Cott. Dr. Benjamin Feingold has also documented his extensive work with children in a number of texts. Dr. Cott, a psychiatrist who practices in New York City and specializes in treating children, carefully monitors both his adult and pediatric patients' diets, eliminating sugar, food additives and preservatives as does Dr. Feingold.

If you read labels you will find that almost all packaged foods contain sugar. There is sugar in ketchup, steak sauce, tomato and spaghetti sauces, soups, breads, frozen and canned vegetables, baked beans, processed luncheon meats, hot dogs and some cheese foods.

287

It is almost impossible to buy anything packaged, frozen, canned or processed that does not contain sugar or salt.

I could never understand adding sugar to soup, bread, vegetables and other such foods. Why eat all the hidden sugars when the taste difference is really not that marked? I would much rather, if I am going to eat sugar, enjoy its very special sweetness in a luscious dessert. If you cannot or will not give up chocolate chip cookies, then forego the hidden sugars in foods. That is what I mean by compromise, selection and balance. There are breakthroughs as more and more food manufacturers become nutritionally aware, and as more and more people demand more wholesome, natural foods. There are tomato sauces without sugar, and Libby and Dole are packing canned fruit in their own juices without sugar. I recently read labels on 12 different brands of bread before I found one which does not contain sugar, corn syrup or honey. It is a thin-sliced rye bread baked by Arnold which has been certified as "legal" by two various diet groups.

The body needs glucose for the cells for sugar is the fuel it runs on. But stay away from simple sugars such as cake, candy, ice-cream and other sweets. They enter the bloodstream too quickly, disrupting delicate body chemistry. They also leech vitamin C, the B-complex vitamins and calcium from the system. Nature provides complex carbohydrates in the form of fresh fruits and vegetables for fuel. Complex carbohydrates go through a slower, more involved process of digestion. They enter the bloodstream gradually without over-stimulating the pancreas. Complex carbohydrates do not cause surges in blood sugar levels which create unnatural cravings for sweets and set off physical and mental aberrations and symptoms which can be frightening.

By making complex carbohydrates (fruits, vegetables and grains) the basis of your diet, and adding the necessary proteins — nuts, soy beans, fish, fowl, meat, eggs, cheese and milk — you have a nutritional program which builds health and prevents disease.

And you can ease into it so gradually that your family will not notice the difference. You will, however, notice a marked difference in the health of your family and your own energies and outlook. Children and adults on a sugar restricted diet are so much more amenable, stable, productive. Children, particularly, do not evidence the tantrums, the "growing pains," so often associated with adolescence, but more likely a result of the enormous amounts of sugar they eat, facts which have been attested to by the research of Doctors Cott and Feingold.

The more you eat of the natural foods, the more delicious they become. As you begin to enjoy what feeling terrific is truly like, you will become disdainful of all those foods which slow you down and drain you of energy.

The following basic diet is the ideal. How closely you stick with it depends on your own motivation and discipline. Do not be discouraged if you do not adopt it fully and wholeheartedly. Just adding various natural foods to your daily regime will be beneficial, and you will eventually begin to eliminate foods which are non-nutritive. Use your creativity and imagination to enhance these suggestions, but remember, the closer you stick to the natural, uncooked, unadulterated food, the healthier it is. It takes time for tastebuds, and psyche to adapt to natural foods, therefore ease into it gradually. Add healthful foods daily and begin to eliminate the sugars, salt, white flour and fantastic concoctions you were raised with and love.

THE BASIC, NATURAL DIET

1—Whole grain cereals. Add 2%, skimmed milk or lowfat yogurt. For additional nutrients and crunchy taste, add: 1 tablespoon wheat germ, 1 teaspoon bran, 1 tablespoon sunflower seeds and 1 teaspoon brewer's yeast.

2—Two citrus fruits per day, or one serving fresh citrus juice and one fresh fruit. (Arthritics should avoid citrus fruit and juices.)

3—Two other fresh fruits. If you choose melons, eat them alone or 15 minutes before a meal. Melons digest more quickly than other foods and should not be eaten along with foods or after a meal.

4—Two servings raw or slightly cooked yellow vegetables.

5—Three servings raw or slightly cooked green and green leafy vegetables.

6—One six ounce glass of fresh squeezed vegetable juice, combining: carrots, celery, parsley, cabbage, beet, cucumber, sweet green pepper.

7—One or two servings sprouts: alfalfa, lentils, mung or soy bean sprouts.

8—One serving potato, corn, brown rice or beans.

9—Three servings protein: fish, fowl, meat, cheese, eggs, soy beans, nuts. Use low fat farmer and cottage cheeses rather than hard cheeses. Limit eggs to three or four per week. Use only the leanest meats, and skin the chickens before cooking. Bake and broil, do not fry. If dieting, keep protein to four ounces at lunch, six ounces at dinner.

10—Two servings whole grain bread with unsalted butter or margarine. Try onion or garlic powder and pepper sprinkled on spreads rather than salt.

If you have no weight problem, or wish to provide nutritious snacks and "fun food" for your family, serve raisins, figs, nuts, and other dried fruits, chopped up, mixed with peanut butter and rolled in coconut. Homemade pop corn, toasted soy beans, whole grain cookies, cakes such as carrot cake and fresh fruit pies made with honey are healthful alternatives. You can even make delicious, sugar-free ice cream!

Combine 1 cup unsweetened frozen strawberries
3 tablespoons frozen orange juice
2 cups yogurt
Blend and freeze

When partially frozen, whip with beater until smooth and return to freezer, or place in small paper cups with wooden sticks and freeze for ice cream pops. You can also vary the flavor with unsweetened, canned peaches, pears and pineapple packed in their own juices, and substitute unsweetened, frozen pineapple juice for the orange juice.

Another bonus healthful cooking brings is a grease-free kitchen. If you bake and broil, you will not have spatter and the grease cleanup associated with frying.

When you cook vegetables use two settings: *High* and *Off.* As a child I hated vegetables because they were soggy, limp, colorless and tasteless. My grandmother boiled everything, and mother was taught by her. At Hygiology I learned how delicious raw and slightly cooked vegetables could taste. I will never forget how spinach, which I dreaded, became a delicious dish and a salad green I love. Use a stainless steel steamer in your pot when you cook vegetables. Put in an inch or two of water, just enough to make steam. Turn the burner to *High;* when steam escapes, turn it *Off* and depending on the vegetable, remove it immediately or shortly thereafter. Broccoli, cauliflower, carrots and beets take a few moments longer than leafy greens. Vegetables are then crunchy, and beautifully green, yellow or orange. When spiced with either tarragon, basil, fresh dill, chives, fennel, garlic or onion powder and a bit of butter or margarine, they taste great! Experiment with herbs and spices instead of salt.

Salt does nothing for the body except help it retain fluids, and tastebuds accustomed to over-salting cannot recognize how delicious unsalted foods can be. Shaking salt all over food is not only harmful but unnecessary. All prepared and processed foods are salted, but people reach for salt shakers nevertheless, before they even taste their dish. Any foods you buy in the market or eat in a restaurant contain more than enough salt to suit your taste. Why add to it? When you cut back on the salt you eat, you will allow the natural flavors to come through.

Hypertension specialists cite the diet of Blacks as slaves as one of the reasons Black people are so genetically prone to high blood pressure. In Africa, their natural diet consisted mainly of grains, vegetables and fruits. As slaves they ate foods highly salted to prevent spoilage. Today their descendents are paying for the slave diet just as your descendants will reflect your dietary habits.

The moment you eliminate salt, sugar and white flour you begin a healthful regime. They are non-nutritive, weight and disease producing and do nothing. . . . except taste great, and that's the problem.

Your reaction is understandable. "Eliminate salt? Did you ever taste unsalted soup?"

I have and it can taste delicious . . . if you season imaginatively with pepper and spices such as fennel, thyme, oregano, basil, chives and onion. If you must have a salty taste, switch to sea salt which at least has some minerals.

If you read labels consistently you will be aghast at the amount of sugar, salt and additives you eat *every day.* The body can assimilate only so much and when you add to the hidden sugars, salt and additives, the cumulative effects of all the other sweets and junk foods you and your family may be eating over a period of time, it is no wonder that breakdowns in health occur. The way you feel and the size of your medical and dental bills are good indications of how nutrition and lifestyle is affecting you and your family. If you are under thirty-five hopefully you will not have experienced any ill effect. But if you lack energy, are subject to frequent colds, acute infections and flareups of annoying illnesses, then you know your body is not functioning healthfully. If you are over thirty-five, it is essential that you begin a program of well-balanced nutritious eating if you wish to enjoy your later years in good health.

When you cook nutritious foods from scratch, not only will you save a good deal of money, you will build a firm foundation of health and longevity for yourself and your family. There are many fine natural foods cookbooks available. Treat yourself to good health by reading them and putting them to use.

SPROUTS

Sprouts not only add a distinctive touch to salads, sandwiches, soups and other dishes, they are important sources of vitamin C, B-vitamins and minerals, as well as containing some protein. Eating them every day assures you of quickly assimilated nutrients, and sprouts should be part of everyone's diet. Many supermarkets and health food stores now feature fully grown sprouts ready for eating. Buy them so that you can start adding them to your diet immediately, but to save money and have a fresher supply, grow your own. It is easy and fun to do.

Buy only unsprayed seeds which you will find most easily in health food stores. Alfalfa, lentils, mung beans and soy beans sprout within a few days. Place a handul of seeds or beans in the bottom of a jar. Cover with a sieve top sprouting lid or with cheesecloth. Wash thoroughly; cover with water and let stand overnight. Rinse seeds the next day in several washings. Turn jar on side so that seeds drain, and place in oven or a dark cabinet. Continue to rinse growing sprouts twice daily. They should be ready to eat in three or four days. Some people toast sprouts lightly to make them crisp.

I remember with amusement how annoyed my daughter was when, as a little girl, I would garnish her peanut butter sandwiches with sprouts. Since it was too messy to separate the sprouts from the peanut butter, she had to eat them. Speaking of peanut butter, you've never tasted *real* peanut butter until you have tried it unadulterated,

292

absolutely natural, with no added salt, fillers or hydrogenization. Unfortunately it is difficult to find such peanut butter unless you shop in a health food store, for few supermarkets carry the natural, unsalted butter made from peanuts only. If you have a growing family consider buying a peanut butter machine. By making your own peanut butter, you will save money in the long run, have a fresh supply with no additives whenever needed, and a fun experience for the entire family.

VEGETABLE JUICES

Drinking six to eight ounces of freshly squeezed raw vegetable juice daily is a quick and easy way to obtain potent vitamins and minerals. For very young children who cannot thoroughly chew raw vegetables, and for older people who also may have difficulty chewing and digesting raw foods, fresh vegetable juice is a healthful and tasty alternative. Many nutritionists recommend raw vegetable juices to alleviate a number of medical problems, and their findings and recommendations have been published. You will find good books on how to combine raw vegetable juices and their therapeutic values in health food stores.

When at home, I drink a daily juice which contains: celery, parsley, cucumber, cabbage, sweet pepper, beet and carrots. On the road I seek out a natural foods store, many of which have juice bars. My three children were raised on fresh vegetable juice and I took my machine on our camping trips. Can you imagine the expressions on the faces of gas station attendants when I would ask to plug in my juicer? It was a three P.M. ritual when my daughter was a baby. I had the vegetables, all scrubbed and ready in a plastic bag and quickly fed them through the machine. What fun mechanics made of me, but when I would give them a taste, they were surprised at how delicious it was. They were also impressed with the way the baby, then only eight months old, would bounce up and down reaching for the orange colored juice.

A vegetable juice machine is a wise investment in good health for a family or the single person. It is an especially thoughtful gift for an older parent. It provides vital, quickly assimilated vitamins and minerals for those too busy to eat large salads and for those who cannot chew or digest raw foods. While juices should never replace eating raw, fresh vegetables, they are an excellent addition to the diet and the perfect alternative for those who resist vegetables.

I have found the Acme stainless steel machine very reliable. It is a heavy duty machine and I have used it for more than twenty years. It survived two camping trips. Today the Acme sells for about $200.00. Many other types of machines are available including more lightweight, plastic models.

YOGURT

Instead of eating high calorie, sugared fruit yogurts, make your own using fresh, unsweetened strawberries, blueberries, apple slices, peaches, pears and cherries in season. Off season use canned, sugar-free, juice packed pears, peaches, pineapple and fruit cocktail. Freeze your fruit yogurts for nutritious sugar free, sherbert-like treats.

Making your own yogurt from scratch is easy and saves you money. While some use a 200 degree oven overnight, I find a yogurt machine far more reliable. They cost only about ten dollars and are well worth the money. I make my yogurt with skim milk powder and a tablespoon of starter from a container of packaged plain yogurt. You will find the texture of homemade yogurt lighter, since you will not add gelatin, and the taste, less tart. If you wish a richer, creamier yogurt, use whole milk, or better yet, raw milk. However, there will be more calories in that yogurt and more butterfat. Yogurt is a fine addition to the diet; it is more easily digested than milk and introduces friendly and beneficial intestinal flora into the digestive tract.

VITAMIN AND MINERAL SUPPLEMENTS

There is much controversy amongst doctors, nutritionists and health practitioners concerning the necessity for vitamin and mineral food supplements. I shall not attempt in this book to explore this controversy. If you eat a well balanced, nutritious diet, get the proper amount of exercise and rest, adopt a positive mental attitude, your body should be able to absorb and assimilate the vitamins and minerals from the natural foods you eat. *However,* few people are on an ideal diet, or are eating *enough* for their needs. Many others have absorption and assimilation problems. I have witnessed first hand the remarkable change in people when they added vitamin and mineral supplements to their diet. *But, they also changed their eating habits.*

Certainly those who smoke and drink alcohol require vitamin and mineral supplementation for the vitamin C and B-complex nutrients leeched from the body by smoking and drinking. Those who live in polluted cities also need supplementation. But supplementation alone will not make a person healthy. *It must be incorporated along with a program of sensible eating, sufficient exercise and rest.*

I take vitamin and mineral supplements daily, prescribed for me by a physician versed in nutritional counseling. There are a number of good books concerning vitamins and minerals and I have listed some at the end of this chapter, but do not attempt to diagnose yourself and your needs. Instead, consult a physician versed in holistic healing and nutritional counseling. For the names of practitioners in your area contact:

International Academy of Preventative Medicine
10409 Town and Country Way Suite 200
Houston, Texas 77024

A WORD OF CAUTION
TO VEGETARIANS ABOUT PROTEIN

It is certainly possible to lead a long and healthy life without eating meat, fish or fowl. However, many vegetarians I have known have too little knowledge about how to combine foods so that they obtain the necessary amino acids. If you are a vegetarian or plan to give up eating animal protein, make sure to read the literature which is available. Some good books are: *"Protein for Vegetarians,"* by Gary Null; *"Recipes for a Small Planet,"* by Ellen Ewald; *"A Vegetarian Diet,"* by S. Moore and M. Byers. Also Rodale Press, Emmaus, Pennsylvania has an extensive catalog of health books, which they will be pleased to send you.

NUTRITION AND THE STUDENT

Sound, healthy nutrition is important throughout your life, and the earlier you begin a habit of eating well balanced, natural foods, the longer you will stay youthful and healthy. While you may think that because you are young you can get away with junk foods, fad diets and on-again-off-again food binges, bad eating habits catch up all too quickly.

There are crucial moments in your lifetime when good nutrition is paramount. As a student, your body and mind need all the vitamins and minerals they can absorb to compensate for the mental and physical energies you expend studying, especially when you are preparing for examinations. Taking tests is stressful and you need a diet high in RNA (ribonucleic acid), vitamins C, and B-complex to nourish brain cells and make you more alert. Complex carbohydrates (fruits and vegetables) will elevate your blood sugar normally, preventing mental and physical fatigue. Protein (meat, fish, fowl, eggs, cheese, nuts) will keep the blood sugar high, and your mind will function in high gear assuring you of better grades.

The poorly nourished cannot concentrate and have problems learning because it is difficult for them to keep their minds focused. Children are often criticized for "not trying." Some call poorly nourished children "genetically disadvantaged" and if generations of diet deficiencies exist in their family backgrounds, this is certainly possible. Good, on-going nutrition begun at an early age would show remarkable results not only in their academic performance but in their personalities and behavior.

As a student, if you rely on coffee, danish, candy bars, and cigarettes to see you through nights of studying and preparing for difficult exams, you set yourself up for unstable blood sugar and fatigue which will result in decreased mental abilities and loss of memory. Your grades cannot help but suffer. Instead of the coffee-danish-donuts-candy bar-routine, switch to peanut butter or sardine sandwiches on whole grain breads (good sources of nucleic acid and B-vitamins as well as protein); celery, sweet pepper, carrot sticks, chunks of raw cabbage and cheeses, (vitamins C, A and protein); apples and nuts, or dried fruits and nuts (complex carbohydrates and protein.)

Before the test, drink a tall glass of orange juice with protein powder or take liver protein capsules. Stay off cigarettes which narrow blood vessels (lessening blood flow to the brain, and oxygen to the brain cells). Avoid all caffeine (coffee, tea, cola drinks, chocolate), which stimulate the pancreas to release insulin. Do not eat simple sugars such as candy, cookies and cake which will give you quick energy and raise blood sugar, but only temporarily. The higher and faster blood sugar leaps, the lower it crashes, and the crash might just coincide with your tests.

The same is true for anyone facing critical decisions, or involved in work which requires a great deal of mental energy. Much has been made of the fact that a number of writers, especially poets, have committed suicide. Others die of alcoholism. Writing drains much mental and nerve energy and writers are notorious for drinking large amounts of coffee, alcohol and smoking excessively. Many others munch constantly, mostly on sweets. Coffee, alcohol, chocolate and sugar cause sharp, unstable rises and falls in blood sugar levels which set off many neurotic symptoms. Smoking narrows blood vessels cutting circulation to the brain. And coffee, alcohol, sweets and nicotine are vitamin B and vitamin C antagonists which leech the system of these necessary, nerve strengthening nutrients. Low blood sugar has been linked to severe depression. In Russia and in some cities in the United States, orthomolecular psychiatrists treat mental illness with diet and vitamins. Could it not be then that the high incidence of suicide in serious writers may be due to these physical causes rather than to the aesthetic and artistic reasons which have been usually associated with their breakdowns?

NUTRITION AND SPORTS

Competitive athletes know the value of well balanced, nutritious eating. For runners, swimmers, skiers, ball players, or any other athlete, good diet can make the difference between winning or losing. If you have a young child who hopes to make the football team, become a gymnast or participate competitively in any sport, pay close attention to what he or she eats. Athletes need a proper combination of complex carbohydrates and proteins, but many young men load up on too much protein to build muscle.

Recently I read of a young man who went into concentrated training for college football. He was eighteen, the star halfback of his high school football team, but he lacked the size needed for college and eventually the pro circuit. He began daily workouts with weights, eating enormous amounts of meat plus protein supplements. By the time he entered college, he had put on fifty pounds, plus a good deal of muscle. He made the college team, continuing to eat large amounts of protein. When he graduated college he was offered a pro contract. At twenty-two years of age, he developed cancer. The last story in our local papers was a plea for funds to aid in his treatments.

The high metabolic rate which the body puts forth to utilize the protein we eat shortens the life span of some cells and causes aging. Excess protein causes the body engine to "idle" faster than normal and since cancer is a disease of abnormal cell growth and activity, could this young man's overloading on protein have triggered the onset of his cancer?

Excess protein is also a dangerous source of energy for athletes because it increases the need for fluids, which an athlete sweats away. Dr. Nathan Smith, professor of sports medicine at the University of Washington in Seattle, discourages athletes from eating too much protein because the nitrogen by-products, a result of protein metabolization, require water so that they can be excreted in the form of urine by the kidneys. If an athlete sweats heavily, he or she can become dehydrated, and according to Dr. Smith many of the deaths which occur on the football practice field happen because athletes, trying to build themselves up on protein, lose water, which prevents them from dissipating body heat. This causes collapse and death from heat stroke.

Excess in any form leads to overload. Overloads lead to imbalance, and nutritional imbalance results in severe health problems.

NUTRITION AND PREGNANCY

Good health habits, nutrition, exercise, rest and a happy frame of mind help assure a healthy mother and a healthy baby. Every spark of life is so precious, it behooves a mother-to-be to give her unborn child the best chance she can! Having and raising a child is the ultimate experience for any woman! It is such an especially beautiful time in a woman's life and it can be so pleasant when there is no discomfort, or pain. I remember my pregnancies with fondness because I felt so great during all of them. I was 36 when I gave birth to my daughter and worked full time almost to the day she was born. I even took my typewriter to the hospital!

Even if you are dilettantish about your diet ordinarily, during the nine months of your pregnancy, forego those foods and bad habits which can make such a difference in the way you feel and the health of your child-to-be. Recent studies cite alcohol, caffeine, nicotine, marijuana and other drugs as causing damage to the fetus. A healthy child is not so much a matter of "God's will," as it is the mother's dedication to the life she carries. There is much less chance for genetic defects if the mother avoids cigarettes, alcohol, pot and other drugs and cuts back substantially if not completely on coffee, tea, cola drinks and chocolates, which all contain caffeine.

Should a woman become ill or uncomfortable during pregnancy and her physician prescribes medication, she should question him closely about possible side effects, especially as they concern the unborn child. Sad lessons have been learned because of thalidomide and D.E.S. Avoid all over-the-counter, non-prescriptive drugs for headaches, colds, nausea and other minor problems, because they too could be harmful.

NUTRITION AND MENOPAUSE

Many subtle, biochemical changes take place in the body of a woman in midlife, which make her especially prone to metabolic problems. Since nutrition affects body chemistry, it is essential that the woman approaching menopause be on a well balanced diet. Hormonal changes affect the nervous system and the glands, with the adrenals, pancreas, thyroid and pituitary particularly vulnerable. High-protein diets and refined sugars are calcium antagonists, drawing calcium from the bones. Calcium absorption decreases with age and the additional calcium lost because of hormonal changes can cause osteoporosis, a disease in which bones become brittle. Many post-menopausal women suffer from this ailment, and a diet high in protein and sugar increases the tendency to osteoporosis and aggravates existing conditions.

Sugar is also a vitamin B and vitamin C antagonist, vitamins which are required for healthy nerves. Thus the mature woman who eats a lot of sugared foods can become excessively nervous and emotional.

Menopausal women *can* be free of annoying symptoms associated with the changes occurring in their bodies and enjoy extraordinary good health with no need for estrogen treatments which increase the risk of breast cancer. A well balanced diet of fresh fruits, vegetables, grains, nuts, poultry and fish keeps the body youthful and functioning with vitality! The more active and involved the mature woman is, the more easily she will coast through this changeable period. It's a great time in a woman's life! Most family responsibilities have lessened. She is freer than ever! She can pursue that which interests her most. Sexually, she is stronger! No longer dependent on birth control, nor fearing pregnancy, she can allow her passions to flow fully. She is at her most beautiful, a fully ripened, interesting woman. Like fully ripened fruit or wine, at her peak!

NUTRITION AND TRAVEL

To travel in high gear, enjoying every moment, super-charged to experience all that interesting travel brings, requires energy, good health and the vitality to bounce back quickly when inclement weather, mixed-up reservations, missed connections and other disappointments occur. If you travel for business, meeting new challenges as well as your timetable requires that you be vigorous, alert and positive. The foods you eat, therefore, while on the road are extremely important. Nothing destroys a journey as quickly as stomach ailments and other acute illnesses.

The following hints will help you stay healthy and hearty.

Avoid fast food places because they specialize in quick cooking, which means deep fat frying, producing high-calorie, high-fat, high-profit foods which are low in nourishment. Save your money instead for better restaurants which offer a wide choice of salads, fish, chicken, meats, fruits and vegetables.

BREAKFAST

Bagging it for breakfast saves you money and also gives you a healthier start on the day because you eliminate high-fat restaurant breakfasts. A nourishing breakfast is such a simple meal to put together. It is easily packed in a small carrier, sack or even your attaché case. Granola, nuts, an apple or banana offer vitamins, minerals and protein. Buy a glass of milk (free on planes) or a container of yogurt. Add granola and fruit for a delicious meal. I much prefer this type of morning meal to horrible airline breakfasts which are high in calories, fats, sugar and taste as plastic as the trays on which they come.

Breakfast at Brennan's is a different matter. All then is permissible. Other than that, there are many healthier alternatives to the bacon and eggs routine. Unsweetened cereals, high in fiber, with some bran content mixed with fresh fruit, and low fat milk or yogurt have less cholesterol and more energy producing properties than grease laden egg dishes. If breakfast is not breakfast to you without eggs and something, switch to poached or boiled eggs with Canadian bacon or ham. You've cut down on the fat calories, but still satisfied your desire. Whole grain breads and muffins have more protein value than white bread and certainly more B vitamins.

About the "Fortified" and "Enriched" breads, Dr. E.V. McCollum of John Hopkins University said: "In the manufacture of white flour, a score or more of essential nutrients present in significant amounts in the wheat kernel are removed. To give such flour supplied with three vitamins and iron so good a name as 'enriched' is misleading."

And why eat only the breakfast menu? The other side of the card has some great foods for breakfast! What about broiled fish and tomatoes, or a large fresh fruit salad and cottage cheese? Make breakfast on the road as interesting an adventure as your journey!

The most memorable breakfast on our two camping trips was the misty morning we were coming out of the Black Hills in South Dakota and stumbled on a back road diner, set next to a tumbling stream. The sign over the door stopped us. It read, "Fresh Trout." Although we had intended to eat fruit, nuts and cereal at a gorge further down the road, we went inside and feasted on trout and pancakes made with fresh blueberries. The taste of that breakfast and the ambience remains a vivid memory that we often talk about.

LUNCH

Many money-wise travelers eat their main meal at lunch when prices are lower. Eating lightly at night is far healthier and while traveling you can often buy dinner in local markets or in cafeterias, where they have wholesome and varied selections. If lunch is to be your main meal, avoid the greasy kid stuff: hot dogs, hamburgers, french fries, fried fish, or cold cuts, and hard cheeses. They are all fattening, high in cholesterol and have less vitamins and minerals than green salads, broiled chicken, fish, lean roast beef, shrimp, fresh fruit. Avoid also anything made with mayonnaise or other dressings: tuna, egg, ham, chicken, shrimp and potato salads and cole slaw. Much better to order a chef's salad or a cutup salad in which you can *see* all the ingredients, *with dressing on the side.* That way you will know if the lettuce is limp.

If weight is no problem, enjoy sandwiches. Sliced turkey, chicken, (not chicken loaf) and roast beef on whole grain breads are better choices than ham and cheese sandwiches, grilled hamburgers and meat loaves. The latter often contain fillers and other ingredients you know nothing about.

Shrimp, crabmeat, oyster and clam cocktails with hot sauce are low-calorie ideas for a light lunch or dinner, along with a green salad and fresh fruit. Raw shellfish can be chancey because many shellfish beds have become polluted with chemicals and other wastes.

Fresh fruit is the best choice for dessert. Cut-up fruit salads often contain sugar, and the fruit in salads may not be fresh.

DINNER

Many journeys and cities are remembered for the food enjoyed and the restaurants visited. If you have saved money during the day by eating from the local markets, you can afford to spend more at night. If you are dieting or have a sensitive stomach, avoid anything fried, covered with sauces or hidden in casseroles. Restaurant cooking is neither low calorie, low salt, nor low sugared. While you can make low calorie sauces, casseroles and desserts at home, you can be assured that Monsieur Chef will put his best foot forward with the richest, most luscious combinations.

Low calorie, healthful foods in fine restaurants are especially tasty because they are good quality. Salads are green and crisp, tomatoes pungent, cooked vegetables top grade, and served crunchy, delicately flavored. Broiled fish (no butter sauce), chicken, shrimp, turkey, lean roast beef and London broil are excellent choices. Fresh fruit and cheese will round out a healthy, nourishing and delicious meal.

Ethnic foods are also good choices: Chinese and Japanese dishes, shish kebabs with chicken, seafood, and vegetables, Greek salads, tropical fruit salads. You can keep super healthy on any journey!

Highly charged, top level executives should be aware of how some salespeople skillfully manipulate them with food and alcohol to help close deals. Heavy, wine-laden lunches make you sluggish, slow your mental processes and lower your defenses! Whenever you have an important decision to make, eat lightly!

NUTRITION AND SCHOOLS, HOSPITALS AND OTHER INSTITUTIONS

Where sound, healthy nutrition is needed most, it is at its worst! The food served in school lunch rooms is unpardonable, and the only way to beat it is to pack your children's lunch and insist they eat it. Good eating habits at home, hopefully, will encourage your children, even though they eat junk foods, to adopt more healthful measures eventually. There is a glimmer of hope with school lunches. Enlightened administrators in some states have removed soda and candy machines and are changing menus. You can help this movement by taking an active role in your local schools and making the lunch room project a major priority!

The situation in hospitals and other institutions is depressing. I firmly believe hospital food is intended to keep you a patient. Insisting on a special menu, as I did the two times I was hospitalized, helps you overcome somewhat, but it is still bad. As for those institutionalized on a long term basis, bring them fresh fruit, granola, whole grain breads and cookies, honey, nuts, pure peanut butter, when you visit.

NUTRITION AND DIET

Every diet works! The only secret ingredient in any diet is *you.* If your discipline is unshaking, you will reap results the moment you cut back on calories and step up your activity. Some diets are soundly based in well balanced eating and bring long-range results, enabling you to reasonably change your eating habits into a lifelong regime. Others are extremely dangerous because they promise you quick results, and do little to change the eating habits which cause you to diet constantly. I tell you two grim tales only to alert you to what can happen to a healthy person, sophisticated in nutrition, who goes on unbalanced diets, even when they are supervised by medical practitioners.

As with many women, weight became more of a problem in my late forties, because of maturing metabolism and changes in my body of which I was unaware. My good friend, Sandy Sprung, and I had written a funny, effective, diet book which featured a well-balanced diet. It detailed Sandy's final triumph in working her way down from over 250 pounds to a svelte 139! At five feet, nine and a half inches tall, Sandy is now truly trim, and she has maintained this weight for seven years! The book was published by Tandem Press in 1973 and is entitled, *Candy, Chocolate, Ice Cream 'N How To Lick 'Em!''* During the writing Sandy would be frustrated because

I could lose weight so easily after a particularly delicious binge or tour.

This ability to lose weight rapidly was ultimately my undoing. My diet was essentially nutritious and my physical activity great. I would rationalize my cheating by declaring, "I burn it off." I felt that the cheating I did was not important, but it was! All the youthful addictions we think are so harmless begin to accumulate and when we hit our late forties, our bodies rebel with a vengeance!

In November 1972, after a heavy lecture schedule and a busy summer of reconstructing the cabin from a weekend retreat to an all year residence, I was horrified to realize that I had gained twenty pounds! How insidiously weight can creep up on you!

I learned about fasting during my years at Hygiology and fasted on a regular basis for many years, my longest fast being seventeen days. I knew how quickly one lost weight on a fast and I had always fasted with good results. I decided this time I would fast under supervision, because I was older, tired from a busy tour and would appreciate the rest. I checked into a fasting spa in Florida run by a naturopath with many years of fasting experience. But he was not prepared for what happened to me. It was not a happy fast. I had many annoying symptoms I had never experienced on other fasts, and I told the director of these. He said, just to hang in there. On the 11th day, reactions were severe and he broke my fast on diluted fruit juice. At five the next morning, I awakened, my hands and feet numb, my eyes blurry. My heart began to race rapidly and suddenly I had crushing chest pains. The director phoned his medical advisor who immediately called for an ambulance. I was rushed to West Palm Beach Hospital where a cardiologist was waiting.

My luck was with me, because the cardiologist was also a board certified endocrinologist and realized what had happened. I had gone into *starvation diabetes* and was close to a diabetic coma. I had never had any indication of diabetes, but I had a hidden tendency to hypoglycemia and this was what the fast triggered.

I was admitted to the hospital for five days with a blood sugar well over 290, and a uric acid level that was "off the charts" as the doctor grimly put it. He was furious that I had not been monitored more carefully on the fast and that my earlier symptoms had been ignored. As soon as I began to eat balanced meals, all the symptoms disappeared and even my glucose tolerance test returned to normal.

Many current books tout fasting as the answer to quick weight loss. Fasting elevates uric acid levels which can be harmful to the kidneys. Fasting also releases toxins into the bloodstream quickly, which your body might not be able to expel as rapidly as needed. Fasting can be beneficial and cleansing, *but not in all cases.* It can seriously affect your health if you have hidden problems such as hypoglycemia. *Do not attempt to fast without expert advice and a thorough medical checkup which should include a glucose tolerance test.*

Fasting for weight loss is not successful in the long run, because the weight one loses on a fast is just as quickly regained. Fasting frequently for weight control leads to a yo-yo syndrome which results in blood sugar disturbances and elevated uric acid levels.

Fad diets are dangerous because they upset body chemistry and unsuccessful because they are not long range. High-protein diets are particularly hazardous, especially for women approaching midlife. In July 1977, I was being considered for a proposed syndicated television show. I needed to be thinner than I was and I did not have much time. I knew I could never attempt to fast again, and while the "On-Off" diet of which Sandy and I wrote is effective, like all good, well-balanced diets it takes time. Nor could I understand why my weight was up. I was jogging daily, eating sensibly, but I had gained. I decided to consult a well known, high-protein diet specialist.

I gave a complete and detailed history to the doctor and his staff. I included the fact I was hypoglycemic and required a balanced proportion of carbohydrates, protein and fat. The prescription had been worked out for me by Dr. Ralph Shaw of Philadelphia, perhaps the nation's leading expert in blood sugar disturbances.

The high-protein priest said the reason for my weight gain was that I was eating too high a proportion of carbohydrate grams. I queried him closely about this, showing him Dr. Shaw's prescription and the diet which had been worked out. He assured me his high-protein program was particularly suitable for anyone with a hypoglycemic problem, that I would experience no reactions and would lose weight safely. Who was I to argue with the great and famous man?

To make a very long and painful story as succinct as possible, it took just seven days on the high-protein diet before I became frighteningly ill. I landed in the hospital with surging bouts of high blood pressure and chest pains. I had never had high blood pressure before. On my first visit to the high-protein specialist my pressure was

130/70, and this after driving two hours, parking my car and walking to his office in 100 degree heat!

Just one week later my pressure was 170/110! I was in the hospital for *nine days* before they could stabilize me! Even though my family phoned the famous man to tell him what occurred, he never called the hospital, never checked on me and I was his well paying patient for whom he should have been professionally responsible. I found out later he was not associated with any hospitals and avoided them.

In the hospital I was put on a balanced diet with a normal proportion of proteins, complex carbohydrates and fats and at the end of my nine day stay, my blood pressure had returned to normal and I passed a cardiac stress test.

That was the summer eleven women my age died as a result of liquid high-protein diets, and while I had not been on a liquid high-protein regime, my symptoms were similar.

Dr. Ralph A. Nelson, associate professor of nutrition at the University of South Dakota, in cautioning people regarding high-protein diets states: "Excess protein causes a higher concentration of urea in the blood. Urea contains the by-products of protein metabolism and is intended to be excreted by the kidneys, and anyone with malfunctioning kidneys or liver could accumulate so much urea they could actually go into a coma or even die."

Is this what happened to me, and to the women who died while on high-protein diets? Protein intake also affects the body's calcium balance, and calcium is an important factor in the function of the muscles of the body. Since the heart is our most important muscle, a loss of calcium can be life threatening. Calcium loss is very substantial among protein eaters, especially women. Dr. Helen Linkswiler, professor of nutritional sciences at the University of Wisconsin, is concerned about women and high-protein diets. "Something seems to be happening in the kidney that promotes calcium loss," she stated in a recent article. "I am most concerned about dieters eating lots of meat. I think low-calcium and high-protein diets are devastating."

A woman's body chemistry is extremely fragile as she approaches menopause and any diet which is unbalanced affects her more than a younger person. All the women who died in 1977 on the liquid high-protein diet were over forty!

Diet and nutrition are indivisible. *Never sacrifice sound nutrition for any diet.* There are many well balanced diets you can choose from. Dr. Neil Solomon proposes a sensible, well balanced regime in his book. The various diet groups: Weight Watchers, TOPS, Diet

Workshop, all are low-calorie, nutritionally sound, long-range plans which help you change your eating habits permanently. The faster you lose weight, the faster it comes back on. The trick is not how much weight you lose, but how long you keep it off, and that means eating well planned, low-calorie, low-fat, nutritious foods for the rest of your life!

Suggested reading:

The Complete Book of Vitamins For Health
                                    Rodale Books, Emmaus, Pa.
The Complete Book of Minerals For Health
                                    Rodale Books, Emmaus, Pa.
Let's Eat Right, Adelle Davis   Harcourt Brace
Let's Have Healthy Children   Adelle Davis New American Library
Feingold Cookbook for Hyperactive Children
                          Dr. Benjamin Feingold, Random House

Psychodietetics, Dr. Emanuel Cheraskin   Stein & Day
Nutrition and Your Mind, George Watson   Bantam
The Psychochemical Response, George Watson   Harper & Row
Supernutrition, Richard Passwater   Pocketbooks
Nutrigenetics, Dr. R.O. Brenna   Signet
New York Times Natural Foods Cookbook, Jean Hewitt
                                              Quadrangle Press
New York Times Natural Foods Dieting Book, Yvonne Tarr
                                              Quadrangle Press
Diet for a Small Planet, Frances Moore Lappé   Ballantine
Recipes for a Small Planet, Ellen Buchman Ewald   Ballantine
Drink Your Troubles Away, John Lust   (self published)
The Ortho-Molecular Approach to Learning Disabilities, Dr. Alan
Cott   Academic Therapy
The Food Depression Connection, June Roth
                                           Contemporary Books
Nutrition and Mental Function, George Serban   Plenum Books
Nutritional Disorders of American Women, Myron Winick
                                                 Wiley & Sons
Malnutrition & Intellectual Development, J.B. Lloyd-Still
                                                    PSG, 1976

18

Relax And Regenerate

Relaxation is an art which frees a cluttered mind, making it receptive and responsive to new discoveries. My ripest thoughts seem to come at the moment I am about to drift off to sleep, when my mind, loosened from a busy day, begins a silent, passive exploration of the unknown. How I wish I could corral those thoughts more efficiently! If I have not fully fallen asleep and have the will, I rise to jot them down. Invariably they are my most provocative and productive ideas.

Few of us have the leisure or the desire to spend our days on mountaintops in contemplation. How then do we control frenetic activity? How do we effect a compromise between what we must do, what we enjoy doing, and the needs of our mind and body to relax, rest and regenerate?

Sleep of course is the most soothing solution.

"What the will and reason are powerless to remove, sleep melts like snow in water," stated British writer, Walter John de la Mare, noted for his poems of childhood.

As children we slept peacefully. Long hours of restful slumber generated our growth. The ability to relax and sleep soundly lessens as we mature. Our minds become taut and stretched like violin strings, and the advice of Arthur Wellesley, the first Duke of Wellington, is painfully apt: "When one begins to turn in bed, it is time to turn out!"

The reaction of the body to rest and relaxation is paradoxical. Healthy, active people who can get by with little rest, relax easily and sleep soundly. The tired, rundown, debilitated person who needs rest most finds sleep as elusive as the snail darter.

Relaxing your mind and insuring that you get enough sleep enables you to meet the challenges that each day brings with a healthy, positive attitude. Physical exercise helps relax the mind and induce sleep. Take a walk after dinner, or turn on the radio or record player and dance around the room. Do the exercises suggested at the end of the chapter on physical fitness. Body movement relaxes muscles and clears the kaleidescopic clutter of the mind. While writing this book, I lengthened my daily four miles of walking to six, adding the two additional miles in the evening. Taking full advantage of my retreat to Florida to finish the text, I spent half my lunch hour swimming 50 to 60 laps. Whenever I became bogged down with an idea that was difficult to transfer to paper, I closed my eyes for a few moments, breathed deeply and let my brain loosen. When I first began to write, I would tire after an hour. Now I can write close to seven hours a day, taking frequent mind breaks, walking at dawn and dusk and swimming at noon.

Taking the time to fit early morning and evening walks into your day enables you to be more efficient, and helps you to relax and sleep peacefully. If you are close to a "Y" or health club, swim during your lunch hour. Many business people are doing this and find their energy levels heightened. If you do not care for swimming, take a walk during lunch to ease tensions. The tautness which begins in the back of your neck and spreads throughout your body eventually takes a terrible toll of your nervous system. Spinal problems, muscle strains, pinging nerves, and chronic disease can all begin with tension.

Exercise and meditation protect your mind and body. Unnatural relaxing agents such as: non-prescriptive anti-depressents, sleeping remedies, pain killers, prescription sleeping pills, Quaaludes, marijuana, and other drugs are not only harmful to the individual taking them, but to their descendants.

I disagree with my young friends that marijuana is harmless, and recent studies have proven me correct. I feel that marijuana should be legalized so as to eliminate the criminal element and give legal sources better control and regulation over its distribution, but smoking marijuana is as deadly as smoking cigarettes. As these young users grow older they will realize how their mental and physical faculties, their health and their potential life span have been harmed by their use of pot.

Wiping the matrix of the mind clean through meditation unleashes it so that it can find its own way. Without fail, better thoughts emerge. My son taught me to meditate after I was released from the hospital following my reactions to the high-protein diet.

Two days before I was discharged, a fire in my mother's home next door killed eight of her breeding poodles, wiped out sentimental possessions as well as publishing stock we stored in our basement. He had flown in from the West Coast. Concerned with the pressures I faced, he took me aside my first day home and instructed me in meditation.

The meditative breathing he taught me has enabled me to relax more easily and to recognize when tensions begin to build. At first it was very difficult to wipe my mind clean. My son cautioned me that the powerful ego of the mind would interfere with intruding thoughts. I was to allow these visions to tumble over each other while I concentrated on the breathing and the movement of my diaphragm. I sat with my hands in my lap, my head relaxed, my eyes closed. I counted the slow intake and outgo of air as it came up from my diaphragm. Soon I lost count. The breathing became slower and shallower. I could actually feel tension flow out of my body. My fingers loosened. My neck, spine, arms, legs and muscles turned liquid. I felt my scalp let go. There was a tingling in my head. My brow seemed to widen and my ears lengthened. I almost fell asleep. Since then I try to meditate daily. Invariably I sleep afterwards for fifteen to twenty minutes, awakening refreshed and regenerated.

You can meditate anywhere! Once on a terrible flight from Reno to Las Vegas, when our plane hit a mountain wave and dropped several thousand feet, while others screamed, I closed my eyes and began to count breaths.

To meditate: Sit relaxed in a chair that gives you good back support, or sit up against the headboard of your bed. Some people cross their feet Indian style. I prefer to keep mine spread with the knees bent. Place your hands in your lap, palms up, fingers loose. Close your eyes. Allow your head to sag naturally. Begin to breathe in (your stomach will move out). Breathe out (your stomach moves in). Concentrate only on these movements and the breathing. Count the breaths. Do not be concerned if you lose count; you will. Allow whatever moves through your mind to play itself out. Think only of the breathing and the counting. Soon you will feel the sensations I described earlier and your breathing will become easy and rhythmic. The pictures in your mind may or may not disappear, it takes time to get results. You may fall asleep. Give in to whatever comes. Eventually, after about twenty minutes you will come out of the meditation or wake up from the sleep. Your pulse will be slower and you will feel rested, at ease.

My mother meditates by reading passages from her Bible, repeating the prayers by rote, over and over. It relaxes her mind and body. For centuries those who prayed concentratedly in religious rituals practiced meditation as they chanted. Often the chanting was combined with rhythmic body movements. The religious experience and participation in prayer does much to free the mind from personal care and is a form of meditation.

Controlled daydreams are another way to relax the mind. How pleasant it is to sit at a desk and turn one's thought to a far-off beach or ski slope, rather than to the work piled thereon. Do not feel guilty about taking a few moments out of the day to muse about something beautiful. Remember that "a mind all logic, is like a knife all blade, it cuts the hand of he who uses it." I think often of these words by the Indian poet Rabindranath Tagore whenever I become uptight about schedules and what needs to be done. Meditative daydreams realistically employed are therapeutic, provided you realize they are a method to escape tensions. Daydreaming constantly without doing, is an illness which requires professional assistance.

Massage in all its varied forms, and loving, fulfilling sex are perhaps the most enjoyable means of inducing relaxation and restful sleep. Whichever methods you choose: exercise, meditation, prayers, daydreams, massage, sex; make time every day to relax, rest and regenerate.

Good health habits encompassing the full spectrum of body and mind nourishment that we have just explored make you a more positive, productive, and happy person. You *can* do whatever you *want* to do, when you have the *physical and mental strength,* the *ability,* the *will* to *unleash the power of your creative potential!*

19

Unleasing The Power Of Creative Potential

Attitude, more than ability unleashes the power of creative potential. If you believe unequivocally that you *can* do it, you will!

I was in Acapulco one January and had swum out with my friend to the raft which bobs in the bay about 100 yards off the Hilton Hotel beach. It was a beautiful day, and the swim was delightful. Just as we approached the raft, my friend, pretending to be a predatory fish, grabbed at my toe. I yelped, and as I opened my mouth, the cap on my front tooth came loose. Horrified, I watched it sink to the bottom.

When my friend surfaced and saw me *sans* tooth he was compassionately gallant, remarking how cute and school girlish I looked. I did not believe him for a moment. I was miserable. We had been invited to a cocktail party that evening at the home of Merle Oberon and I very much wanted to meet this remarkable woman. I was not about to go without a front tooth! I began to dive, but I had no goggles and could see nothing. The water was over forty feet deep and I could only get about halfway down before having to surface for air.

We headed back to shore, my friend laughing. He thought it very funny. As we came out of the water, Harry yelled to the Mexican beach boys in front of the hotel, "Ten dollars American if you find the lady's tooth!" He made me open my mouth to show them!

More than a dozen bronzed men dashed into the surf. Harry and I swam out with them and showed them about where we thought it might be. Within minutes a grinning brown face appeared and in his hand was my cap! I could not believe it! He wore no goggles, dove only once, and there it was! Holding the cap aloft and laughing uproariously he headed for shore. On the beach the diver ceremoniously handed the cap over to me, amidst the laughter and astonishment of the crowds which had gethered. Turning to me, Harry said, "You see, Judy, anything is possible with ten dollars American!"

I, who am so positive about most things was truly astounded. To find such a small item, in such a big bay, in continually shifting water and sand, and to find it so quickly was amazing!

The young men who swam out into the bay did not question the possibilities. They had *confidence* in their abilities and could see no reason for not trying. I am sure they would have kept on trying until they eventually achieved success.

If you believe you *can* do something, you will *develop* the ability to do it, even if you *cannot* do it at the very beginning! This confidence, this belief, is the first step to creativity. Motive, means and opportunity help strengthen creative accomplishment, and *audacity* puts it over the top!

For some, developing confidence is a torturous, slow growth. Those with reserved, cautious natures build confidence by searching their inner selves and continually testing their reactions and abilities. They fear making mistakes.

Others, with a carefree spirit of adventure, achieve confidence more easily through the "oops" method of trial and error. I've learned a good deal from my daughter. Whenever she makes a mistake, she laughs and says, "Oops," and tries again. I thought I had a spirit of adventure, but it pales beside hers. The "oops" attitude keeps you young, because nothing ever becomes so serious that you won't give it a whirl. This is what opens the door to creativity.

When you laugh at yourself, your inhibitions, your faults, and your feeble attempts, *anything is possible.* This is the secret to *unleashing the power of creative potential!*

Everyone has an inherent capacity for creativity, and creativity emerges more from abstract ideas and intuition than reason. Reason can be tyrannical, telling you . . . *"you can't do that."* Intuition cries, "ANYTHING IS POSSIBLE!" Do not allow reason to chain your creative urges! *Dare to do! Experiment!* Each experiment becomes an experience and each experience generates and strengthens your creative expression giving you the courage and impetus to continue!

May you enjoy unleashing the power of your creative potential all the days of your life!